MOVEMENT
FUNDAMENTALS

Janet A. Wessel

Michigan State University

3RD EDITION

MOVEMENT FUNDAMENTALS

figure

form

fun

PRENTICE-HALL, INC., Englewood Cliffs, New Jersey

MOVEMENT FUNDAMENTALS: *figure, form, fun*
3RD EDITION/ Janet A. Wessel

13–604504–9
13–604512–X

Library of Congress Catalog Card Number: 78–103562

Current printing (last digit):
10 9 8 7 6 5 4 3 2 1

PRINTED IN THE UNITED STATES OF AMERICA

Prentice-Hall International, Inc., London
Prentice-Hall of Australia, Pty. Ltd., Sydney
Prentice-Hall of Canada, Ltd., Toronto
Prentice-Hall of India Private Limited, New Delhi
Prentice-Hall of Japan, Inc., Tokyo

foreword

This new edition of MOVEMENT FUNDAMENTALS, which emphasizes individual differences as well as human similarities, will be welcomed by many college women and their teachers.

Like earlier editions, it evidences the fact that Dr. Wessel's own understanding of the anatomical, physiological, psychological, and social implications of many forms of movement is both broad and deep; and it also evidences her talent for relating her own scientific understanding to the needs, interests, habits, and concerns of college women.

Accordingly, this new edition of MOVEMENT FUNDAMENTALS can make a substantial contribution to each college woman's understanding of herself by guiding her exploration of her own capacities for movement, by showing her how she may maintain and improve her own bodily functioning, and by introducing her to a wide variety of movement activities which can make all the years of her adult life more satisfying and enjoyable.

Eleanor Metheny
Los Angeles, California
January 1970

70352306

preface

Today discoveries in many fields of knowledge about the ways a person learns and acquires ideas and action patterns are revolutionizing educational theory and practice at all levels. These discoveries and related theories have led to a dramatic transformation of many fields of study: the identification of significant information and skills deemed of most worth in the subject, and the integration of acts and concepts into an organized, cohesive structure for sequential development by the learner. Current research in health-fitness and exercise has led to widespread recognition of the necessity for regular, suitable physical activity throughout life. Indeed, facts and concepts gained from studies focused on the psychological and sociological, as well as on the biological basis of physical activity, provide new insights in selecting, planning, and designing purposeful physical activity or movement patterns for developing and maintaining personal well-being throughout life. Personal experiences in teaching in college-level programs and in reseach related to exercise and health for girls and women led to the writing of this book.

The book has been developed to emphasize the personal nature of physical activity and the very real value of regular, suitable physical activity for *making the most of self*; effectively meeting and adjusting to the demands of a rapidly changing, complex society; and gaining joy, pleasure, and satisfaction in all life experiences. This book reflects the position that each person ultimately formulates her own values for physical activity, values that will determine her choices and the extent to which she engages in such activity throughout her life. Further, it is based on the belief that each student is not only capable of assuming personal responsibility for her own self-development and educational growth but also that she *desires to do so*. The underlying theme of this book is that a physically educated person understands her physical self and the *why* and *how* of physical activity; that she has the skills to meet her personal needs and interests in her particular environment; and that she accepts responsibility for developing and maintaining her physical potential, not only for self enhancement but also for her family and the betterment of society.

In order to insure that the book may be used effectively in different college and university settings, the material presented is adaptable to various methods of course organization such as team teaching, closed circuit television, and laboratory experimentation. These materials represent an in-depth approach to problem-solving for individualized instruction in the college program. To this end the individual laboratory experiments were constructed. Each student will have the opportunity to intelligently evaluate her physical self-image and the consequences of her movement or physical activity behavior: body shape, body function, and health-physical fitness; motor performance; and attitudes toward herself and physical activity. To provide the student with sufficient background for selecting and designing personal action plans, general conditioning principles and principles of movement in skilled performance are presented. Certain facts and concepts of the functional-structural components of various body segments are discussed concisely in relation to techniques (*the how to*) for achieving specific outcomes. For experimentation by the student in applying these principles and techniques, examples of action plans for designing personal programs and analyzing movements in work and play are included. Documentation of the materials presented and additional sources should enable each student to gain insight into kinds of available data, direction of research efforts, and avenues for further study. In the Glossary at the end of the book each term that has a specialized or technical meaning is defined for the reader.

Three other features of importance are included in this revision: Women In Competition, Problems Related to Health and Physical Activity, and Role of Physical Activity for Children and Youth and in Later Years. It is hoped that this information—whether assigned or read and discussed voluntarily with others—will stimulate young women's interest in athletic events, the beneficial effects of early motor experiences in the home, the new curricula or new image of physical education in schools, and in the need to maintain optimal levels of physical activity throughout life for health and personal well-being.

It may not be feasible to use all the materials or all the individual laboratory experiments described in this book in a particular college course. However, by selecting those activities compatible with specific course objectives, desired student outcomes, and the facilities that are available, the materials should be adaptable to various college or university programs.

It is hoped that this book will make a significant contribution to contemporary college-level programs for women. To this end, a determined effort was made to emphasize significant data on the effects of physical activity or the lack of it on major health problems and personal well-being. The book seeks to integrate into a meaningful whole the facts and concepts underlying the foundations of movement fundamentals in the physical education program—facts and concepts that have traditionally been presented in separate courses. It seeks to present a personal approach to learning experiences through up-to-date problem-solving techniques that will not only be valuable now but may also serve as a practical guide throughout the years. Each student should be in a position to evaluate intelligently her physical self-image and the consequences of her movement behavior in modern living, and have the knowledge and skills to design a personal program. Having these, the responsibility of maintaining optimal levels of suitable physical activity is *hers*.

Though designed primarily for use by college students in contemporary physical education programs, the individual experiments and the action plans are directed toward all women, regardless of age, occupation, or educational background. The material presented should be of particular importance to the professional student in Health Science—namely, nursing, physical and occupational therapy, and Health Educators. Graduate students in physical education will find it helpful in refining many of their own concepts and in translating the objectives of physical education into meaningful learning experiences for the student. And those organizing new programs related to preventive medicine such as "Well Mother Clinics" should find the book helpful.

I am indebted to the many students and colleagues whose interest, cooperation, and encouragement helped to make this revision of the book possible. Especially do I wish to express appreciation to the Administration and the women's faculty at Michigan State University for their support, cooperation, and faith in the program developed for college women.

My special thanks go to Brian Petrie for his help in editing the manuscript and securing pertinent reference materials, in designing attitude measures, and in helping to write the chapter dealing with psycho-social factors that influence participation; and to Frances Koenig for her contribution of the chapter on women in competition.

J. A. W.
East Lansing, Michigan

contents

laboratories

Experiments, Exercises, Conditioning Programs, Records

Part

1

self-image
and
physical
activity

some introductory

discussion

THE ROLE OF PHYSICAL EDUCATION

a concept

1 *The physically educated person today.* Are you physically educated? To answer "yes" because you have taken courses in physical education has no more justification than to claim that you are an educated person because you have a degree or diploma. When applied to a field of study, the term "educated" implies a degree of mastery of the content (knowledges and skills) deemed most important for attaining the ultimate goals of that study. For physical education, the ultimate goal is mastery of content—the use of the body as an efficient, skillful, and graceful instrument of the *self*. Being physically educated then, means:

> *Optimal development of one's body or physical potential, which will*
> —meet the movement exigencies at all stages of life effectively
> —make childbearing a safe and natural process
> —prevent chronic disease and delay the onset of aging per se
> —put a brake on overweight and the current "epidemic" of fatness
> —curb emotional stresses and release tensions
> —help one meet the exciting challenges of the changing role of women
>
> *Self-awareness and recognition of*
> —the uniqueness of one's body, its capabilities and limitations
> —the joy and exhilaration in skillful and efficient use of one's body
> —oneself as a moving being who needs and desires activity and mobility
> —motivation, with the inner being as the driving force for achievement of one's potential
>
> *Acceptance of responsibilities for self, for family, for society, for*
> —personal physical development and maintenance
> —recognition of the cultural forces that influence participation and levels of aspiration
> —intelligent manipulation of environment for the well-being of all.

These goals do not come from exposure to isolated facts, or from a conglomeration of physical activities or movement experiences, or even from selected experiences that are not intellectually challenging. It is evident that the unique contribution of physical education to the development of the *total self* is attained through movement. Based upon this premise almost all physical education programs stress the need to remain physically active throughout life. However, there are great differences of opinion on how this goal should be reached.

a position

What shall be taught in the physical education program? Some instructional programs are based on the concept that if a person is proficient in a skill and enjoys it she will continue this activity and remain active throughout her life. Unfortunately, however, evidence to date does not seem to support this contention. Many young women entering college are proficient in team games. They participate because they enjoy the challenge, the comradeship with other young women, and the excitement. But on leaving the college environment, they often find that continuing to engage in these activities is impractical and, more importantly, that these activities are no longer meaningful avenues for self-expression. Instruction in leisure-time sports and games should theoretically resolve this problem. But does it? Will the young woman continue to participate regularly if she has been fortunate enough to select an activity that appeals to her—one in which she has the capabilities and talents to achieve a reasonable degree of skill? The answer is probably no. Because her responsibilities increase, pressures multiply, and social patterns change, her level of participation, which was motivated by a desire for pleasure, tends to diminish. The usual reason given is simply "I just don't have the time." It may also be true that the activity she selected satisfied all her needs except one—the biological. To insure that students do not overlook the physiological effects of activity, physical education programs should include a fitness or conditioning course. Too often, procedures border on indoctrination and regimentation of training and fail to provide the young woman with an intelligent basis, a built-in capacity, for determining the action she should take in regard to herself within the environmental alternatives of her own life situation, present and future.

How, indeed, can we program physical education in such a way that each young woman has the opportunity to become physically educated and understands her need to remain physically active throughout her life? The common denominator of all physical education programs is movement, or physical activity, but this does not imply that organized activity experiences are programmed merely for the *sake of activity*. Movement experiences are the tools or media through which desired outcomes deemed most important are attained. Teaching not just the *what*, but the *why* and the *how*, is the essence of physical education in the present for the future. The development of skill is no more important than the development of the ability to learn to play and to enjoy movement and the challenges inherent in personally satisfying activities; to interact and relate to others; and develop and preserve one's own well-being through purposeful choices in movement behavior and intelligent manipulation of one's environment throughout life. To take these steps for personal development one must have knowledge and understanding of the factual information and concepts of purposeful activity in modern living, and competence in using such information.

The logical answer is that the content (the why and how) as well as the skills of physical activity belongs in the instructional program. Because such knowledge is essential for attaining desired outcomes, it is most efficiently learned in organized experiences in school and college, for no other public agency provides such instruction for all. At a general level a reasonable degree of mastery of *content in physical education* means that each person has developed sufficient understanding and knowledge of

> Body structure and function and ways to evaluate body performance
> How the body is affected by movement behavior (physiological and psychological effects of physical activity)
> How much and what kind of physical activity is best
> A wide variety of skills, so that selection of an activity suitable to meet one's needs and interests is possible
> Principles and techniques for effecting desired changes and designing and selecting exercise programs
> Environmental influences on movement behavior and alternative channels within the socio-cultural milieu and physical environment
> Competition and athletics, and the woman's role in these areas.

a case

A personal-program approach to physical education. This book emphasizes the personal approach to physical education. The young women in our colleges represent a cross section of the abilities and aspirations of the nation. Each young woman has her own personal interests, goals, and level of aspirations; each differs in her likes and dislikes; and each has unique capabilities, talents, and limitations. Some love the challenge of competition and find satisfaction in pitting their skills against other young women and men, against previous personal performance, or against the environment itself. Others engage in activities because they enjoy social relations with other young people—for the sheer pleasure of socialization. Others hope to enhance their physical appearance and to gain peer acceptance. And then there are those who do not enjoy any kind of activity remotely resembling physical exertion, effort, or "sweat"; but they too must find channels for meeting psychological and sociological needs.

Everyone needs activity to fulfill a common, biological need. Obviously, the activity needs of all these young women cannot be met by a uniform program of instruction in physical education. Nor can the needs of our country be met by such a program. Traditional theories of physical education that advocate a uniform program for all ignore the unique nature of each individual and of the different activity forms created by man, the diversified nature of *American life*, and the environmental alternates. Equal physical education opportunity for all, YES; the same physical education program for all, NO. A common body of knowledge, skills, and values representative of the content of physical education deemed most important, YES. A common need for regular vigorous physical activity for all young men and women at all stages of life regardless of personal preferences, YES.

Thus the question, "What shall be taught in college physical education classes for young women?" constitutes a central issue in attempts to cope successfully with this diversity of abilities, interests, and needs. Stated in behavioral terms the question becomes, "What should the graduate be able to do that she could not do if she had not gone to college?" At a specific level then, the college program based on a personal approach is designed to enable each young woman to

> *Appraise* accurately her body structure and functions and *evaluate* realistically her physical image, likes and dislikes of activity, strengths and limitations, and present activity practices
>
> *Select* the kinds of activity that are most suitable for her needs, interests, and level of aspiration
>
> *Design* an activity program that allows her to attain adequate levels of physical activity of her choice
>
> *Acquire* experiences and reasonable proficiency in some leisure-time activity of her choice
>
> *Recognize* that motivation is an inner force and that she must take the responsibility for her movement behavior and for what she does with her own life
>
> *Make* decisions about the role of physical activity in her life—for self, for her future family, and for the American way of life in which she believes
>
> *Accept* the responsibility of maintaining optimal levels of physical activity in her life.

It is in answering the question, *"Who is physically educated today?"* that your reactions to these seven statements are important. Do you have these knowledges, abilities, skills, and values? If so, one can assume that you have cultivated movement as a fundamental condition of your life. You have attained the desired outcomes. We in the profession fervently encourage you not only to make the decision to remain physically active throughout your life but also to *follow through*, regardless of the pressures, the responsibilities, the changing social patterns, and all other time-consuming tasks that make up your life.

PHYSICAL ACTIVITY IN MODERN LIVING

the situation

In the past few years many technological, social, and material changes have occurred; no one doubts that even more drastic alterations are in the

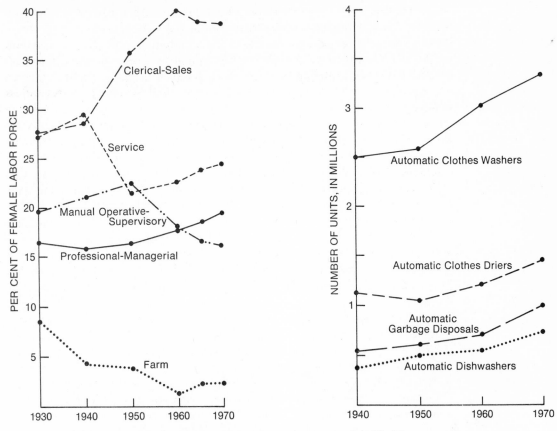

Figure 1.1 Changes in Activity Demands in the Home and at Work*
Left, the structure of the female labor force; *right*, increasing use of labor-saving appliances.

offing. The application of scientific knowledge and automation has produced marked changes in the physical effort or requirements for muscular activity in daily living. Such technological gains have reduced the demands for muscular effort in the performance of work on the farm, in industry, in the office, in the home, and even in leisure. Figure 1.1 illustrates these trends.

Predicting events of the future is no longer solely within the realm of the science fiction writers. Such prestigious organizations as General Electric, the Sperry Rand Corporation, the American Academy of Arts and Sciences, the Ford Foundation, and the Stanford Research Unit are currently engaged in making prognostications for the years up to 2000. They have come to a level of

*Adapted from: D. L. Kaplan and M. C. Casey, *Occupational Trends in the United States, 1900 to 1950*, Bureau of the Census, Working Paper No. 5 (Washington, D.C.: U.S. Dept. of Commerce, 1958); E. D. Goldfield, *Statistical Abstract of the U.S., 1963*, Bureau of the Census (Washington, D.C.: U.S. Dept. of Commerce, Government Printing Office, 1963); E. D. Goldfield, *Statistical Abstract of the United States, 1966*, Bureau of the Census (Washington, D.C.: U.S. Dept. of Commerce, Government Printing Office, 1966).

agreement on many details of future life. The home, for instance, will become the focus for many different forms of automated machine application. Food preparation will be automated, with a small computer storing desired menus for the week and then preparing the food on demand. Already, some stores are experimenting with fully automated supermarkets. The shopper pushes buttons to denote her purchases, and the goods are delivered to the checkout counter, wrapped and with the cost totalled. The necessity of going to the store at all may be eliminated in the future by sending coded data stating household needs over telephone wires to the store computer, which would then assemble the goods for delivery and charge the householder's account. Programmed machines would also take care of house cleaning by filtering the air and attracting dust particles to a collecting device. (Of course, we may or may not choose to accept these devices.)

Even the leisure pursuits that characterize our culture at the present time seem to be preponderantly inactive or sedentary. One of the major trends in leisure time has been the increase in the number and following of spectator sports. It is now possible to be one of twenty thousand spectators at a hockey game, one among a hundred thousand at a football game, or one of many thousands watching *others* play what is often regarded as one of the best "carry-over" sports—golf. Spectator sports provide an opportunity for many thousands who watch in person or via TV to give vent to their feelings and "let off steam" in a socially acceptable manner. As such, their value is great. However, this vicarious excitement generated by other people's activity is many people's *only* contact with sport and exercise. Spectator sports may provide some measure of cathartic release and emotional involvement, but it is only through personal involvement—the doing as well as the feeling—that one will benefit from physical activity.

Our highly mechanized society and industry have not only taken away the daily demands for physical effort or muscular activity but also tend to provide a rationale for inactivity in one's daily life. Walking is regarded as old fashioned. An individual's rejection of physical exercise, of "sweat," on the basis that life should be effortless and air conditioned, is accepted by many as a perfectly legitimate attitude. Yet, while this social attitude may appear to be logical to those who equate modernity with physically inactive work and sedentary forms of recreation, it seems unlikely that drastic reductions in muscular activity in life styles can take place without adverse effects.

medical reasons for physical activity

Until recent years, faith in the health values of regular physical activity was founded almost exclusively on tradition and the subjective opinions of people who were convinced that exercise made them feel better. Over the past decade, medical personnel and researchers have become increasingly interested in the value of regular exercise as a preventive for major health problems, particularly cardiovascular disease and obesity. Though it is difficult to find incontrovertible proof, there is a growing body of evidence that directly or indirectly supports the contention that certain medical conditions may be "deficiency diseases," the deficiency being a lack of regular physical activity. A number of physicians and investigators have become convinced (1, 2) that lifelong regular exercise can help in

> Curbing obesity, or excessive fatness
> Putting a brake on the current "epidemic" of coronary artery disease and strokes
> Releasing tensions and emotional stresses
> Delaying the debilitating effects of aging
> Preventing orthopedic disabilities and postural pain.

In a position paper of the American Medical Association the following statements were made.

> Vigorous exercise reasonably applied under rational conditions will not damage young healthy hearts (2).
> Proper exercise as a way of life helps to keep healthy hearts healthy and prevents the onset of cardiovascular disease (2).
> Proper exercise as a way of life may help to lessen the severity of cardiovascular disease and make recovery more likely (3).

Much of the scientific basis for the belief in the health protection value of regular exercise has come from the use of exercise in rehabilitation. Exercise has helped in speeding the recovery of surgical and maternity patients; in preventing phlebitis, clots, embolisms, kidney stones, and loss of calcium from the bones of bed patients; in restoring physical and mental health in elderly invalids; and in physical reconditioning of those who have had strokes, arthritis, injuries, and neurological and orthopedic disorders (4). An examination of current scientific literature shows an increasing number of research studies on the effects of specific exercise and decreased daily physical activity on body function. Both here and abroad a number of laboratories are doing experimental research on the specific physiologic effects of exercise on the cardiovascular-respiratory system. Numerous statistical studies of selected population groups have been concerned with the incidence of heart disease and overweight, and the level of physical activity in daily life. Despite large gaps in scientific knowledge of the role of exercise in health and disease, many prominent authorities believe that the human body may be "disease imperiled" if optimal levels of physical activity are not maintained in daily life. The term "hypokinetic disease" was coined by two prominent medical authorities (5) to represent such medical or health conditions.

How much scientific basis is there for a belief in the preventive or health values of exercise? In Chapters 17 and 18 we present research evidence that exercise tends to prevent two major health problems, obesity and heart disease. These data can aid you in reaching logical conclusions on the role of exercise in the prevention of disease, which you can then interpret in light of your own physical endowment, environment, and personal needs.

personal reasons for physical activity

A changing environment demands individual adaptation. While adaptability to new circumstances is one of the outstanding qualities of the human being, it does require energy or vitality, a physical potential, to function effectively within the inherited endowment of the individual and the particular social-cultural-physical environmental conditions. No one denies that there are many diverse forces in daily living that diffuse your energy or physical potential, e.g., improper diet, rest, and sleep; too much tension or emotional stress; illness or chronic conditions. The focus of this book, however, is on how physical activity in modern life can maximize your energy, your physical potential. This is not to negate the health values of physical activity but to present personal reasons for physical activity as a basis for designing personal action plans.

The beneficial effects to the individual in improved physical appearance, better body function, improved performance of skills involved in work and play, and the feeling of personal well-being and self-esteem, although difficult to quantify, provide immediate justification for optimal levels of regular physical activity in modern living. Each individual, given her hereditary endowment, has the capacity to improve her figure, her body function, her skill level within her cultural milieu, unless prevented by a serious debilitating medical condition or environmental circumstances beyond her control. Such a viewpoint assumes that everyone is born with certain capacities or potentialities that can be advanced or retarded by the individual's perception of her physical self-image in the total situation as well as by social-environmental influences. Implicit in this position is the belief that an optimal level of physical activity in daily life is one of the essential ingredients in developing and maintaining physical potential; that high levels of energy or vitality in all aspects of life are necessary. From this point of view, an individual's physical activity—the physical expression of the self—is conceived as an integrative process involving the self—the mind, the emotions, and the body. Based on this postulate, active use of the muscles has an important role that exceeds the mere function of locomotion or sitting down in a chair or pushing a button or manipulating a machine. Muscular activity influences, directly or indirectly, the circulation, respiration, metabolism, and hormonal balance of the body. Besides providing the stimulation necessary for organic function and tone, it affects our bone structure, our body shape, and even our body weight. Last but not least in any sense of the word, it is an outlet for our emotions and tensions, and makes us feel recreated and refreshed. From this position, it can be further postulated that the mind, the body, and the emotions each affect one another and, in turn, are affected by each other in the physical expression of self.

No single activity is sure to develop or maintain your physical potential. There is no one way, no single action plan, to fit the personal needs of every individual. There is an endless variety of physical activities involved in all the patterns that make up your life. In Table 1.1 we classify all physical activities into four basic groups based on movement patterns to show the relative contribution of each kind of activity to your physical potential.

TABLE 1.1 Positive Approach to Physical Activity in Daily Life

Movement patterns	Primarily involving	Contribution to your physical potential
Muscular tone (strength, muscular endurance)		
Stoop-lift Pull-push Hold-reach Throw-strike	Legs-back Arms-shoulders Hands-fingers	Physical appearance Efficient movement (free and easy; energy saving) Improved motor performance
Elastic tone (flexibility)		
Bend-extend Turn-twist Stretch-reach	Trunk Legs-feet Arms-hands Head-neck	Efficient movement (free and easy; energy saving) Improved motor performance
Organic tone (stamina, cardiovascular-respiratory endurance)		
Walk-run Jump-hop Swim-skate Bike May be combined with arm movement patterns	Internal body systems (circulation, respiration, digestion, elimination)	Generalized muscular tone Weight control Increased energy reserves Improved body functions
Psychosocial tone		
All movement patterns in work play	Skilled performance or body mastery	Feeling of worth (sense of achievement; joy and pleasure of belonging) Refreshment Relaxation Release of tensions

Since our highly mechanized society has taken away the demands for daily physical activity, each individual will have to find new personal and socially acceptable reasons for changing her daily living habits to include optimal levels of regular physical activity and thus maximize her energy or physical potential. Rather obviously, each individual will need to develop the capacity to adapt to or direct the changes occurring in her mode of living if she is to channel her talents and physical activity to make the most of her physical potential. To acquire this capacity she must not only have a knowledge of physical activity and be able to perform skillfully, but also be aware of, and able to, evaluate her present status. This assessment of physical potential is basic to any action plan—either on an individual or a class basis. Although physical potential is difficult to measure in terms of energy or vitality, there are certain definitive, measurable characteristics that reflect the kind and extent of regular physical activity in your mode of living (see Table 1.2, p. 12).

The individual laboratory experiments in Chapter 2 provide an opportunity for self-assessment. Information on *how* to develop your physical potential will be found in Part II, and examples of action plans for designing personal conditioning programs will be found in Part III.

TABLE 1.2 Assessment of Physical Potential

Bodily Conditions	Measurable Descriptive Characteristics	Physical Potential
Functional status of the body	*Health-physical fitness* Strength Muscular endurance Flexibility Cardiovascular-respiratory endurance	Function
State of the body build or physique	*Body shape* Weight Fatness Body proportions Posture	Figure
Quality of body move-ment	*Motor performance* Power Agility Speed Coordination	Form

references and sources for additional reading

1. "Exercise and Fitness," *Journal of the American Medical Association*, CLXXXVIII (May 4, 1964), 433.
2. Wolffe, J.B., "Prevention of Disease Through Exercise and Health Education," in *Health and Fitness in the Modern World*. Chicago: The Athletic Institute, 1961.
3. Bauer, W.W., and V.V. Hein, *Exercise and Health*. Chicago: American Medical Association, 1958.
4. Wessel, J.A., and W.D. Van Huss, "Therapeutic Aspects of Exercise in Medicine," in *Science and Medicine of Exercise and Sports*, ed. W. R. Johnson. New York: Harper & Row, Publishers, 1960.
5. Kraus, H., and W. Raab, *Hypokinetic Diseases*. Springfield, Ill.: Charles C. Thomas, Publisher, 1961.

Brown, R., Jr., and G.S. Kenyon, eds. *Classical Studies on Physical Activity*. Englewood Cliffs, N.J.: Prentice-Hall, Inc., 1968.

Slusher, H.S., and A.S. Lockhardt, *Anthology of Contemporary Readings in Physical Education*. Dubuque, Iowa: William C. Brown Company, Publishers, 1966.

Steinhaus, A.H., *Toward an Understanding of Health and Physical Education*. Dubuque, Iowa: William C. Brown Company, Publishers, 1963.

the physical inventory:
an appraisal
of physical potential

THE PHYSICAL IMAGE

2 Every girl conceives of herself as a unique person or *self*, different from every other individual. This self-image is composed of many parts, each of which has a hierarchy of traits or behaviors, some of greater value to the person than others. The self is made up of all that goes into the individual's experiences. It is a composite of her thoughts and feelings; her view of what she is, what she has been, what she might become; and her attitude about her present status and future expectancies. The individual's personal awareness and self-evaluation of the characteristics that make up her body and her movement behavior, and her feelings toward these characteristics constitute the physical or body image.

The basic approach to self-awareness and evaluations of the body image is through self-assessment. Such evaluations are specific in nature. Each individual will be asked to appraise her physical self-image within a specific context: (*1*) her figure or body shape, (*2*) her body function or health-physical fitness, and (*3*) her movement form or motor performance. The physical image, the person's concept of self, may vary widely from objective fact and the way others see her. To help each girl acquire an accurate self-appraisal of her physical capabilities and potentialities is the primary objective of this chapter. Measures of attitudes toward body image are presented on pages 47–52. Additional measures of movement form in fundamental patterns of work and play will be found in Chapter 10, Analyzing Movements in Work and Play.

THE PHYSICAL INVENTORY

There are three major components that make up one's physical potential: figure, function, and movement form. Each of these components is composed in turn of measurable items or subcomponents that can be measured either quantitatively or qualitatively, by using a battery of evaluation tools and techniques for *self-assessment*. These methods range from crude assessment by visual appraisal to quite refined objective analyses. Each major component and its subcomponents will be presented as laboratory experiments in this chapter, according to the following organization plan:

> Section A: *figure*. Body shape to be measured in terms of build, weight, proportions, and fatness.
>
> Section B: *function*. Health-physical fitness to be measured in terms of strength, muscular endurance, flexibility, and cardiovascular-respiratory endurance.
>
> Section C: *motor performance*. Physical performance to be measured in terms of speed, coordination, power, and agility.

You should be particularly interested in this portion of the text since it provides information that will be most important in understanding yourself: in building a realistic profile of your self-image and present status. This understanding is basic to any *action plan* (either on an individual or class basis), and will help you to make decisions about the role of physical activity in your immediate life. The benefits of improved appearance, greater health-physical fitness, better social acceptance, and feelings of personal well-being, although difficult to quantify, loom larger as immediate justifications for physical activity than the more delayed expectations of reduced incidence of disease and increased longevity.

LABORATORY IN SELF-ASSESSMENT

section A: appraisal of figure

This section is divided into four parts, each with its own experiments or exercises and tables for recording your scores. In the first experiment you will appraise your *weight* and *fatness* by comparing yourself to standard levels. The second provides a subjective rating scale (Expt. 2a) and anthropomorphic measures (Expt. 2b) to help you determine your basic figure or *body type*. In the third experiment we suggest average *proportions* for you to compare to your own figure. The fourth experiment, which deals with *posture*, includes illustrations of good and bad posture and space for you to record your characteristics.

> *Experiment 1: Appraising Body Weight and Fatness.* In assessing your nutritional status, basic measurements of your height, weight, and fatness are needed. How these may be taken and interpreted as measures of obesity are described herewith. By definition *overweight* is overheaviness in contrast to *obesity*, which refers to fatness.
>
> *Height-weight tables.* Actual weight in relation to a selected standard for age, sex, and height is the most commonly used criterion of *caloric overnutri-*

tion. The individual's weight is determined and then compared with a height-weight standard. There are two kinds of standards. One is based on average weights for height, age, and sex—average findings for a population in which weight increases with age. The other kind of standard is the so-called ideal, desirable, or best weight. This is based on the concept that once growth in height ceases there is no biological need to gain weight. In general, for women an increase over the desirable weight at age 22 is a warning of potential obesity, and preventive measures should be immediately activated: diet and physical activity.

Many height-weight standards are available. In Appendix C you will find new data on average weights for women by age and height. The maximum average weight occurs between the ages of 55 and 64, with a relative gain with increasing age. These data are based on a nationwide probability sample; therefore, they are considered accurately descriptive of the height and weight patterns of women in the United States. Despite this fact, the use of this or any other table to indicate obesity (excess body fat) without making other assessments of fatness may be misleading and inaccurate. A comparison of your weight with a height-weight standard gives an estimate of the *degree* of overweight or underweight. It does not give an index of fatness per se, unless the degree of overweight or underweight is excessive. You may be overweight relative to the chosen standard on the basis of your bone structure or musculature and yet not be obese. Conversely, you may be of average weight and yet be excessively fat if you have relatively small bone or muscular components. Judgments of fatness should not be determined only by the degree of relative overweight or by the percentage of overweight alone.

Total body fatness.   To determine whether you are too fat is rather simple and does not require scientific acumen—just look in the mirror! A realistic appraisal of your nude body is a fairly reliable guide for estimating fatness. If, however, your appearance fails to give you a clear answer, there is the "pinch test." At least half the body fat is found directly underneath the skin. At many locations on the body (see Figure 2.1, p. 19)—the back of the arm, the side of the lower chest, just below the shoulder blades, at the top of the iliac crest, halfway between the umbilicus and pubis, to name a few—a fold of skin and subcutaneous fat can be lifted between the thumb and forefinger so that it is held free of underlying muscle and bony structure. If you pinch more than one inch, this is an indication of excessive body fatness. The ruler test is another simple indicator of body fatness. When one is lying flat on her back and is relaxed, the surface of the abdomen between the flare of the ribs and the pubis is normally flat or concave. A ruler placed on the abdomen parallel with the vertical axis should touch both the ribs and pubis.

A technique of a more scientific nature is available for determining body fatness. The amount of subcutaneous fat may be measured by pressuring a skinfold caliper on certain selected sites on the body (see Figure 2.1, p. 19). The skinfold measure to be obtained is the doubled thickness of the pinched, folded skin with the attached subcutaneous fat tissue. The triceps and sub-scapular skinfold measurement (below the shoulder blade) are recommended by the Committee on Nutritional Anthropometry (1). The upper arm or triceps

TABLE 2.1 Triceps Skinfold Thickness Indicating Obesity

Age	Skinfold
yr	*mm**
16	25
17	26
18-19	27
20-24	28
25-29	29
30-50	30

Adapted from C. C. Seltzer and J. Mayer, "A Simple Criterion of Obesity" (3).
*25 mm = 1 inch

seems to be the most representative single site for estimating overall fatness in individuals, regardless of fat patterning.

From nine years of age on, fat accounts, in females, for a higher percentage of total body weight than in males. Body fatness increases with age, and women of all ages above nine are, on the average, fatter than men. There are no real norms for most population groups. There is sufficient evidence, however, to calculate the minimum triceps skinfold thickness in millimeters that would indicate excessive fatness relative to age and sex. Table 2.1 presents obesity standards based on triceps skinfold thickness.

Experiment 2: Appraising Figure or Body Type. Your constitutional body or figure type is inherited. You have probably recognized different body types all your life without giving them a name. We say, "Betty is just skin and bones," "Marge is just like a butterball," or "Jane is as solid as a rock." A more scientific method for classifying body types has been developed by Dr. William Sheldon and his colleagues (4). It is based on estimating the relative predominance of inherited body characteristics; bone structure, muscularity and the amount and distribution or pattern of fat deposits. Sheldon utilizes these three principal components (fat, muscle, and bone) to designate body types as the endomorph (soft, fat type); the mesomorph (husky, muscular type); and the ectomorph (thin, frail, linear type). Sheldon derived the names for these primary components from the three basic embryonic layers: endoderm, the inner layer, which develops principally into viscera; the mesoderm, the middle layer, principally muscle and bone; the ectoderm, the outer layer, principally skin and nerves (4).

Subjective rating scale. Each person's basic body type is unique. Yet all persons have the three basic components in varying degrees. The relative amount of each can be rated on a simplified scale of from 1 to 7. The body type of a person, then, is designated by three numbers: the endomorphic component is always given first, followed by the mesomorphic and ectomorphic components (4).

Women are much more endomorphic than men; consequently, at all ages they are heavier in proportion to stature. Somatotypically speaking, there are perhaps ten times as many men who reach 5 in endomorphy as women who reach 5 in mesomorphy. Men have been found to vary from 1 to 7 on the scale, but women vary only from 1 to 6. Also, it is very rare for women to reach 1 on the scale in endomorphy. Note that you may use halves to describe body type, such as 3½, 4½, 5½, 6½. The sketches below illustrate the three extremes in body types as well as the most common type for women.

Some research workers have linked personality characteristics with body types. (5) Other investigators consider body type to be a long-range predictor of potential health problems; e.g., the obese type is associated with heart disease, diabetes, and surgical risk.

A person's basic figure type remains relatively constant throughout life. However, you can make marked changes within your body type, particularly in regard to fat—the most unstable component—and muscle. There is a range within which changes—positive or negative—can be made; the limits are unknown. Logically, you can, through knowledge and action, achieve a desirable level of health-fitness, a better physical appearance, and feeling of personal well-being regardless of your basic body type.

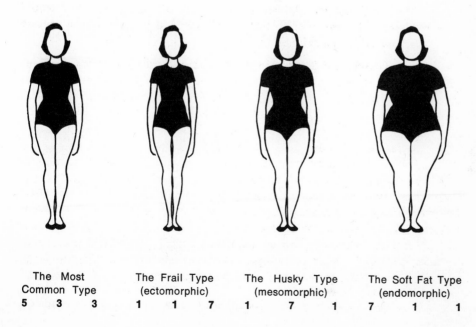

The Most Common Type			The Frail Type (ectomorphic)			The Husky Type (mesomorphic)			The Soft Fat Type (endomorphic)		
5	3	3	1	1	7	1	7	1	7	1	1

	Extremely Thin	Average	Most Obese
Endomorph	Low in fat tissue Small front to back dimensions of trunk		Large fat deposits Thick abdominal region, cheeks, hips, thighs
	1 2	3 4 5	6 7

	Extremely Underdeveloped	Average	Extremely Developed
Mesomorph	Muscles with poor tones Muscles squeezed or pushed in contracted state—arms, buttocks, calves, thighs		Muscles large and firm with good tone in biceps, buttocks, calves, thighs, abdomen
	1 2	3 4 5	6 7

	Extremely Thick and Heavy	Average	Extremely Thin and Frail
Ectomorph	Bones of ankle, knee, elbow, wrist joints		Linear skeleton with small wrist, ankle, knee, and elbow joints
	1 2	3 4 5	6 7

Objective analyses of the principal components of body type. Ectomorphy is estimated by bone measurements as follows.

1. Biacromial width: The subject should relax her shoulder muscles and hold the entire shoulder girdle in a neutral position with no evidence of rounding or excessive bracing of the shoulders. The arms of the measuring instrument are then placed so that they press firmly against the outer aspect of each acromial process of the shoulder blades (scapulae). Read this measure of shoulder width in inches.
2. Bi-iliac width: This measurement is taken between the outer aspects of the iliac crest (top of the pelvic or hip bone). Make sure there is firm pressure against the bone. Read the measure in inches.
3. Ankle girth: Take this measure with the tape around the crests of the two side bones of the ankle. Record the measure in inches.
4. Wrist girth: This measure is taken around the crests of the two bony processes at either side of the wrist. Take the measure in inches.

The endomorphic component is estimated by skinfold measurements. Use a skinfold caliper (see Figure 2.1) as follows.

1. Pinch a fold of skin and subcutaneous tissue firmly between the left thumb and forefinger; pull the full fold away from the underlying muscle, and hold during the entire time the measurement is being taken.
2. The calipers are then applied to the fold about one centimeter below the fingers.

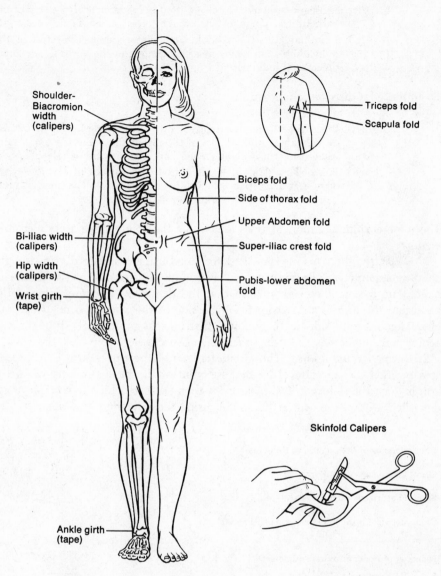

Figure 2.1 Sites for Skinfold, Caliper, and Tape Measurements

3. The handle of the calipers is released and the dial is read to the nearest one-half millimeter.

4. Take the measurement twice to obtain a stable reading.

Measurements are made at the following sites.

(*a*) Triceps. This measure is taken of the skinfold located midway along the back of the right upper arm. The arm is flexed at a 90° angle with no muscle tension, and the skinfold is lifted parallel to the long axis.

the physical inventory: an appraisal of physical potential   **19**

(b) Subscapular. This skinfold is lifted perpendicular to the skin of the back from a point just below the left shoulder blade (scapula).

(c) Suprailiac. Lift the skinfold immediately above the crest of the right ilium (hip bone) at a slight angle to the vertical axis along the normal fold line.

To appraise fat distribution measure:

(d) Biceps. With the arm relaxed, lift up the skinfold that is located directly above the midline of the biceps muscle of the upper arm. Allow the arm to hang freely while the measure is taken.

(e) Pubis. This skinfold is lifted from the surface of the lower abdomen at a position 3 inches below the navel. The muscles must be relaxed while measuring the skinfold.

The mesomorphic component is estimated by the following muscle measurements.

1. *Grip strength.* This measure is determined using a standard grip-strength hand-dynamometer. The measure we seek is of the strength of the dominant hand. The dynamometer is held so that the dial faces into the palm of the hand and the arm is kept away from the side of the body. Do not lock your elbow against your side, as this allows other muscle groups to be brought into action and invalidates the grip strength measurement.

2. *Biceps circumference.* The circumference of the upper arm is measured at a position directly above the highest point of the biceps muscle when the arm is tensed and flexed. The measure is then corrected for the amount of fat deposited around the arm at this point, using the following equations:

Circumference of the upper arm (in inches) :   _____ (a)

Skinfold at biceps (in millimeters)   :   _____ (b)

Skinfold at triceps (in millimeters)   :   _____ (c)

Circumference of the upper arm (in centimeters)
  = (a) _____ X 2.54 =   _____ (d)

Diameter of upper arm (in centimeters)
  = (d) _____ ÷ 22/7 =   _____ (e)

Bicep + Tricep Skinfolds (in centimeters)
  = (b) _____ + (c) _____ ÷ 10 =   _____ (f)

Average fat thickness
  = (f) _____ ÷ 2 =   _____ (g)

Diameter of upper arm corrected for fat thickness
  = (e) _____ - (g) _____ =   _____ (h)

Circumference of upper arm, corrected for fat thickness (in centimeters)
  = (h) _____ X 22/7 =   _____ (i)

Circumference of upper arm, corrected for fat thickness (in inches)
  = (i) _____ X 0.394 =   _____ (j)

Experiment 3: Appraising Body Proportions. Symmetry of body proportions contributes a great deal to a shapely figure. To be well-proportioned according to average measurements based on dress size, a woman's waistline should be 8 to 10 inches smaller than her bust circumference. The abdomen should measure 1½ to 2½ inches less than the bust. Hip measurements are usually 1 to 2 inches larger than the bust. Full hips measure 3 to 4 inches larger, while slim hips measure the same as the bust. Your calf should be 4 to 5 inches larger than your ankle. Your thigh should be 10 to 13 inches larger than your ankle.

Experiment 4: Appraising Posture. Posture is simply defined as the relative arrangement of the body segments; *good* posture combines a minimum expenditure of energy to maintain body balance with a minimum of joint-muscle strain. Your body alignment may also reflect your general attitude—your moods, thoughts, and feelings. Think how often we "take a firm stand," "pull ourselves together," or "straighten up!"

At present we have no device for measuring the attitudinal or expressional component of posture. We are therefore most interested in the *symmetry* of body lines and the relative *balance* of body segments. The body is composed of many movable segments: it is never considered a solid structure. The important body segments for analyzing posture are shown below.

Body Segments	Balanced	Unbalanced

1. Head and Neck

2. Trunk (back-shoulders-chest)

3. Pelvis

4. Legs-Knees

5. Feet-Ankles

In assessing posture, these segments are evaluated from the back and side views. Examine the illustrations of good and bad posture on the next page before attempting to assess yourself. Remember that your posture is more than a static vertical stance, the upright position. It might be conceived of as the point of departure for all your movements; as an expression of your *self*—your attitudes toward yourself and the world around you; and perhaps as an expres-

BALANCED POSTURES: Position of best balance for body segments for work and play with minimum expenditure of muscular energy and minimum amount of strain on joints and ligaments. Result: graceful, easy motion.

Back View
Line of gravity passes:
1. Through midhead
2. Midtrunk
3. Midwaist
4. Midankle

Side View
Line of gravity passes:
1. Tip of ear
2. Center of shoulders
3. Slightly behind center of hip
4. Slightly in front of center of knee
5. In front of ankle joint

Balanced	Unbalanced	Balanced	Unbalanced	

	hollow back	*fatigue slump*

Head erect
Body symmetrical
Shoulders level
Spine straight
Hips level
Legs straight
Feet parallel, toes point forward
Weight equally distributed on both feet and toward outer half of each foot

Head tilted
Body asymmetrical
One shoulder high
Spinal column curves sideward
One hip is high and protrudes
Kneecap turns out or in
Ankles roll inward
Feet point outward
Weight unequally distributed on feet and on inner border of foot

Head up, chin level
Chest easy
Shoulders easy
Abdomen flat
Back curves normal
Pelvis balanced
Knees easy
Body line perpendicular through weight center

Head back, chin up
Chest high
Shoulders back
Abdomen protuberant
Back curves accentuated
Pelvis tilted forward
Knees forward
Body line zigzags

Head forward, chin forward
Chest sags
Shoulders forward and in
Abdomen sags
Back inclined to the rear
Pelvis pushed forward
Knees back
Body line zigzags

sion of your total life experience—your habits of activity, nutrition, and rest, as well as your biological endowment. Record your characteristic postural lines on the forms provided. (In Chapter 15 you will find additional experiments to help you discover more about the attitudinal components of posture.)

How close is your self-image to your physical self? Do you feel fit and attractive when you're happy, small and underweight when you're depressed? The record forms below give you an opportunity to assess your figure *objectively*. Perhaps you have always considered yourself overweight, but find that losing a few pounds does not improve your appearance. You may discover that you look heavier than you are because of uneven distribution of fat or poor posture. Exercises—not dieting—will help *you* to improve your figure. Fill in each form carefully, comparing yourself to averages when appropriate. This information will give you a realistic self-image on which you can base a personal action plan.

RECORD: Height and Weight and Skinfold Measurements (expt. 1)

Date taken _____

Directions: Height is the distance from the soles of the feet to the top of the head. It should be measured without shoes. Stand erect with your heels and shoulder blades touching the wall; hold your head so that your line of sight is horizontal. Record your weight as nude body weight, is possible. (If not, make appropriate correction for weight of clothing.) See Appendix C for table of average weight for your height.

Triceps skinfold (see Figure 2.1) is measured midway at the back of the upper right arm (as determined with a steel tape, midpoint between the tip of the acromion and that of the olecranon) flexed at 90°. When skinfold is measured by a partner, manually, or with skinfold calipers, the arm should hang freely. See Table 2.1 for averages.

Weight

Age (years) _____ Height (inches) _____ Weight (lbs) _____ Average Weight (lbs) _____

Difference between your
weight and average _____ lbs $^{over}_{under}$ $\times$ 100 = _____ % over- or under-weight

Weight Continuum

:	:	:	:	
Markedly under-weight (40% below)	Underweight (20% below)	Acceptable (10% above/below average)	Overweight (20% above)	Markedly over-weight (40% above)

Body Fatness

Triceps Skinfold Continuum

:	:	:	:	
Thinness (5 mm)	Thin (11 mm)	Average (18 mm)	Plump (24 mm)	Fatness (28 mm)

Date taken ————————

Rate your body type and have several others rate it also. Review the ratings and record the best estimates. Use the simplified scale of 1 to 7 to rate each of the primary components. Circle the number for each component below, and record the best estimates for your basic figure type. The following descriptions should help you.

The Soft, Fat Type (Endomorph)

May lack muscle tone. No sharp corners. Rounded contours with well-developed fat pads of abdomen, buttocks, thighs, wrists, neck, hips, and upper arms. Predominance of weight in the center of the body. Small feet, hands, waist, and ankles. Capacious stomach, likes practically all foods. Physical performance is slow with poor agility, strength, and power in moving the body. Sometimes susceptible to strain in lower back and feet. Most women find themselves at 5. Circle your number on the scale below. Your triceps skinfold measure should aid you. (See Laboratory Experiment 1.)

Extremely thin	Average	Most obese
1 2	3 4 5	6 7

The Husky Type (Mesomorph)

Characterized by squareness, hardness, and ruggedness of body. Lacks concentration of mass in the center of the body. Chest large, waist slender, strong arms and legs, with relatively large girths of arms, calves, and thighs. Muscles well developed, firm, and hard. Relatively large-boned with short or moderate height. Likes practically all foods. Physical performance is good in many events calling for maximum strength, power, agility, and balance. Most women are 3. Circle your number on the scale below.

Least husky	Average	Most husky
1 2	3 4 5	6 7

The Frail Type (Ectomorph)

Frail body with thin, small dimensions of **trunk, chest, and hips.** Generally has short trunk, long, thin underdeveloped arms and legs. Long, narrow feet and hands. Long and slender neck and narrow chest. Muscles thin and underdeveloped. May lack muscle tone. May have marked curves in dorsal and lumbar (back and lower back) regions. Uses more energy just sprawling than the average individual uses during work. Physical performance is lacking in strength and power for maximum force. May be fast but lacks agility. Circle your number on scale below.

Least frail	Average	Most frail
1 2	3 4 5	6 7

Record best estimates of your basic figure type:

Endomorphic	Mesomorphic	Ectomorphic
( )	( )	( )

RECORD: Profile of Basic Figure or Body Type Measurements (expt. 2b)

Date of 1st trial _____   2nd trial _____

Directions: Circle your scores in red. Connect all circled test scores with a
solid red line. For retest period, circle your scores in blue. Connect all circled
scores with a solid blue line.

Measurements	Least (25th percentile)	Average (50th percentile)	Most (75th percentile)
Fat component			
Triceps skinfold *(mm.)*	11	15	18
Subscapular skinfold *(mm.)*	10	12	17
Suprailiac skinfold *(mm.)*	11	17	26
Total (3 measures)	32	44	61
Muscle component			
Grip strength/body weight ratio	0.54	0.60	0.67
Grip strength dominant hand *(lbs.)*	66.0	75.0	85.0
Biceps (corrected for fat) *(in.)*	6.2	7.1	7.8
Bone component			
Bi-iliac width *(in.)*	10.5	10.9	11.3
Biacromial width *(in.)*	12.3	13.8	15.2
Ankle girth *(in.)*	7.7	8.0	8.3
Wrist girth *(in.)*	5.5	5.7	5.9
Additional fat measures			
Biceps skinfold *(mm.)*	5.0	9.0	12.0
Pubis skinfold *(mm.)*	8.0	19.5	31.0

RECORD: Body Proportion Measurements (expt. 3)

Directions: Bust measurement is taken over a properly fitted bra. Your partner should circle the tape over the maximum curve of your bust and bring it around back under your arms. Be sure the tape measure is level across the back and under the arms. The tape should be firm but should not indent. Your partner should read the tape by crossing it and reading the measurement at the point where it crosses. Your waist measurement is taken at the smallest part of your waist. Your partner should circle the tape around from your back, pulling it snugly, but not tight. Your abdomen measurement is taken to include the curve of the abdomen at the level of the greatest roundness as seen from the side. Your partner should circle the tape around you from the side. She should read the measurement at the side. Your hip measurement is taken around the lower hips at the largest part of your buttocks. Your partner should circle the tape around you from the side. Be sure the tape is firm but does not indent. Your thigh measurement is taken around the upper part of the leg, close to the crotch, which will include the largest area of the thigh, in a standing position. Your partner will take the measurement from the front. Your calf measurement is taken at the fleshiest part of the calf, in a standing position. Your partner will take the measurement from the front. Your ankle measurement is taken just above your ankle bone, in a sitting position. In the final analysis, let the mirror be your guide!

Body Proportions for Symmetry

Body Regions	Actual Measurements	Ideal or Proportional Measurements	Difference (actual vs. ideal, + or –)
Bust			
Waist			
Abdomen			
Hips			
Thighs			
Calf			
Ankle			

Fat Distribution Pattern

check one

Proportional, evenly distributed   _____
Centrally distributed (middle portion of body)   _____
Disproportionately distributed (lower portion of body   _____

RECORD: Postural Measurement—Side and Back Views (expt. 4)

Directions: Obtain pictures of your standing posture, both side and back views, and attach them to the space provided below. Analyze your postural lines by assessing each segment of your body according to the descriptions given below. Check your characteristics in column 1. Then have a friend rate your standing posture and mark these results in column 2. (For the most accurate picture, wear a leotard in both of these experiments.) Compare the two ratings. Any item checked in the unbalanced sections indicate a need for further consideration: check with your instructor.

Side View

Your picture

	Balanced	1	2	Unbalanced	1	2		1	2
Body line	Perpendicular through weight center			Zigzags			Zigzags		
Head and chin	Level			Head back, chin up			Head forward, chin down		
Shoulders	Easy			Back			Forward		
Chest	Easy			High			Sags		
Back curves	Normal			Accentuated			Inclined to back		
Abdomen	Flat			Protruding			Sags		
Pelvis	Balanced			Tilted forward			Pushed forward		
Knees	Easy			Forward			Back		

Front View

Your picture

	Balanced	1	2	Unbalanced	1	2
Body line	Symmetrical			Asymmetrical		
Head	Erect			Tilted		
Shoulders	Level			One shoulder high		
Spine	Straight			Curves sideward		
Hips	Level			One hip high, protruding		
Legs	Straight			Knees turned in or out		
Feet	Parallel			Toes pointed in or out		
Weight	Evenly distributed, toward outside of feet			Unevenly distributed, on inner border of feet		

As a further check, compare the photograph of your side view to the illustration of body segments above. Check your head and neck, trunk (back, shoulders, and chest), pelvis, legs and knees, and your feet and ankles. If you find that you are markedly unbalanced in any of these areas, you might consult with your instructor or other professional personnel.

section B: appraisal of body function

The test exercises in this section will enable you to assess your present functional status and to see how you compare to other college women. Your health-physical fitness profile is a composite of your scores in four different areas.

1. *Total body strength*: the ability of the muscles to exert a force against a resistance or object. Exercise 1: grip strength of the dominant hand.
2. *Muscular endurance*: the ability of the muscles to sustain a continuous strenuous activity. Exercise 2: bent knee sit-up; and dorsal curl; flexed arm hang or push-ups.
3. *Flexibility or range of motion*: the degree of movement you are capable of in gross body movements. Exercise 3: trunk-hip flexion and back extension tests.
4. *Cardiovascular-respiratory endurance*: the capacity of the body, through efficiency of the heart, lungs, circulatory, and respiratory systems, to continue an activity that is above the level of normal function, and to recover rapidly when that activity is concluded. Exercise 4: two-minute step test and 600-yard run/walk.

Precise descriptions of these exercises follow. Record your scores on the Profile Record that follows exercise 4.

Exercise 1:   Tests of Strength

Grip. Stand on both feet with the entire arm away from the body. Place the dynamometer in the palm of your preferred hand with the dial toward the palm and set at zero. Grip the dynamometer as tightly as possible without touching any other object with either hand or arm. Read your score on the dial.

Grip/Weight. Divide the best score you made on the grip strength test (in pounds) by your body weight (in pounds) for an estimate of total body strength per unit weight.

Exercise 2: Tests of Muscular Endurance

Sit-Up—Abdominal Test. Lie in supine position with knees bent and feet flat on the floor. Put your hands on your shoulders with elbows pointing toward your knees; have a partner support your feet. On signal, curl trunk far enough forward to touch the point of elbows to the knees. Return to your starting position, but do not let head touch. You may stop and rest if you wish.

Score: total number of correct movements (up and down) in 30 seconds, or total number of times you can perform the test correctly. Maximum numbers is 50.

Dorsal Curls. Lie face down on the floor with your hands behind your neck. Your partner sits across your thighs and presses down on your buttocks to prevent movement. Raise your head and shoulders from the floor by arching your upper back as far as possible and then lower to the floor. Repeat as often as possible in 30 seconds.

Score: total number of correct movements (up and down) in 30 seconds.

Push-Ups—Arms and Anterior Shoulder. Assume a prone position with knees bent at a right angle and hands on floor under shoulders, fingers pointed straight ahead. Push up to a position where arms are straight, body straight from head to knees, head up, weight supported on hands and knees. Lower body until chest touches floor. Do not allow hips to bend or abdomen to sag. Repeat promptly and continue.

Score: total number of correct upward movements. Maximum number is 50.

Flexed Arm Hangs. Adjust a chinning bar so that its height above the floor is equal to your standing height. Use an overhand grasp of the bar (the backs of your hands face you, your fingers over the top of the bar). You are assisted to a position where your chin is above the bar, arms fully bent, and chest close to the bar. One trial is allowed. The tester calls out the seconds aloud.

Score: the total period of time that you can maintain the position. Time is recorded to the nearest second; the clock stops when chin touches the bar or head is tilted back.

Trunk-Hip Flexion. Stand on a chair with toes even with the front edge and against the sides of a scale. With the knees straight let your arms and trunk relax and hang forward, fingers in front of the scale. Bob downward three or four times. Each time reach equally with the fingers of both hands down the scale.

Score: the lowest point you reach in a series of bobbings. Your partner will keep her eyes down on a level with your reach and read your score. (A variation of this test is simple reaching with your finger tips toward the floor, keeping your knees straight. You pass if you touch the floor.)

Back Extension. Lie face down on the floor clasping your hands together above your hips. Raise your head and shoulders from the floor by arching your upper back and pulling with your arms. You must keep the lower corner of your ribs on the floor.

Score: The vertical distance from the top of your sternum (suprasternal notch) to the floor. The measurement is taken by your partner placing one end of a string on the notch before you start to lift. The string is pulled taut and straight to the floor while you are at the top of your extension. Your partner measures the string from finger tip to finger tip on a ruler.

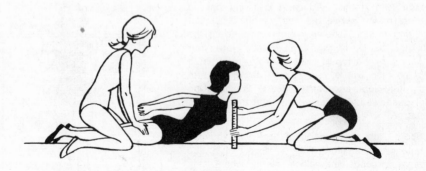

Two Minute Step. Sit quietly for 5 minutes and then check your pulse for 30 seconds. Then stand and face a 17-inch high bench. The proper stepping sequence is: step up with the right foot, then up with the left foot; step down with the right foot, down with the left foot. Step up and down in this manner thirty times a minute for 2 minutes. At the end of this period stop, sit down and relax.

Score: 60 seconds after you stop stepping begin to record your pulse (below the bone at the bend of the jaw is best). Count the number of beats for 30 seconds. The total number of pulse beats in 30 seconds is your score. The better your physical condition, the faster your body will recover from exercise. The lower your pulse rate during this period after exercise, the greater your cardiovascular-respiratory endurance.

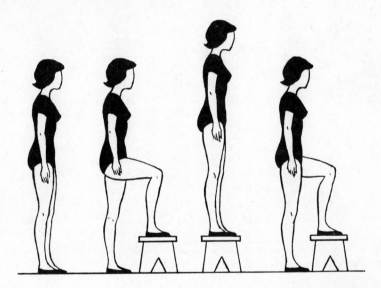

600 Yard Run-Walk. Take a position for a standing start behind the take-off line. The starter will give the following commands: "Get on your mark. Get set! Go!!!" If possible, you should run the full distance; however you may intersperse walking with running.

Score: The starter counts the seconds elapsed aloud. The count heard immediately after you cross the finish line is recorded. One trial is given.

Date of 1st trial _____   2nd trial _____

Directions: Circle your scores in red and connect these rates with a solid red line. After your second trial, circle your retest scores in blue and, again, connect these values with a solid line.

Find how you compare to other college women by looking for your percentile score in column 1. Interpret these as follows: if you rank in the 85th percentile for a specific test, 15 per cent of the college women in your group ranked higher than you, 85 per cent ranked lower. In general, the 50th percentile and below are considered minimal functional status. Obviously it is difficult to determine just how much is optimal!

Percentile Rank	Muscular Strength		Muscular Endurance				Flexibility		Cardiovascular-Respiratory Endurance	
	grip strength	grip/ weight	sit-ups	dorsal curls	push-ups	flexed arm hang	trunk-hip flexion	back extension	step-test*	walk-run
	lbs.		*30 sec.*	*30 sec.*	*total*	*sec.*	*in.*	*in.*		*min./sec.*
100	110	0.87	26	46	40	80	11.0	21.0	41	1:52
95	98	0.79	23	45	36	45	6.0	17.0	47	2:09
90	94	0.74		44	30	36	4.0	16.0	54	2:20
85	91	0.71	21	43	25	28	3.2		55	2:25
80	88	0.69	20	42	22	24	2.7	15.0	57	2:27
75	85	0.67		41	20	20	2.2			2:33
70	83	0.65	19	40	18	18	2.0	14.0	60	2:35
65	81	0.64		39	17	16	1.8			2:40
60	79	0.63	18	38	16	14	1.5		62	2:42
55	77	0.61		36	14	12	1.4			2:45
50	75	0.60		35	12	11		13.0	63	2:47
45	73	0.59	17	34	11	10	1.3		64	2:53
40	71	0.58		33	10	9	1.0	12.0	65	2:55
35	69	0.56		32	9	8	0.5			2:59
30	68	0.55	16	31	8	7	0.2		68	3:05
25	66	0.54	15	30	7	6	0.0	11.0	69	3:09
20	64	0.52	14	29	6	5	-0.5		70	3:15
15	62	0.50	13	28	5	4	-1.7	10.0	72	3:26
10	60	0.49	12	27	4	2	-2.2	9.0	80	3:40
5	58	0.46	9	26	2	0	-3.5	8.0	88	3:56
0	49	0.37	0	25	0	0	-10.0	6.0	< 2 min.	5:02

*Thirty-second pulse count starting one minute after the exercise ceases

section C: appraisal of motor performance

In this section we present test exercises that will enable you to assess your motor performance and to see how you compare to other college women. Your motor performance profile will be a composite of your scores in four different events.

1. *Power*: Speed in performing a unit of work; rapid muscular contraction to produce explosive movement. Exercise 1: standing broad jump and vertical jump.
2. *Agility*: rapidity and ease in changing direction while moving quickly. Exercise 2: shuttle race.
3. *Speed*: maximal achieved over a short, standard distance. Exercise 3: 50-yard dash.
4. *Coordination*: Integration of visual judgment with a series of muscular movements to perform a task.

Record your scores in the exercises that follow on the Profile Record at the end of this section.

Exercise 1:   Tests of Power

Standing Broad Jump.   Stand on the take-off board with toes curled over the edge. Take off from both feet at the same time: jump as far forward as you can.

Score: the distance from the edge of the take-off board to the nearest heel or part of your body touching the ground. The best of three trials is counted. You may swing your arms and flex your knees in preliminary movements if you desire.

Vertical Jump.   Stand with your side to the wall on which the measurement board is placed, feet together. Rub a little chalk on the fingers of the hand closest to the wall and reach up as high as possible without lifting your heels; leave a mark from your fingers on the board. Stand back and see how far you were able to reach. Then jump as high as you can from a standing start and leave a mark on the measurement board by touching it when you have reached your maximal height from the floor.

Score: the distance in inches between your standing score (reaching height) and your jump score. The best of three trials is counted. You may use whichever hand you prefer so long as it is the closest to the wall when you reach and jump. You may also crouch and bend your knees before you jump.

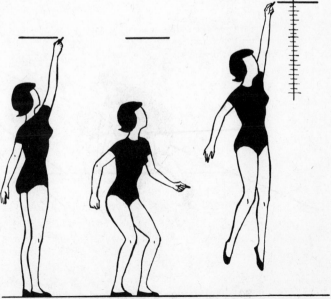

Shuttle Race. Stand behind the starting line ready to go. On signal run to the forward line, pick up one block, bring it back and put it down behind the starting line. Run back and get the second block and run as fast as you can with the block back over the starting line.

Score: time in seconds for you to complete the shuttle race. Better of two trials.

30 feet

Exercise 3: Test of Speed

50 Yard Dash. Assume a starting position behind the line. On signal run as fast as you can to the finish line 50 yards away.

Score: time in seconds for you to run the 50 yards. Better of two trials.

50 yards

Basketball Throw. Stand anywhere you like behind the throwing line (you must not step on or cross this line when throwing). You may throw three times in any way you wish.

Score: the distance from the throwing line to the spot where the ball touches the floor. Your longest throw is the one that counts. (The same test may be performed with a softball.)

Wall Throw. Stand behind the throwing line facing the wall. Throw a basketball against the wall, catch it, repeat again as quickly as possible. You must stay behind the line all of the time. You can throw the ball any way you like.

Score: the number of times you hit the wall in 15 seconds.

PROFILE RECORD: Motor Performance (exercises 1-4)

Directions: Circle your scores in red. Connect all circled scores with a solid red line. For the retest, circle your scores in blue. Connect all circled scores with a solid blue line. (See the Profile Record in the previous section for an explanation of the percentile column.)

| Percentile Rank | Power | | Agility | Speed | Coordination | |
	Standing Broad Jump	Vertical Jump	Shuttle Race	50-Yard Dash	Softball Throw	Basketball Throw
			min./sec.	*min./sec.*	*ft.*	*ft.*
100	7'10"	21"	7.5	5.7	184	73
95	6'6"	19"	10.2	7.3	115	59
90	6'3"	18"	10.5	7.6	103	53
85	6'1"	17"	10.7	7.7	96	50
80	5'11"	16"	10.9	7.8	90	47
75	5'10"	15"	11.0	7.9	86	46
70	5'8"	14"	11.1	8.0	82	44
65	5'7"	13"	11.2	8.1	79	43
60	5'6"	12"	11.3	8.2	76	42
55	5'5"	11"	11.5	8.3	73	41
50	5'4"	11"	11.6	8.4	70	40
45	5'3"	10"	11.7	8.6	67	39
40	5'2"	9"	11.9	8.7	65	38
35	5'0"	8"	12.0	8.8	62	37
30	4'11"	7"	12.1	9.0	59	36
25	4'10"	6"	12.2	9.1	57	34
20	4'8"	5"	12.4	9.2	54	32
15	4'7"	4"	12.6	9.4	51	30
10	4'5"	3"	12.9	9.7	47	28
5	4'1"	2"	13.4	10.1	42	25
0	2'3"	2"	17.3	13.7	5	21

TABLE 2.2   Equipment Needed for Various Physical Appraisals

Measures	Equipment Needed
Anthropomorphic Measures	
Height/weight/fatness	Scales, wall rule, skinfold calipers
Body type	Tape measure, skinfold calipers
Body proportions	Tape measure
Posture	Camera for posture photos
Health-Physical Fitness Measures	
Strength	
grip strength	Dynamometer
Muscular endurance	
sit-ups	Stopwatch
dorsal curls	Stopwatch
push-ups	
flexed arm hang	Chinning bar, stopwatch
Flexibility	
back extension	Yard rule
trunk-hip flexion	Bench with yard rule set vertically on front
Cardiovascular-respiratory endurance	
two-minute step test	Step or platform 16-inches high, stopwatch
600-yard run/walk	Stopwatch and measured track
Motor Performance	
Power	
standing broad jump	7 ½ foot mat marked off at 2-inch intervals, solid takeoff board, and yard rule
vertical jump	Scale marked off in 1-inch intervals and attached to wall
Agility	
shuttle race	Space 30 feet long. Two blocks
Speed	
50-yard dash	Measured track and stopwatch
Coordination	
basketball throw	Space 80 feet by 20 feet, with parallel lines every 5 feet in front of throwing line; basketball
softball throw	Space 50 yards long, softball, and steel measuring tape

references and sources for additional reading

1. Committee on Nutritional Anthropometry, Food and Nutrition Board, National Research Council, "Recommendations Concerning Body Measurements for The Characterization of Nutritional Status," in *Body Measurements for Human Nutrition*, ed. J. Brozek. Detroit: Wayne University Press, 1956, p. 10.

2. National Center for Health Statistics, *Weight by Height and Age of Adults* in *United States, 1960–62. Vital Health Statistics*. PHS Publication No. 100—Series 11, No. 14, May 1966. Washington, D.C.: Government Printing Office, 1966.

3. Seltzer, C. C., and J. Mayer, "A Simple Criterion of Obesity," *Postgraduate Medicine*, Vol. 38, No. 2 (1965), A 101–7.

4. Sheldon, W. H., S. S. Stevens, and W. B. Tucker, *The Varieties of Human Physique*. New York: Harper & Row, Publishers, 1940.

5. Parnell, R. W., *Behavior and Physique*. London: Edward Arnold (Publishers) Ltd., 1958.
6. Scott, M. G., and E. French, *Measurement and Evaluation in Physical Education*. Dubuque, Iowa: William C. Brown Company, Publishers, 1959.

sources for physical appraisals

American Association for Health, Physical Education and Recreation, *Youth Fitness Test Manual*. Washington, D.C.: American Association for Health, Physical Education and Recreation, 1965.

Mathews, D. K., *Measurement in Physical Education*, (3rd ed.). Philadelphia: W. B. Saunders Co., 1968.

psycho-social factors
influencing participation
and performance levels

A PROPOSITION

3 No matter what psychological and sociological factors influence participation and performance in physical activities, it must be realized that each individual can achieve greater success in certain physical activities than in others. Such capabilities depend upon your body build, which is largely determined by hereditary endowment, and also on the present status of your body shape and function. Body build is also likely to influence your participation and performance levels, as well as your choice of activities. Indeed, the choice of a physical activity that is not suited to your present body build and physical condition may lead to frustration and a heightened sensitivity to your lack of success. Passivity and complete withdrawal from all physical activity, as well as feelings of isolation and rejection by one's peers, may result from such an experience. Body build as a factor in selecting physical activities will be discussed in greater detail in Chapter 16.

If your participation and performance levels in physical activity were based purely on your individual potentialities, then activity selection would be a simple matter. However, this is not the case. Many psychological and sociological factors mediate between the independent factor of basic physical capacity, and actual participation and performance. These factors all affect one's level of aspiration, participation, and achievement. Here, *aspiration level* is defined as the individual's perception of her potential in terms of choice of physical activities and of her capacity for quality performance in such activities. Aspiration level is subject to redefinition at any time in either an upward or downward direction. It is influenced by many psycho-social factors that act as intervening variables between basic physical capacity and actual participation and performance.

| Basic Physical Capacity | → | Aspiration Level as Mediated by Psycho-Social Factors | → | Participation and Performance Levels |

These factors act upon a person's perception of her abilities and capacities and may operate favorably or unfavorably toward participation and performance levels in physical activity. The factors that form the basis of the following discussion are depicted in Table 3.1.

TABLE 3.1 Factors that Influence Participation and Performance Levels in Physical Activity

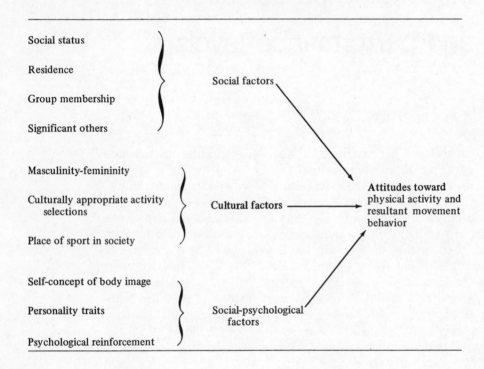

Each of these factors influences not only participation and performance patterns of women but also society's ideological position toward women in physical activity.

PSYCHOLOGICAL FACTORS

body image

The body image component of the self-concept is the mental image an individual has of her body in terms of physical appearance, bodily functions, motor performance, and capacity for participation in different physical activities.

Body image is learned, and can best be visualized as the sum total of all the assessments that an individual makes of herself and her body in relation to her perceptions of the opinions that other people, particularly her friends, have of her. This image functions as a frame of reference and influences the thoughts and feelings of what a girl is, what she has been, what she might become, and her present assessments of herself and her capacities for future change. That is, each person has a set of expectancies and self-evaluations that can influence physical traits and movement behavior. As the body image is an internalization of many factors—her own assessments, her perceptions of how others judge her physical appearance and capabilities, and knowledge of the verbalized judgments of people significant to her (significant others)—it is possible for a certain amount of discrepancy to be manifest (1).

In this sense, it is possible for an individual to have an unrealistic body image. She may have a negative attitude toward her appearance and capabilities; she sees faults or limitations where none exist. Conversely, she may have an excessively positive attitude toward her body, which is out of step with her actual physical potential.

Considering body image in relation to the possibilities of kinds of participation and performance levels, as well as achievement in different physical activities, it is obvious that the perception of her body is an important determinant of a girl's movement patterns. A girl with a negative perception of her body image would be unlikely to participate in any physical activity, even though her body capabilities would enable her to perform well.

What is important then is what an individual thinks about her own body, and, for this reason, one must be able to determine the association between perceived and ideal body images. Rating scales for this are included at the end of this chapter. By comparing your median scores, you can determine the magnitude of the discrepancy that exists between your ideal and actual body image.

The body image undergoes constant redefinition. The change, whether positive or negative, comes from your personal awareness and evaluations, and from your motivations and expectations. Societal attitudes may facilitate change in either direction. Each individual is growing up within a particular cultural milieu and needs to continually integrate all her reactions and responses to the varied situations and individuals in her life. As she participates in physical activity, she is constantly evaluating her experiences against a framework of societal expectations and the attitudes others have toward her movement behavior. She develops a set of values and expectations associated with society's image of the female and what physical activities and levels of performance are positively supported within the limitations of that role. Various types of learning experiences, success and failure, reward and punishment, motives and drives, expectations and conflicts, all act upon the individual to effect what she participates in and to modify her levels of performance and achievement (1).

In summary then, if one conceives body image as a system of personal actions and tendencies to such, then body image will be a facilitating or limiting factor in the individual's liking for, participation in, and performance in physical activity. There are many types of activities that society does not consider "feminine." In this respect, body image is judged against a set of social expectations, proscriptions, and participation characteristics specific to a given culture. The major determinant of sporting participation patterns is the sex-role standard by which a girl modifies her behavior in keeping with socially defined, sex-appropriate participation norms. She wishes her behavior, participation, and appearance to be consistent with the standard that represents the "ideal social image," or her perception of it.

personality factors

Personality may be defined in many ways. In general, it is regarded as being the individual's personalized and characteristic way of responding and behaving toward stimuli. These responses are a result of past experience and learning, although some geneticists believe that much of an individual's personality is passed on by heredity, pointing to differences in behavior at birth that carry over to later life. Environmental factors, however, must be taken into account as modifiers of such characteristics. Each individual, then, is born with a definite set of potentialities that may be developed or retarded by environmental and social conditions.

Individuals differ in temperament, motivation, sociability, and adjustment. These characteristics operate to enhance or retard an individual's physical activity potential. The differences between introverts and extroverts, leaders and followers, the sociable and unsociable, and those with high and low emotional stability in terms of physical activity participation patterns are well substantiated (2, 3).

Cavanaugh (4) found that the emotionally well-adjusted tend to participate in more recreational activities. Beck (5) found that general motor ability, social adjustment, and acceptance were related. Girls with a high degree of motor ability were higher scorers on dominance, self-reliance, sociability, and communality, while the low motor ability group was characterized as retiring and unresponsive, but cooperative (6). Extroverted, self-confident, socially and emotionally adjusted students with high political interests, leadership potential, and ability to like people were often found to be athletically inclined. Introverted, theoretically and aesthetically inclined girls who were less well adjusted socially, but more capable of accepting the consequences of their actions, and more liberal, were found to be disinclined toward competitive athletics (2, 7).

It would seem that the sports participant may choose her competitive sport on the basis of her personality. However, these findings are subject to disagreement: some studies have not indicated any difference between athletically inclined and disinclined girls. There have been few personality differences determined that can differentiate between the normally active and the sedentary; although it would be expected that an individual's personality traits could mediate against participation in physical activity and toward selection of certain types of activities and sports.

The gregarious, aggressive, and achievement-oriented girl may choose a rigorous team sport, in which her aggressiveness can be expressed in socially accepted behavior; this would help her be more adjusted in other aspects of her life. The introspective girl might gravitate to sports requiring repetitious, solitary training for the mastery of basic skills in which she competes with herself and "the elements," rather than others.

It would surely be an error to believe that certain types of sport lead to the development of distinct personality traits among the performers. No such cause-and-effect relationship has been substantiated. Most of the elements of personality are well formed by the age of seventeen, and by this time the self-image is reasonably stable. A girl's perception of her capabilities in physical activity has been internalized to a great extent by this age, but, as discussed above, it is still subject to change. She would probably assess new sports and activities on the basis of how well she might like them and how well she thought she could perform. These decisions are largely made on the basis of how well the activity suits personal characteristics, but here too, social factors—the desire to make new friends, acquire social skills, or take up a popular new sport—operate in the decision-making process.

psychological reinforcement

If an individual takes up a new activity and finds she performs well in it, very likely she will continue with that activity. If she knows that her performance is good and she receives pleasure and the plaudits of her friends and significant others, then such recognition is called *reinforcement*. Reinforcement may be positive and favorable to the individual or negative and unfavorable. The most powerful type of positive reinforcement is success. Success in an activity not highly regarded by her group may stimulate a girl to develop an entirely new group whose members appreciate her performance, and she may choose not to publicize her activities in that sphere to the members of the original group.

Just as success is a powerful reinforcer, failure is a strong negative stimulus against participation, unless the activity is so highly regarded by the group that a girl decides to persevere until she has mastered the task. Here, the significance of the activity itself is the strong motivating factor.

SOCIOLOGICAL FACTORS

Women have made slow but steady progress in gaining full acceptance and equality in physical activities over the years. However, many myths, legends, biases, and beliefs that are still held by many, women included, act to prevent or discourage participation in various specific types of sporting and recreational activities.

The values held by our society regarding female participation are converted into action patterns through the effects of peer and societal pressure, perceived social roles, and historical factors.

Cultural sex-typing defines acceptable male and female behavior, the activities that are proper for people from various social strata, and those appropriate for people of different ages. In this century women have had much success in redefining socially accepted ideas of "proper" feminine behavior. It started out as the acceptance of women's participation in a few activities. However, the quality of their play was restricted by the bulky clothing they wore. Gradually, women were able to wear clothes appropriate to their activities and games, yet it wasn't until 1941 that they could wear shorts at Wimbledon and Forest Hills in championship tennis matches.

In America the first game played by mixed groups was croquet, which became popular before the Civil War. Archery and lawn tennis were next, being accepted in the 1870's, while cycling came in vogue about 1890. Women did not compete in the first modern Olympic Games in 1896, but they did participate in equestrian events in 1900. Figure skating for men and women took place in the 1908 Olympics, and swimming and diving were introduced in 1912. Track and field events were closed to female competitors until 1928. Additional discussion of women in competition is presented in Chapter 4.

the peer group

A peer group is made up of individuals of the same age and usually, but not necessarily, of the same sex. This group defines the activities, attitudes, values, and social behavior of the group through consensus or through copying the beliefs of opinion leaders. If behavior approved for group members inclines toward specific choices of physical activity, then virtually all members of the group will have positive feelings toward physical activity. If activity is poorly regarded, then those who participate in it will be considered deviants from accepted group practices. The penalty for deviation from peer group attitudes may not be severe, or it may result in complete exclusion from the group.

The peer group plays an important part in deciding acceptable types of behavior for those in the 9 to 16 year age group (with some variation before and beyond these years). After this stage, membership and occupation groups become more important, but peer groups still define acceptable and unacceptable behavior for their members to some degree throughout life.

Peer groups also operate at the university level. As this environment places large numbers of people of approximately the same age in a similar situation, students tend to group together along lines of mutual interest, association, or housing. Peer groups develop that are as strong as those in high school in approving certain types of behavior, course selections, activity, and amount of skill to be attained.

The tremendous interest in football on college campuses indicates a strong positive evaluation of the sport. For freshmen this results partly from peer group pressure, but also because it is traditionally defined as proper for students to like football. Spectating at basketball, baseball, and soccer matches is not usually given the same high evaluation and positive identification, and so there is less participation.

The same situation prevails with participation in intramural and recreational sports. The peer group plays a tremendous role in deciding upon the acceptability of certain activities for members of the group. Fortunately, the group sanction for certain sports is not usually severe; it may be expressed as mild amusement or the belief that each individual has the right to select her own way within certain limits.

social roles

Much of the difficulty women have had in achieving equality of opportunity has been due to the lack of a major say in deciding upon the definitions of femininity and masculinity. Traditionally, men have decided what is feminine, in terms of figure, movement patterns, characteristics, participation patterns, and appropriate performance levels. Women have been attempting to have a greater voice in developing such definitions and have succeeded to a large extent over the last twenty years.

The social role of women incorporates many variables, such as age, body build, appearance, and achievements. It has, of course, been traditional for women to get married and have children, thereby validating one important aspect of their identity. Over the last decade or so, however, women have found that it is increasingly possible to develop and validate their identities in other areas of life and still be regarded as indisputably female. They are becoming more successful in the business world, rising to high positions in government, and breaking records in sports, without being regarded as any less feminine.

It is true that many sports and activities are considered unfeminine by women as well as men. Women who may be attracted to such sports are not given great esteem by other women. Perhaps this is because they are capitalizing on traits of their body structure and personal characteristics (competitive drive, aggression, dominance, etc.) that society regards as masculine.

It is also strange that, although physical activity and sport are widely accepted in the United States, they are not considered acceptable for older people. Women are as much in need of exercise in later years as men, especially after menopause when hormonal protection from some aspects of coronary heart disease diminishes. It is important that some form of attitude change program be instituted and that women be encouraged to redefine their social role to include the necessity for exercise at older age levels.

The peak period for acceptance of physical activity in women is from about ages twelve to fifteen. After this participation in and enjoyment of strenuous physical activity appears to diminish and stabilize at a lower level. However, active women who participate skillfully in a variety of sports without losing their elegance or femininity are quite common in the upper levels of society. What a pity that more women don't copy their activity as they do their fashions!

In the United States new conceptions of the role of women in society have usually originated in the upper levels of society and filtered down. Sports that were previously the exclusive province of men have been taken up by wealthy women and have since become widespread. The introduction of croquet, tennis, and billiards as suitable games for women to play shows this pattern. Of course, when new sports and games are introduced, their costs are usually high. But, as the sport becomes accepted, the unit cost of facilities and equipment drops until almost anyone may compete. Golf and skiing are examples of such trends.

Residence is also an important factor: some people cannot participate in certain sports because appropriate facilities are not available in their area. People in rural areas usually do not have the same scope of selection of sporting and recreational pursuits (either commercially or in schools) as those in urban areas, particularly in the suburbs. People living in inner city areas are also poorly provided with recreational facilities and a wide choice of school sports programs.

SOME CONCLUDING REMARKS

Your selection of recreational activities and your attitudes toward physical activity are usually developed through the integration and interaction of a number of vastly different factors. Many of these are latent and do not seem to be obvious reasons in accounting for your behavior. Their effect is strong nonetheless. You should be aware of these positive and negative factors, and decide what is best for your emotional, social, and physical development. The health and fitness benefits of physical exercise are well established and you should certainly not allow social pressures to keep you from participating and striving to improve your performance in activities you enjoy and in which you can excel. Perhaps of equal importance is your personal involvement in community, neighborhood, and school programs—part of each person's social responsibility, not only for self, but for family and country as well.

LABORATORY: YOUR ATTITUDES

Understanding the complex psychological and social influences that figure in your choice of physical activities and your subsequent level of achievement will only help you to cope with these pressures if you are aware of *your own* feelings. The experiments that follow are tools for measuring your attitudes toward yourself and towards physical activity in general.

In Experiments 1 and 2 you record your ideal and actual body image. Experiment 3 is a comparison of these scores to help you locate the areas of greatest discrepancy. Ask yourself whether it is possible to improve your situation. Are you being fair in your evaluation of yourself? Discuss discrepancies with friends and instructors. In the 4th experiment you will measure your feelings toward physical activity itself. Can you see what social pressures influence your attitude?

Definitions. Ideal Body Image: This is your assessment of your body *as you would like it to be.* Body image and the discrepancy or similarity between the ideal and actual perception an individual has of her body are closely related to the overall concept of self. Actual Body Image: This is your assessment of your body and its potentialities *as you believe them to be at this time.*

Appraisal of Attitudes

Directions for Completing the Semantic Differential Scales. These scales are a refinement of those developed by Kenyon in connection with the ideal and actual body image (8). Each is made up of a number of word pairs. These pairs are opposites and one is placed at each end of a continuum. The concept you are to evaluate is in the box at the top of the scale.

If you feel that the word at one end of the continuum is very closely related to the concept at the top of the scale, circle the number closest to that word, i.e., 1 or 7, on the line beside the word.

If you feel that the concept lies midway between the two words or if you feel that the words do not relate to the concept at all, then circle the middle number, i.e., 4.

If you feel that the concept is slightly related to one word, then circle one of the numbers between the midpoint and the extreme position; i.e., circle either 2, 3, 5, or 6, depending on which word is related to the concept and how strong you feel the relationship is.

Judge each relationship separately in turn and make a quick decision, as the first impression is the important one here.

Link all the circled numbers with straight lines.

Scoring. The numbers you have circled are not additive in the statistical sense, so in order to get an indication of the strength of your body image you have to determine your median score. The *median* is the score above and below which 50% of your responses lie; it is the midpoint of your responses, not the average.

In each case, scores should be arranged in increasing order of magnitude, and the response *at* the midpoint (total number of word sets, plus one, divided by two: n + 1 / 2, is your score. If two or more numbers are tied at this position, the median lies at the fraction midway between the tied numbers.

The lower your median score, the more positive is your attitude toward the concept.

Count the number of times you have circled each particular number, and place the total in the appropriate box under "Response."

Locate the position that the median should occupy (where there are 15 responses, the median is the midpoint, i.e., the 8th score counting cumulatively from 1).

If, as is most likely, the median is one of several numbers that are numerically the same, i.e., occupy the same Frequency of Response box, then the median will be fractionally greater than the number of the response. For an example, if the scores are:

Frequency of Response	1	2	3	4	5	6	7	Median Score = 3.88
	2	1	3	4	2	3	0	

the median is the 8th number from the 1, but this number is a 4, and there are four 4's. The responses to 4 occupy the numerical space from 3.5 to 4.5, with 3.5 being the lower limit of the interval. The following formula is then used to determine the median.

$$Mdn = I + \left(\frac{\frac{N}{2} - F}{f_m}\right) i$$

Where:

I = the lower limit of the interval which contains the median (in this example it is 3.5)

$\frac{N}{2}$ = the number of scores divided by 2 (in this example it is 7.5).

F = the number of scores below the lower limit of the interval that contains the median (in the example it is 6).

f_m = the number of scores contained within the interval which includes the median (in this example it is 4).

i = the length of the class interval (here it is 1.0).

Then:

$$Mdn = 3.5 + \frac{(7.5 - 6)}{4} 1$$

$$= 3.88$$

Profile. A special profile form is provided to allow you to record your scores and to determine the relationship between your ideal and actual body image. *Note* that all the lines on this profile commence with 1 on the left of the chart, whereas the direction of the numbers on the continua was varied.

Experiment 1: Ideal Body Image

> **My Body:** *as I would like it to be*

No.		Scale	
1.	Coordinated	1 : 2 : 3 : 4 : 5 : 6 : 7	Uncoordinated
2.	Rigid	7 : 6 : 5 : 4 : 3 : 2 : 1	Flexible
3.	Weak	7 : 6 : 5 : 4 : 3 : 2 : 1	Strong
4.	Graceful	1 : 2 : 3 : 4 : 5 : 6 : 7	Awkward
5.	Flabby	7 : 6 : 5 : 4 : 3 : 2 : 1	Shapely
6.	Relaxed	1 : 2 : 3 : 4 : 5 : 6 : 7	Tense
7.	Beautiful	1 : 2 : 3 : 4 : 5 : 6 : 7	Ugly
8.	Tall	1 : 2 : 3 : 4 : 5 : 6 : 7	Short
9.	Light	1 : 2 : 3 : 4 : 5 : 6 : 7	Heavy
10.	Large	7 : 6 : 5 : 4 : 3 : 2 : 1	Small
11.	Masculine	7 : 6 : 5 : 4 : 3 : 2 : 1	Feminine
12.	Hard	7 : 6 : 5 : 4 : 3 : 2 : 1	Soft
13.	Attractive	1 : 2 : 3 : 4 : 5 : 6 : 7	Unattractive
14.	Rugged	7 : 6 : 5 : 4 : 3 : 2 : 1	Delicate
15.	Active	1 : 2 : 3 : 4 : 5 : 6 : 7	Sedentary

Response

Frequency of Response (N = 15)	1	2	3	4	5	6	7	Median Score = _____

Experiment 2:   Actual Body Image

My Body: as it is now

#	Left	Scale	Right
1.	Coordinated	1 : 2 : 3 : 4 : 5 : 6 : 7	Uncoordinated
2.	Rigid	7 : 6 : 5 : 4 : 3 : 2 : 1	Flexible
3.	Weak	7 : 6 : 5 : 4 : 3 : 2 : 1	Strong
4.	Graceful	1 : 2 : 3 : 4 : 5 : 6 : 7	Awkward
5.	Flabby	7 : 6 : 5 : 4 : 3 : 2 : 1	Shapely
6.	Relaxed	1 : 2 : 3 : 4 : 5 : 6 : 7	Tense
7.	Beautiful	1 : 2 : 3 : 4 : 5 : 6 : 7	Ugly
8.	Tall	1 : 2 : 3 : 4 : 5 : 6 : 7	Short
9.	Light	1 : 2 : 3 : 4 : 5 : 6 : 7	Heavy
10.	Large	7 : 6 : 5 : 4 : 3 : 2 : 1	Small
11.	Masculine	7 : 6 : 5 : 4 : 3 : 2 : 1	Feminine
12.	Hard	7 : 6 : 5 : 4 : 3 : 2 : 1	Soft
13.	Attractive	1 : 2 : 3 : 4 : 5 : 6 : 7	Unattractive
14.	Rugged	7 : 6 : 5 : 4 : 3 : 2 : 1	Delicate
15.	Active	1 : 2 : 3 : 4 : 5 : 6 : 7	Sedentary

Response

Frequency of Response (N = 15)	1	2	3	4	5	6	7	Median Score = _____

Experiment 3: Body Image Profile

Directions: Circle the numbers you chose for your ideal body images and link these scores in one color, then do the same with your scores for actual body image in another color. This is your attitude profile.

Word Group Number	Scores
1	1 : 2 : 3 : 4 : 5 : 6 : 7
2	1 : 2 : 3 : 4 : 5 : 6 : 7
3	1 : 2 : 3 : 4 : 5 : 6 : 7
4	1 : 2 : 3 : 4 : 5 : 6 : 7
5	1 : 2 : 3 : 4 : 5 : 6 : 7
6	1 : 2 : 3 : 4 : 5 : 6 : 7
7	1 : 2 : 3 : 4 : 5 : 6 : 7
8	1 : 2 : 3 : 4 : 5 : 6 : 7
9	1 : 2 : 3 : 4 : 5 : 6 : 7
10	1 : 2 : 3 : 4 : 5 : 6 : 7
11	1 : 2 : 3 : 4 : 5 : 6 : 7
12	1 : 2 : 3 : 4 : 5 : 6 : 7
13	1 : 2 : 3 : 4 : 5 : 6 : 7
14	1 : 2 : 3 : 4 : 5 : 6 : 7
15	1 : 2 : 3 : 4 : 5 : 6 : 7

Locate on this profile those areas where the greatest discrepancies are perceived. Ask yourself whether it is possible to improve the situation as it is now. Also, are you being fair in your evaluation of yourself? Discuss discrepancies with your friends and instructor.

Experiment 4: Attitudes Toward Physical Activity

1. Good   1 : 2 : 3 : 4 : 5 : 6 : 7   Bad

2. Ugly   7 : 6 : 5 : 4 : 3 : 2 : 1   Beautiful

3. Muscle-bound   7 : 6 : 5 : 4 : 3 : 2 : 1   Slimming

4. Coordinated   1 : 2 : 3 : 4 : 5 : 6 : 7   Uncoordinated

5. Desirable   1 : 2 : 3 : 4 : 5 : 6 : 7   Undesirable

6. Dirty   7 : 6 : 5 : 4 : 3 : 2 : 1   Clean

7. Smooth   1 : 2 : 3 : 4 : 5 : 6 : 7   Jerky

8. Thrilling   1 : 2 : 3 : 4 : 5 : 6 : 7   Dull

9. Worthwhile   1 : 2 : 3 : 4 : 5 : 6 : 7   Worthless

10. Unhealthy   7 : 6 : 5 : 4 : 3 : 2 : 1   Healthy

11. Masculine   7 : 6 : 5 : 4 : 3 : 2 : 1   Feminine

12. Coarse   7 : 6 : 5 : 4 : 3 : 2 : 1   Elegant

13. Fashionable   1 : 2 : 3 : 4 : 5 : 6 : 7   Unfashionable

14. Fit   1 : 2 : 3 : 4 : 5 : 6 : 7   Unfit

15. Relaxed   1 : 2 : 3 : 4 : 5 : 6 : 7   Tense

Response

Frequency of Response (N = 15)	1	2	3	4	5	6	7

Median Score = _____

references and sources for additional reading

1. Wessel, J.A., and H. Webb, "Body Image, Culture and Females in Sports." Paper presented at the 1st International Congress of Psychology of Sport, Rome, Italy, 1965.
2. Sperling, P. A., "The Relationship Between Personality Adjustment and Achievement in Physical Education Activities," *Research Quarterly*, Vol. 13 (October 1949) 351–63.
3. Ragsdale, C. E., "Personality Traits of College Majors in Physical Education," *Research Quarterly*, Vol. 3 (October 1951), 243–48.
4. Cavanaugh, J. O., "The Relation of Recreation to Personality Adjustment," *Journal of Social Psychology*, Vol. 15 (February 1942), 63–74.
5. Beck, J. H., "The Relationship Between General Motor Ability, Social Adjustment and Social Acceptance of Junior High School Girls." M. A. thesis, State University of Iowa, 1956. (Microcard BF698)
6. Ferguson, B.A., "Personality Differences Between Adolescent Girls of High and Low Motor Performance," cited in *Completed Research in Health, Physical Education, and Recreation*, Vol. 6 (October 1964), 49.
7. Booth, E.G., Jr., "Personality Traits of Athletes as Measured by MMPI," *Research Quarterly*, Vol. 29 (May 1958), 127–37.
8. Kenyon, A.K., *Values Held for Physical Activity by Selected Urban Secondary School Students in Canada, Australia, England and the United States*. U.S. Office of Education, Contract S-376. Madison, Wis.: University of Wisconsin, February 1968.

Cratty, B.J., *Social Dimensions of Physical Activity*. Englewood Cliffs, N.J.: Prentice-Hall, Inc., 1967.
Ulrich, C. *The Social Matrix of Physical Education*. Englewood Cliffs, N.J.: Prentice-Hall, Inc., 1968.

women and competition

SOME MISCONCEPTIONS

4 There are increasing numbers of opportunities for girls and women to compete in sport activities at all levels of skill. What the American public once considered unladylike and physically detrimental is now accepted as appropriate and healthy—perhaps even necessary for women who need to achieve individual excellence in athletics. Perhaps the changing image of the woman athlete in our culture is the primary force behind this change in attitude (1).

Two misconceptions regarding competitive sports for girls and women played a major role in deterring participation. It is only recently that these ideas have been proven erroneous. *First, sports masculinize the girl or woman who competes.* Current medical opinion (2, 3) is that sports participation has no masculinizing effect on the body. This is not to say that women who participate in sports do not exhibit such personality traits as aggressiveness, independence, extroversion, self-assurance, or venturesomeness—traits often culturally defined as "masculine." Several cross-sex comparison studies show that highly skilled athletes of both sexes possess these traits, but they are more indicative of general competitive excellence than of masculinity (4, 5).

There is probably a small percentage of female athletes with so-called male characteristics in body build, behavior, and customs before participation in sports (2). These, however, are not the result of sports participation. Women supposedly masculinized by sports are probably in fact those who excel because of natural android tendencies that endow them with smaller hips, wider shoulders, higher centers of gravity, and similar body characteristics. Genetic makeup rather than competitive sports experience must take the credit.

The second misconception is that girls and women are unable to withstand the emotional stress inherent in competition. Actually, all scientific evidence points in the opposite direction. Girls and women have been found to be as emotionally stable as men. They appear as well equipped to handle stressful situations in sports contests as men who participate in the Olympics—in fact, some evidence suggests that competition itself increases emotional stability. Girls with more competitive experience tend to be more emotionally stable (5, 6). Even over extended periods of time, girls from 12 to 16 show no apparent nervous symptoms due to either hard training or competitive experiences (7). Rather than competitive contests bringing about undue emotional stress, it is quite possible that they may actually help to dissipate stress (8). This phenomenon, "working it off," when situations are especially bothersome or cause anxiety and tension is discussed in Chapter 9.

COMPETITION AT SCHOOL AND COLLEGE LEVEL

Direction for providing competitive experiences for girls and women in schools and colleges has come from the Division for Girls' and Women's Sports (DGWS). This is the only organization in our country concerned exclusively with the promotion and administration of sports programs for girls and women. The Division, which is part of the American Association for Health, Physical Education, and Recreation, has written rules, published standards for competitive events, and trained and rated officials in a number of sports for many years. Traditionally, most educational institutions have looked to DGWS for guidance in planning and administering sports programs for girls and women.

New impetus for expanding competitive experiences in high schools and colleges came in 1963 when DGWS published its revised *Statement of Policies for Competition in Girls' and Women's Sports.* This was followed in 1965 by guidelines for conducting girls' interscholastic and women's intercollegiate sports activities. Most likely, these guidelines or proposed minimum standards are reflected in the program of your institution if intercollegiate sports are offered (9–11).

Your college probably offers an intramural program in which all competition is between teams from within the institution; interdorm, intersorority or intergroup organization is common. In many colleges and universities, intramurals are organized and directed by the Women's Athletic Association or Women's Recreation Association. It is possible that the WAA or WRA is a member of your state and/or national Athletic and Recreation Federation for College Women. ARFCW's purpose is to help athletic and recreation associations to run more effective programs in colleges. It works toward this end by sharing ideas through meetings, conventions, and publications.

Many colleges also offer an informal extramural program where an occasional sports event will be attended by a team or group that may have practiced together several times before. Usually these competitions are sports days when three or more colleges bring a team or several teams to participate in a designated sport. Often, each team will play two shortened games, and the day will end with a coke hour sponsored by the hostess school. Frequently, state ARFCW's will see that a sports day is held annually for each sport commonly played in the area. This assures institutions without intercollegiate programs and colleges in remote regions of having at least one interschool event to climax their season.

It is becoming more common, especially in certain sections of the country, to offer intercollegiate programs in women's sports. Because of the organizational and administrative problems involved, such a program should be the responsibility of the department of physical education for women within the university or college. Student assistance is frequently utilized in the program.

Intercollegiate teams are selected solely on the basis of skill, and they practice regularly to prepare for a scheduled series of games against teams of similar skill. Scheduling may be done by the coach or manager or if the college belongs to a regional or state conference scheduling for all sports may be done at an annual conference meeting.

As competitive opportunities for women increase, the skill level of individuals and teams improves. If you are a superior gymnast or swimmer or a member of a highly skilled volleyball or basketball team, competing in the regular intercollegiate program probably does not fully meet your need to excel. To meet such situations the Division for Girls' and Women's Sports Executive Council formed the Commission on Intercollegiate Athletics for Women (CIAW) in 1966. Prior to this, no single organization was authorized to guide and set controls for women's intercollegiate sports.

The CIAW has a multiple purpose: to provide information on the conduct of women's intercollegiate athletics to institutions that request assistance; to encourage competitive collegiate events at local, district, and regional levels; to sanction state, district, or regional competitions, thereby assuring participants that recommended DGWS standards are met; and to sponsor closed national intercollegiate tournaments as the need for such competitions becomes apparent. Tournaments in golf, archery, bowling, gymnastics, track and field, swimming, badminton and volleyball are among those held annually. Further information on the CIAW can be obtained by writing to the DGWS Commission on Intercollegiate Athletics for Women; AAHPER; 1201 Sixteenth St., NW; Washington, D.C. 20036.

INTERNATIONAL COMPETITION

National collegiate tournaments meet the needs of all but the most highly skilled woman athletes. Provision, however, has been made for the relatively small number of women ready to compete in collegiate sports at the international level. The U.S. Collegiate Sports Council (USCSC) officially represents our country in the International University Sports Federation (FISU[1]). The FISU organizes summer and winter student games every two years for the purpose of promoting international understanding among its 53 member countries. DGWS has a representative on each USCSC games committee in sports in which women's teams are sent (basketball, fencing, figure skating,

[1]The official names of the sports federations are in French; this accounts for the discrepancy between the English title and the initials.

gymnastics, tennis, skiing, swimming, track and field, and volleyball). Women participated in the summer games at Tokyo (1967) and at Lisbon (1969), and in the winter games at Innsbruck (1968) and at Finland (1970), and will compete in increasing numbers in future games. Participation is open to all full-time undergraduate and graduate students who are U.S. citizens and who hold amateur status in the sport in which they compete.

All the types of competition mentioned above are "closed" events, in that only bona fide college students may participate. Other groups that sponsor closed competition are high schools, junior highs, recreational departments, industries, the Amateur Athletic Union, YWCA's, Catholic Youth Organizations, Jewish Welfare Board groups, and many other similar organizations sponsor athletic programs for girls and women. Any time participation is limited to members of an organization, the competition is termed "closed," and its sponsoring group is completely autonomous in setting up rules and regulations.

In open competitions members of various organizations match their skill against the best of other groups. These competitions may be at the district, regional, national, or international level, and whenever they are held, they must come under the direct jurisdiction *or* receive the sanction of the recognized governing body for the particular sport.

For each sport there is only one recognized national governing body. This is the U.S. member of the International Amateur Athletic Federation, which is recognized by the International Olympic Committee (IOC). The IOC, for example, recognizes the International Volleyball Federation (FIC) as the rules and policy-making group for international competition. The U.S. member of the FIC is the United States Volleyball Association; therefore, the United States Olympic Committee officially recognizes the USVBA as governing body for all open competition for men and women in volleyball. Likewise, for basketball the IOC recognizes the International Amateur Basketball Federation (FIBA) as the international governing body, and since the Amateur Athletic Union is the U.S. member of that group, it governs open competition in men's and women's basketball in the U.S.

Primary responsibilities of sports-governing bodies are to develop, sanction, and supervise open competition at the local, regional, and national level; approve arrangements for all international sports competition (both open and closed events); and to certify to the appropriate world governing body that U.S. athletes are amateur and eligible according to national and international regulations. Such clearance must be given all athletes participating in the Olympic Games, Pan-American Games, Maccabiah Games (restricted to members of the Jewish faith), World University Games (under FISU auspices), International Military Sports Council Games (CISM), world championships, and all other international competitions.

In addition, sports-governing bodies may approve open competitions sponsored by groups or organizations ordinarily permitted to hold only closed events. For instance, if a college wishes to sponsor an open basketball tournament and invite noncollege teams, it must secure the sanction of the Amateur Athletic Union (the governing body for basketball) to guarantee to participating athletes that the event will be conducted in accordance with established regulations and that they will not jeopardize their amateur status by participating.

It is becoming more and more vital that women competing in closed or open competition be thoroughly familiar with the amateur standing regulations of the organization for which they play *and* with those of the national governing body for the particular sport. Regulations vary from sport to sport, and many women have inadvertently lost their amateur standing by accepting small fees for officiating, teaching, or coaching. To ascertain what is permissible in a particular sports activity, a college athlete should check the rules and regulations with her coach and should resolve any doubt with the sports-governing body.[2]

College women who meet eligibility requirements of the governing body, may enter competition at the local, state, regional, or national level. Ordinarily, such requirements include membership or registration with the governing organization and, in the case of regional or national competition, exhibiting proficiency as shown by an outstanding season's record or through placing in state or area tournaments. Most top-notch women athletes endeavor to get as much experience as possible in open events for several reasons. In many cases teams representing the U.S. in international competitions (other than the World University Games sponsored by FISU) are selected at national tournaments sponsored by the governing bodies. The national open is the best route to selection for the Olympic Games and Pan-American Games, since it affords the best single occasion to compare the talents of top women performers. In many cases the Olympic Games Committee (whose members decide on the method of selecting teams for both the Olympics and Pan-American Games) attend the national open. Here they select a squad of outstanding athletes to receive further coaching at a training camp; the U.S. team is subsequently chosen from those who attend the camp. In some sports a woman cannot attend such a training camp if she does not participate in the national open tournament, and in all sports the vast majority of those selected for teams do participate in the nationals.

OLYMPIC COMPETITION

Since the Modern Olympic Games were revived in 1896, there has been increased participation by women in the official competitions open to them—athletics (track and field), canoeing, equestrian sports, fencing, gymnastics, shooting, swimming and diving, volleyball, and yachting. Table 4.1 gives some indication of the growing interest of women throughout the world in the highest levels of competition (12).

You may be interested in the fact that a large proportion of the women athletes in U.S. Olympic delegations are students, and some—especially the swimmers—are still in high school.

In the 1964 Tokyo games, 58 of the 81 U.S. women participating were still pursuing studies, and all 15 gold medals won by U.S. women were taken by

[2]A list of sports-governing bodies appears at the end of this chapter.

TABLE 4.1 Modern Olympic Games

Site of Games	Year	Number of Women's Sports	Women Athletes
Summer Games			
Athens, Greece	1896	0	0
Paris, France	1900	1	6
St. Louis, U.S.A.	1904	0	0
London, England	1908	3	36
Stockholm, Sweden	1912	3	57
Antwerp, Belgium	1920	3	63
Paris, France	1924	3	136
Amsterdam, Netherlands	1928	4	290
Los Angeles, U.S.A.	1932	3	127
Berlin, Germany	1936	4	328
London, England	1948	5	385
Helsinki, Finland	1952	5	518
Melbourne, Australia (including equestrian events in Stockholm, Sweden)	1956	6	384
Rome, Italy	1960	5	537
Tokyo, Japan	1964	8	732
Mexico City, Mexico	1968	14	884
Munich, West Germany	1972	8*	—
Winter Games			
Chamonix, France	1924	1	13
St. Moritz, Switzerland	1928	1	27
Lake Placid, U.S.A.	1932	1	30
Garmisch-Partenkirchen, Germany	1936	2	76
St. Moritz, Switzerland	1948	2	90
Oslo, Norway	1952	2	123
Cortina d'Ampezzo, Italy	1956	2	146
Squaw Valley, U.S.A.	1960	3	159
Innsbruck, Austria	1964	4	225
Grenoble, France	1968	5	235
Sapporo, Japan	1972	5	—

*Women's archery and basketball may be added to this number.

students. At the Innsbruck Winter Games the same year, all but 4 of the 20 women competitors were still in school. (For a breakdown by sports, see Reference 12 and Table 4.2.)

Figure 4.1 illustrates the recent improvement in women's performance in swimming, the sport in which the most dramatic changes have occurred.

In general, the youthful age of U.S. athletes also holds true for the Pan-American Games, which were first held in 1951 in Buenos Aires, Argentina.

TABLE 4.2 Women Participants in 1964 Olympic Games

Sport	Number of U.S. Women Participating	Number of Students
Athletics (Track and Field)	20	12
Canoeing	3	2
Equestrian Sports	6	5
Fencing	5	0
Gymnastics	7	5
Shooting	0	0
Swimming	28	27
Volleyball	12	7
Yachting	0	0
Figure Skating	6	6
Luge (Tobogganing)	2	0
Skiing	6	6
Speed Skating	6	4
total	*101*	*74*

All the countries of North, Central, and South America are invited to enter the Games, which are held every four years and are modeled after the Olympics. (For further information see References 12 and 13.)

YOUTH PROGRAMS AND SOME FUTURE PLANS

In the last two decades, perhaps the most significant single factor in the development of youthful talent, especially in swimming and track and field, has been the Age Group programs sponsored by the Amateur Athletic Union and inaugurated in 1951. Volunteer leaders and directors of AAU district associations conduct varied sports activities year round for boys and girls. Age categories are 10 years and under, 11 to 12, 13 to 14, and 15 to 17, and competitions take place in each class. Roughly 3,000 to 5,000 girls start to swim competitively at the age of eight, and by the time they are ten these girls are equaling the top performances of the champions of 1948. By the age of 15, their number has increased to approximately 200,000. All of the 12 women's swimming medalists in the Tokyo Olympics were developed through the Age Group program, and in 1966 a 16-year-old Los Angeles swimmer, Patty Caretto, swam the 1500-meter freestyle faster than the men's Olympic champion had in 1952 (14).

With all due credit to better coaching and improved techniques, it is still impossible to overlook the importance of this AAU program. Another important development in seeking out future champions and giving them competitive experience at an early age is the AAU Junior Olympics program, begun in 1949. District AAU associations annually guide and supervise competition in as many events as facilities and interest allow: swimming, track and field, and gymnastics are the most common.

Figure 4.1   Improvement in Women's Swiming Records, 1900 to 1965*

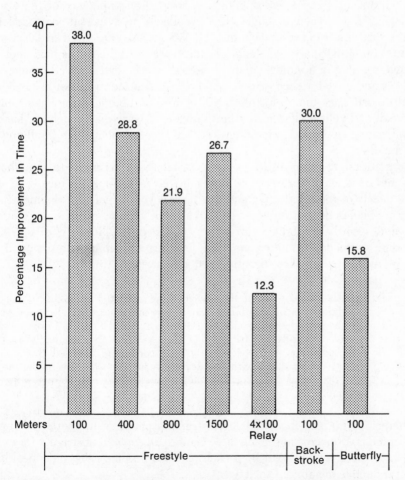

*Adapted from: J. Hodskins, and V. Skubic, "Women's Swimming Records: Analysis and Predictions," *Journal of Sports Medicine and Physical Fitness*, 8(2):96–102, 1968.

In 1967 the regional winners in swimming and track were invited to Washington, D.C. to compete in the Junior Olympics championships. These nationals were limited to boys and girls 13 to 17 years of age in swimming and 14 to 17 in track. Nearly 500 of the very best young athletes competed; 18 former Junior Olympic records were surpassed, and 4 others equaled.

Although a great many young people compete in Age Group and Junior Olympic programs, thousands of others receive most, if not all, of their initial training through school physical education and athletic programs. The United States Olympic Committee and other interested organizations, therefore, have become vitally concerned with developing sound sports programs in schools and colleges.

As a consequence, the Women's Board of the U.S. Olympic Development Committee was created in 1961. Together with the Division for Girls' and Women's Sports, the Women's Board has endeavored to help the American public better understand the role of competition in our culture, to provide information on the organization and administration of athletics to physical education teachers and coaches, and to improve the competence of those who coach girls and women in high schools, colleges, and recreational agencies.

Since 1963 the Women's Board and DGWS have cosponsored five National Institutes on Girls' Sports at which selected teachers and coaches have met for intensive training in a variety of sports activities. The first stressed gymnastics and track and field; the second, diving, fencing, advanced gymnastics, kayaking, and advanced track and field; the third, figure skating and skiing; the fourth, basketball and volleyball; and the fifth, advanced basketball coaching, basketball officiating, gymnastics judging, and advanced coaching and judging of track and field.[3]

Those attending these institutes have, in all cases, returned to their home states and conducted workshops to disseminate the information received.

The effects of these institutes and the various youth-sport development programs are being felt constantly as the skill level of young women in our country rises, and records are broken in each new meet. In all our efforts toward expanding sports opportunities, we need a pattern of competition designed for women. Such a pattern has recently been summarized (16).

> It should (1) permit the development of stated values including the physical, social, emotional and health outcomes, (2) allow the game to be played and directed by the players, not the coach, (3) studiously avoid the frills and fringes that surround the men's games, (4) avoid the adulation and special privileges commonly afforded the athlete, (5) concern itself with the development of good taste in the matter of dress and behavior and hence add to and not detract from the feminine image.

Whether or not the increased interest and proficiency in sports will bring home more gold medals in the Olympic Games, *we know* that striving for excellence in a sports activity will help each of us to become a happier, healthier, more productive member of society.

[3]Proceedings of the Institutes available from AANPER, 120 116th Street N.W., Washington, D.C.

Sports-Governing Bodies for Women's Sports

In this list sports-governing bodies recognized by the International Amateur Athletic Federation, which officially designates the U.S. member of the International Sports Federation, are designated by an asterisk. Those recognized as governing agencies for non-Olympic sports are marked with a ‡.

Archery*: National Archery Association, 23 E. Jackson Blvd., Chicago, Ill. 60604

Athletics (Track and Field)*: Amateur Athletic Union of the U.S., 231 W. 58th St., New York, N.Y. 10019

Badminton‡: American Badminton Association (c/o Virginia B. Lyon, Sec.-Treas., 1330 Alexandria Drive, San Diego, Calif. 92171)

Basketball*: Amateur Athletic Union of the U.S., 231 W. 58th St., New York, N.Y. 10019

Bowling‡: American Bowling Congress, 1572 E. Capitol Dr., Milwaukee, Wis. 53211

Canoeing*: American Canoe Association, 400 Eastern Street, New Haven, Conn. 06500

Equestrian Sports*: American Horse Shows Association, 40 E. 54th St., New York, N.Y. 10022

Fencing*: Amateur Fencers League of America (c/o William Latzke, 33 62nd. St., West New York, N.J. 07093)

Field Hockey‡: United States Field Hockey Association, 107 Schoolhouse Lane, Philadelphia, Pa. 19144

Figure Skating*: United States Figure Skating Association, 575 Boylston St., Boston, Mass. 02116

Golf‡: United States Golf Association, 40 E. 38th St., New York, N.Y. 10016

Gymnastics*: Amateur Athletic Union of the U.S., 231 W. 58th St., New York, N.Y. 10019

Lacrosse‡: United States Women's Lacrosse Association, 107 Schoolhouse Lane, Philadelphia, Pa. 19144

Luge (Tobogganing)*: Amateur Athletic Union of the U.S., 231 W. 58th St., New York, N.Y. 10019

Riflery*: National Rifle Association of America, 1600 Rhode Island Ave. NW, Washington, D.C. 20036

Skiing*: United States Ski Association, (Gloria Chadwick, Exec. Sec., Broadmoor, Colorado Springs, Colo. 80900)

Softball‡: Amateur Softball Association, (Don E. Porter, Exec. Sec., 11 Hill Street—Suite 201, Newark, N.J.)

Speed Skating*: U.S. International Skating Association, Box 464, Rt. 2, Kenosha, Wis. 53140

Swimming and Diving*: Amateur Athletic Union of the U.S., 231 W. 58th St., New York, N.Y. 10019

Synchronized Swimming*: Amateur Athletic Union of the U.S., 231 W. 58th St., New York, N.Y. 10019

Tennis*: United States Lawn Tennis Association, 51 E. 42nd St., New York, N.Y. 10017

Yachting*: North American Yacht Racing Union, 48 Wall St., New York, N.Y.

Volleyball*: United States Volleyball Association, Grand Central Branch, YMCA, 224 E. 47th St., New York, N.Y.

references and sources for additional readings

1. Key, Katherine, "Value in Sports and Athletics As They Relate to Personal and Social Value Systems." Paper presented at Midwest AAHPER Convention, Chicago, Ill., April 1965.
2. Erdelyi, G.J., "Gynecological Survey of Female Athletes," *Journal of Sports Medicine and Physical Fitness*, Vol. 2 (September 1962), 174–79.
3. Russell, James C. H., "Girls' Sports as Viewed by the Physician," *Sports for Girls in Wisconsin Secondary Schools*, Vol. 9 (October 1964).
4. Kane, J.E., and J.L. Callaghan, "Personality Traits in Tennis Players," *British Lawn Tennis*, Vol. 3 (July 1965), 10–13.
5. Ogilvie, Bruce, "What Is An Athlete?" *Journal of Health, Physical Education, and Recreation*, Vol. 38 (June 1967), 48.
6. Ulrich, Celeste, "Measurement of Stress Evidenced by College Women in Situations Involving Competition." Doctoral dissertation, University of Southern California, 1956.
7. Astrand, P.O., *et al.* "Girl Swimmers," *Acta Paediatrica Supplementum*, 147, 1963.
8. Ulrich, Celeste, "The Tomorrow Mind," *Journal of Health, Physical Education, and Recreation*, Vol. 35 (October 1964), 17.
9. Division for Girls' and Women's Sports, "Guidelines for Interscholastic Athletics for Junior High School Girls," *ibid.*, Vol. 37 (September 1966), 36.
10. ——, "Statement on Competition for Girls and Women," *ibid.*, Vol. 36 (September 1965), 34.
11. ——, "Statement of Policies for Competition in Girls' and Women's Sports," *ibid.*, Vol. 34 (September 1963), 31.
12. United States Olympic Committee, *The Olympic Games*. New York: United States Olympic Committee, 1967.
13. United States Olympic Committee, *Olympic Pictorial 1967 U.S. Pan-American Team Trials*. New York: United States Olympic Committee, 1967.
14. Schoenfield, Albert, "Age Group Teens Dominate Women's Swimming World," *Amateur Athlete*, Vol. 38 (August 1967), 19.
15. United States Olympic Committee, *Quadrennial Review 1961–1965*. New York: United States Olympic Committee, 1965.
16. Scott, P. M., *Food for Thought*. In Fourth National Institute on Girls' Sports. Washington, D.C.: American Association for Health, Physical Education and Recreation, 1966.

Part

2

developing
physical
potential

physical conditioning

5 Regular participation in physical activity is one of the major keys to personal success in the most important game of all—*life*. If movement patterns in work and leisure do not demand an optimal level of energy expenditure in both the amount and kind of physical activity then conditioning the body through supplementary exercises may be required. The exercises and the methods you use will depend upon the physical and physiological changes needed to achieve improvements. With each conditioning program specific changes will be described. It is important to emphasize here that improvements in flexibility, strength, tone, endurance, relaxation, and motor performance are attributable to specific physical and physiological changes that occur in response to increased demands placed upon the cells, tissues, organs, and systems of the body. But these improvements are not ends in themselves. Evaluation is a state of mind; therefore, the improvements are *means to achieve goals*, and to be effective, a training program must incorporate both *soma* and *psyche*.

There are many goals that motivate individuals to engage in training programs. They may be specific or general in nature. Here are some goals stated by girls and women.

> To have a better figure
> To lose body weight
> To have better posture
> To improve general physical condition
> To relax and release tensions
> To have fun and feel refreshed
> To get in condition for a specific sport activity
> To become more proficient in a specific sport
> To gain a sense of achievement

Whatever the goals, anyone who aspires to *look better, feel better* and *do better* must recognize the inevitability of expending energy and expending it wisely to achieve desired outcomes. To insure the success of any training program—*to make it safe, beneficial,* and *enjoyable*—certain facts and concepts relative to exercise must be considered.

FACTS AND CONCEPTS RELATIVE TO EXERCISE

Exercise Requires Overload to Produce Desired Effects. Exercise, work, workload, and energy expenditure are synonymous in the physiological sense. By expending energy, the physiological processes become *elevated* in response to increased demands placed upon the cells, tissues, organs, and systems of the body. In order for improvements to occur, these demands must be greater than those usually encountered in day-by-day living. *Overload* may be defined as any demand, or resistance, that exceeds those levels ordinarily experienced in daily life. This phenomenon of the body adapting to the demands or stresses placed upon it is known as the Law of Use and Disuse: *function begets function.* The present level of your physical performance (body shape, function, and control) merely reflects the specific adaptations you have made to the level of physical activity (amount and kind) habitually required in work and leisure. Increased physical activity of the right kind and amount will bring about improvements in the range of joint motion, strength, tone, size, and endurance of skeletal muscles, and give the cardiovascular-respiratory system the ability to sustain physical stress without undue fatigue. Inactivity produces the opposite effects: a decrease in range of joint motion; a lack of tone, strength, and endurance of the skeletal muscles, along with atrophy (wasting) of these muscles; and a decline in the efficiency of the cardiovascular-respiratory system.

The primary focus of a training program is to produce physical and physiological changes that improve strength, flexibility, endurance, and coordination. To accomplish this, you may progressively increase the demands or intensity of the overload (workload) by increasing the:

> *Amount of resistance* (lift heavier loads or apply greater force);
> *Rate of work* (perform the exercise in a shorter period of time);
> *Duration of work* (lengthen the work period while maintaining rate of work);
> *Duration of rest intervals* (shorten the rest periods or the time between defined exercise).

The rate of improvement is directly related to the intensity of the workload. This means that the closer the overload is to maximum, the faster the rate of improvement. Overload, however, should be applied gradually; it takes time for the body to adapt without *excessive* muscle soreness or fatigue.

Exercise Adaptations are Specific to the Type of Training Used. Exercise adaptations are far more specific than was previously recognized. Training for strength, flexibility, endurance, and coordination in sport and work tasks tends to have a highly specific quality. (The body adapts in specific ways to the type of overload used.) It follows, therefore, that you must clearly define the areas in which you need to improve and the type of overload required before designing a training program. In general, the following types of overload are commonly used to bring about improvement in:

Strength: Resistance, weight lifted or muscular tension exerted

Flexibility: Resistance, force exerted by opposing muscle groups to produce movement or body positions held to lengthen or stretch muscles

Endurance: Duration, repetitions increased while maintaining the rate of work; rest, decrease rest time between work periods

Speed: Rate, increase rate of work; rest, decrease rest time between work periods.

These techniques for applying overload are broad examples; specific techniques for designing training programs will be presented later in this chapter.

Exercise Adaptations Require Repetition and Regularity. It is not necessary to expend a great amount of time to achieve specific adaptations or to improve general physical performance. However, the human body is much too complex to derive lasting benefits from exercise that is completed in a few seconds. There is no "ultimate," all-encompassing training program that can be completed within seconds: improvement requires *systematic repetition* of suitable physical activity (kind). Repetitions of short duration at the level of overload (intensity) required to increase demands placed on the body are essential. This fact is of particular significance in endurance and motor skill training. Training, in effect, cannot be divorced from learning; that is, repetition reinforces patterns of responses, and these responses are specific to the type of overload used. Regularity (frequent short periods of physical activity at desired levels of intensity) is more beneficial to continued improvement than infrequent periods of longer duration. Simply stated, don't become a weekend athlete or go on repeated crash training programs. Such regimens are a waste of time and energy.

The benefits of frequent short periods of exercise include: (*a*) less fatigue and muscle soreness and stiffness; (*b*) continued improvement (rate of improvement is greater); (*c*) enhanced motivation as improvements occur—interest, drive, will to persevere to achieve goals. A properly formulated training program can produce desired adaptations within a short period of time, since improvements in strength, tone, endurance, and coordination are accomplished through cumulative beneficial exercise.

Exercise Adaptations Require Motivation: Setting Personal Goals. Motivation is difficult to separate from goals. Exercise or movement is the physical expression of the self which is governed by thought processes and guided by inner drives. Cells, tissues, and systems of the body cannot evaluate the improvements made through training. Evaluation and decision-making are psychologically and sociologically motivated. Any training program should therefore focus on the achievement of specific goals and the form of exercise that involves both *psyche* and *soma*. Experimentation with different approaches to training for specific goals should be undertaken. This is one reason for writing this book. Motivation—the will to persevere, to exert effort or expend energy—is essential regardless of how skillfully the training program is formulated. Therefore, if maximal benefits are to be realized, each individual must establish her own goals. She must realistically evaluate her *self*—her *physical self-image*. She must decide upon her needs for physical activity in her life and the reasons behind those needs, and then she must establish goals. During the training program progress toward these goals should be evaluated regularly. The positive reinforcement that comes from attaining immediate success is of primary importance for maximum motivation. Success breeds success. This is the success syndrome; i.e., You tend to repeat those activities that are enjoyable and in which you achieve success.

$$\begin{array}{ccccc} \text{your} \\ \text{heredity} \end{array} + \begin{array}{c} \text{your} \\ \text{intelligence} \end{array} + \begin{array}{c} \text{physical} \\ \text{energy} \\ \text{potential} \end{array} + \begin{array}{c} \text{motivation} \\ \text{(will to do)} \end{array} = \text{YOU}$$

Exercise Adaptations Are Unique to the Individual. The essential physiological changes that take place in the body as the result of training are well known. Evidence indicates that women respond physiologically to training in the same way as men. For this reason, women should not be denied their biological heritage of vigorous physical training and its benefits.

It is important to emphasize here that the response (the amount and rate of improvement) is unique to the individual. Certain factors account for this. Present physical condition, past experiences in training, body build, motivation, and age all contribute to the uniqueness of individual responses.

(*a*) In a given training program individuals who have had previous experience tend to improve faster than those embarking on such a program for the first time (1). Training appears to form specific patterns for future responses to training. Perhaps this hypothesis is related to the concept of specificity of training.

(*b*) Individuals at the top level of physical performance improve more slowly than those at lower levels. Variations have been found in the rate of increase in the strength of different muscle groups in the same individual. Muscle groups used most strenuously in daily activity showed only slight increases compared with muscle groups seldom used (1)—here again, the Law of Use and Disuse.

(*c*) Women are less responsive to strength and power training than males (2). This has been attributed to the quantity of muscle tissue. The relative muscle mass of the average adult female is 35%, whereas that of the average male is 41% (3). In addition, the protein catabolic effect (protein is used up in the performance of vital processes rather than for muscle mass) limits the trainability of women with respect to muscle bulk and strength development. Furthermore, many women fear that strength training may result in larger or more bunchy muscles. They are also concerned that cessation of activity will lead to unsightly weight increases. No real evidence has been found to substantiate these concerns. However, individuals (both men and women) with a high mesomorphic component appear to be subject to greater increases in strength and/or muscle tone.

(d) Women are more responsive to flexibility training than men. This is attributed to restrictions placed upon men by their greater muscle masses and larger bone structures. Women with a high ectomorphic component and linear build appear to be most responsive in flexibility training.

(e) Women are as responsive to most endurance training as men (4); physiological adjustments are equal. Only in endurance activities where power (strength per unit of time) is an important factor do sex differences show. This undoubtedly reflects the lesser strength of women. Women with a high mesomorphic component appear most responsive to this type of endurance activity training.

(f) Physical performance measurements, in general, improve rapidly from early childhood to a maximum between the middle teens and about 30 years of age, followed by a slow decline during maturity and a more rapid decline with increasing age (5). Unfortunately, scientific evidence concerning responses of aging individuals to various kinds of training is very scanty. One might hypothesize, however, that responses to training would be greatest during the period when physical performance measures were at there maximum.

Exercise Adaptations Are a Lifelong Possibility.

While training effects may be highest during a relatively short period of one's life, it should be emphasized that age alone is not the determining factor; the habitual repetition of suitable physical activity is of far greater importance. Research at the Human Energy Research Laboratory at Michigan State University on the health-fitness of girls and women ages 20 to 69 supports this concept (6). Age per se did not appear to influence levels of strength, range of motion, amount of body fat or body weight, and cardio-respiratory efficiency as much as the habitual physical activity. This concept has been effectively summarized by one authority (7): "At least one aspect of aging, the decline of efficiency, can be inhibited by 25 years and more, provided there is systematic and lasting application of suitable physical training." Often a performer can continue in competition or enjoy participating in games and sports because she maintained a training program despite her advancing years. Research workers have concluded that habitual physical activity can aid in preserving youthful body contours, in maintaining organic vigor and the general suppleness of the body, and in delaying the onset of degenerative conditions associated with aging. Ultimately, a pharmacopeia of exercise will be written to identify the types of overload required to acquire specific adaptations throughout life. Exercise benefits are not the panacea for all aging effects; however, they are valuable tools for emotional release, improved performance capacities, greater efficiency, feelings of well-being and refreshment, and relaxation and pleasure. Each benefit is valuable in its own right; together they make a significant contribution to health-fitness that cannot be ignored by any intelligent individual. The facts are clear: the decision is yours.

Use Table 5.1, a summary of these concepts, as a guideline in designing a personal conditioning program.

TABLE 5.1 The Conditioning Principles

Key Concept	Generalization
Overload	In order for improvement to occur demands must be placed on the body that are greater than those usually encountered (overload).
	The type of overload may be: amount of resistance, rate of movement, duration of work or rest intervals.
	The nearer the intensity of the overload is to maximum, the faster the rate of improvement.
	Progressive overload is the key that permits the body time to adapt to increased demands without excessive muscle soreness or fatigue.
Specificity	The type of overload and the form of exercise or movement used produce specific adaptations.
Repetition and regularity	Repetitions and regular application of exercise at the level of overload required to produce desired improvements are necessary.
	Frequent periods of exercise are essential for continued improvements.
Motivation	Personal goals that are realistic and attainable must be established. Willingness to persevere to ultimate goals is related to the success syndrome.
Individuality	Individuals are unique in their responses (amount of and rate of specific improvements).
Maintenance	Benefits of exercise are a lifelong possibility when a systematic and lasting application of suitable physical activity is built into one's daily life.
	Less energy and time are needed to maintain desired levels of performance than to attain them.

Conditioning is purposeful physical activity: It involves action with a purpose or goal. Techniques for implementing the given principles to improve your health-fitness and motor performance components are presented in the next section.

DESIGNING SPECIFIC CONDITIONING PROGRAMS

A physical conditioning program is composed of exercises and sports and games organized into a planned and progressive program designed to develop health-fitness and the motor capabilities of your body. The overall objective is to develop girls and women who are psychologically and physically capable and ready to:

perform their chosen life work

achieve the desired level of proficiency in their chosen lifetime sports

derive fun and pleasure from vigorous physical activity

gain a sense of achievement from health-fitness through physical activity that is enjoyable

look their best.

To reach this goal, physical conditioning activities must be aimed at: (1) developing *strength* in adequate amounts to perform efficiently (to use minimum effort) all required tasks; (2) providing muscular tone and firmness to body contours; (3) developing *flexibility* in joints to give freedom and ease of motion and prevent vague aches and pains; and (4) providing sufficient *endurance* to sustain activity over a period of time with cardiovascular-respiratory efficiency. Strength, flexibility, and endurance are the primary components in health-fitness. Separately or in combination, they are also primary components in developing a better figure. In addition, these components, along with specific activities, provide the basis for improving motor performance, power, agility, and balance.

Before you embark on a training program, three important concepts should be discussed: warming up, retrogression, and types of muscular contraction.

Warming up Produces Psychological and Physiological Benefits. Any activity conducted with submaximal effort may be considered a warm-up exercise. During such exercise beneficial physiological adjustments to more strenuous exercise take place. These adjustments are known as the immediate effects of exercise: heart rate is increased, blood pressure is raised, blood is diverted from less active to more active tissues, and blood and muscle temperatures are raised. The body, as a total entity, needs time to mobilize its resources, to meet the demands of additional overload or stress. And, psychologically, you need time to prepare yourself for these additional demands.

The most effective types of warm-up are activities that warm up the whole body, i.e., increase heart rate, increase rate and depth of breathing, and raise muscle and blood temperatures. Some activities that have been used to accomplish this include: running in place, jumping jacks, knee bends or squat thrusts, arm and shoulder movements involving movements through the full range of motion, and hip and leg activities such as toe touching. Whenever possible the warm-up should be related to the specific form of exercise or performance to follow event, so that a practice effect may be simultaneously achieved, e.g., throwing a ball; swinging a bat, a hockey stick, golf club, or tennis racket.

Retrogression Precedes Improvement. The phenomenon of retrogression is reflected in the fact that the body requires a certain amount of time to adapt to the increased demands placed upon it in the training program. Fatigue, whether psychologically or physiologically produced, is inescapable. In any program focus is directed not on the inevitability of fatigue, but rather on delaying its onset. The two distinct stages that you will experience in any training program are the adjustment stage (followed by a period of retrogression), and the slow improvement stage.

The *adjusting stage* normally lasts from one to two weeks. This stage is called the toughening period and is particularly encountered by individuals unaccustomed to the physical activity. During this period, muscular pain or discomfort may be experienced. The pain may occur during the exercise or immediately following it and may persist for several hours. When muscular tissue is overloaded to any degree by unaccustomed activity, the waste products, or metabolites, produced by the exercise collect more rapidly than the blood can remove them. These metabolites build up in muscle tissue and tissue spaces and irritate the nerve endings. Muscle soreness is probably due to the accumulation of waste products or to ischemia (temporary anemia) of muscle tissue. This kind of pain is not much of a problem. It can be relieved by stopping the exercise or by a short rest following the exercise. A second, more serious kind of pain produces a condition of localized muscle soreness or "lameness" usually some 24 to 48 hours after the exercise. This delayed soreness was thought to be caused by microscopic ruptures of muscle fibers and fascia. More recently, however, a new explanation has been proposed—a spasm theory (7:258). According to this theory, the pain is caused by localized muscle spasm or cramp. It is postulated that the ischemia produced by unaccustomed activity produces pain; this brings into play more reflex muscular responses that in turn, create greater local muscle tension and causes further ischemia. In addition to fatigue and soreness, you may feel depressed, that you want to quit—that "it's just not worth it!" Disturbed, restless sleep may also follow over-exercise.

You can avoid these problems first, by warming up properly before beginning to exercise; second, by starting your conditioning program at a low level of overload and increasing the intensity gradually, perhaps each week; and third, by keeping in condition! However, it may be impossible to avoid all delayed muscle soreness. If so, a brief period of passive stretch exercises (static flexibility conditioning) has been shown to bring relief. Assume a position that places the muscles and fascia to be lengthened in the greatest possible stretch. Hold this position for two 2-minute periods with a 1 minute rest period intervening. Repeat three times daily (7:260).

The *improvement stage* generally lasts about six to ten weeks. After you have passed through the toughening stage, both mind and body will undergo improvement. Blood circulation in the muscles increases, and the body as a whole becomes more efficient in meeting the demands placed upon it. In a sense, the body has learned the pattern of response and mobilizes its resources to meet these demands. The actual length of the improvement stage depends for the most part on the beginning level of performance and the frequency of exercise periods. Improvement will be rapid the first few weeks, but as a higher level of skill and conditioning is reached, it becomes less noticeable. It is not unusual to hit a plateau,—a period in which improvement is "nil." Sometime between the sixth and tenth weeks, you probably will reach your peak level of performance. The most important points to remember in this stage are: be consistent, be regular. Individual differences account for the amount of improvement and rate of improvement. Evaluate your improvement and rate of improvement. Evaluate your improvement in terms of your *self*.

TABLE 5.2 Five Concepts of Exercise

Exercise	Type of Muscular Contraction	Conditioning Program
1. Isometric exercise	Muscles contract isometrically, without appreciable shortening, to exert tension or force against an immovable resistance.	*Static strength* Isometrics
2. Isotonic exercise	Muscles contract isotonically, shortening and lengthening, to exert force to produce movement of body parts.	*Dynamic strength* Calisthenics Weight lifting
3. Stretch exercise (a) Active	Muscles contract isotonically to produce movement through the full range of motion at specific joints to exert force against the resistance of opposing muscles that are to be stretched or lengthened.	*Dynamic flexibility* Calisthenics
(b) Passive	Muscles contract isotonically to place the body in a static position for maximum lengthening of muscle groups to be stretched.	*Static flexibility* Held positions
4. Aerobic exercise	Muscles contract isotonically to exert force to produce total body activity that lasts longer than a minute; it demands oxygen and forces the body to deliver and use it (aerobic – with oxygen).	*Endurance* Walking, running, swimming, bicycling, jumping rope, jumping
5. Anaerobic exercise	Muscles contract isotonically to exert maximum force (strength x speed) for less than one minute. Demands energy to be supplied without the presence of oxygen (anaerobic – without oxygen).	*Power/Speed* Sprints (running, swimming), fast movements with moderate weights (jumping)

Types of Muscular Contraction Provide the Basis for Conditioning Programs. Skeletal muscles are startlingly efficient machines for converting chemical energy (food) into mechanical energy (work, movement, or exercise) in response to impulses conducted by the nervous system. There are *two types of muscular contraction* (isotonic and isometric) each of which has been used separately or in combination as the basis for exercises in conditioning programs to improve strength, endurance, and flexibility.

The material in the next chapter is presented to guide you in the design of a specific program to meet your physical performance needs. Techniques of implementation (how to apply principles) and examples of conditioning exercises are included. Examine the techniques and exercises. Decide upon exercise objectives relative to your needs. Then you will have the foundation for designing a personal program.

references and sources for additional reading

1. Muller, E.A., and W. Rohmert, "Die Geschwindigkeit der Muskelkraftzunahme bei isometrischen Training," *Arbeitsphysiologie*, Vol. 19 (1963), 403–19.

2. Hettinger, T., *Physiology of Strength*. Springfield, Ill.: Charles C Thomas, Publisher, 1961.

3. Tuttle, W.G., "Women Are Different From Men," *Science Digest*, Vol. 14 (September 1943), 69–72.

4. Astrand, P.O., *et al.* "Girl Swimmers—With Special Reference to Respiratory and Circulatory Adaptation and Gynecological and Psychiatric Aspects," *Acta Paediatrica* (Stockholm) Suppl. 147, 1963.

5. Norris, A.H., and N.W. Shock, "Exercise in the Adult Years with Special Reference to the Advanced Years," in *Science and Medicine in Exercise and Sports*, ed. W.B. Johnson. New York: Harper & Row, Publishers, 1960, pp. 466–490.

6. Wessel, J.A., D.A. Small, W.D. Van Huss, D.J. Anderson, and D.C. Cederquist, "Age and Physiological Responses to Exercise in Women 20–69 Years of Age," *Journal of Gerontology*, Vol. 23, No. 3 (1968), 269–78.

7. De Vries, H.A., *Physiology of Exercise for Physical Education and Athletics*. Dubuque, Iowa: William C. Brown Company, Publishers, 1966.

Howell, M.L., and W.R. Morford, *Fitness Training Methods*. Toronto, Canada: Canadian Association for Health, Physical Education and Recreation, Inc., 1965.

Karpouich, P.U., *Physiology of Muscular Activity*. Philadelphia: W.B. Saunders Co., 1967.

techniques for
improving muscular tone:
strength and
muscular endurance

6   *Definitions.* There are three types of muscle tissue in the body cardiac muscle, of which heart muscle is composed; smooth muscle, such as that found in the walls of blood vessels; and the voluntary (sometimes called striated or skeletal) muscle responsible for physical activity or movement. Skeletal muscle is our concern here. *Muscular strength* can be defined as the ability to exert force to overcome a resistance, while *muscular power* is the ability to exert explosive force (which is related to the strength and speed of the movement). *Muscular tone* is reflected in the firmness of a muscle to palpation and, in general, is related to physiological condition (the elasticity of muscular tissues and the state of contraction of the muscle). *Muscular endurance* is the ability to continue physical activity and resist fatigue in local muscle groups involved in a specific muscular movement.

SOME FACTS ABOUT SKELETAL MUSCLES

The voluntary or skeletal muscles make up about 38–40% of the body weight in women. There are approximately 434 muscles in the human body, but only 75 pairs are used in movement. Muscles operate as teams. All movements involve cooperation among many muscle groups, that is, movement patterns (such as running, jumping, throwing, walking, pulling, and pushing) and local movements at joints [such as flexion (bending), extension (straining), and rotation (turning-twisting)], require the action of many muscles. The effectiveness of such movements depends upon the neuro-muscular system. Understanding the structural and neuro-muscular organization of individual muscle fibers is basic to understanding strength.

A single muscle is composed of many thousands of muscle fibers (cells). Each fiber is filled with a liquid protein solution called *sarcoplasm*, which is surrounded by a thin cell membrane called *sarcolemma*. Each fiber is wrapped in a sheath of connective tissue. A whole muscle is formed by bundles of a dozen or more fibers collected together and covered or wrapped in connective tissue. The whole muscle is attached to bone by means of tendons, which stem from the connective tissue sheath surrounding the whole muscle (see Figure 6.1).

Whole muscles vary in length, size, and shape. These structural variations result from the different functions of muscles. When range of motion and speed are the chief functions, the bundles of muscle fibers are arranged parallel to the long axis of the bone with tendons at each end (fusiform or spindle shaped arrangement). When strength/power or maximum force is the prime requirement, muscle fibers are short, and the bundle of fibers are placed at an oblique angle to the tendon. This is the pennate arrangement. One has only to examine a muscle chart of the human figure to perceive the relation of muscles to the formation of body contours and to movement functions (See Figure 6.2.)

Muscles are nourished by thousands of miles of hairlike capillaries, which transport food and oxygen and carry off the waste products of metabolism. This profuse network of capillaries, as well as the nerve fibers supplying muscle tissues, is in the connective tissue supporting the muscle fibers. Peripheral nerves contain both sensory and motor nerve fibers. Each motor nerve fiber (neuron) serves a single bundle or "squad" of muscle fibers through motor end plates. At its end, the motor nerve fiber divides into a large number of twigs. Each twig has a motor end plate, which is embedded in the sarcolemma of an individual muscle fiber. This arrangement provides each muscle fiber with direct communication to the central nervous system. Sensory (afferent) nerve fibers are equipped with specialized endings that are located around muscle fibers, tendons, and joints. These specialized endings are stimulated by the

Figure 6.1 Muscle Fibers and Structural Arrangements and Attachment of Skeletal Muscle*

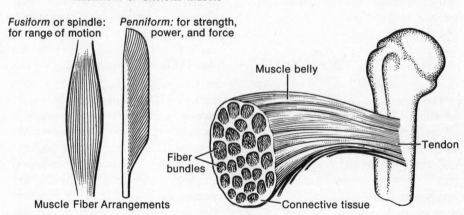

*Adapted from K.F. Wells, *Kinesiology*, W.B. Saunders Co., Philadelphia: 6th edition, 1966.

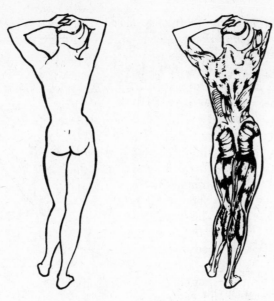

Figure 6.2

contraction of muscle fibers, the stretching of muscles and tendons, and changes in joint positions. Learning a skill partly involves training the higher center—the brain—to properly interpret signals transmitted from the sensory nerve endings. (This awareness of body positions in space and amount of muscular force to be exerted are components of what is known as *kinesthesia* or *kinesthesis*.)

The strength of contraction of a muscle depends on the number of muscle fibers involved. Because they are isolated, individual muscle fibers are innervated separately from each other. When a muscle fiber contracts in response to impulses conducted by a motor neuron, it contracts maximally. This is known as the *All-Or-None* law. Muscle fibers are arranged in bundles or squads; each squad of fibers is served by a single motor neuron (see Figure 6.3). When a motor neuron "fires," or is stimulated and conducts impulses, all the muscle fibers to which it is connected contract maximally. (The term commonly used to describe this neuromuscular organization is the *motor unit*. That is, the motor neuron together with the muscle fibers it innervates or serves comprise the motor unit.) If only a few motor units are "firing," the force or tension exerted by the muscle is slight. To increase the force, more motor units would have to be brought in or recruited to cause more muscle fibers to participate in the task. Changing the frequency of motor unit firing will also produce an increase in muscle force.

The force exerted by a muscle contraction in response to impulses conducted by the nervous system is known as *strength*. Muscle is said to be contracting *isometrically* when the tension or force increases but the length of the muscle is unchanged. Muscle shortening and lengthening while tension within the muscle remains unchanged is *isotonic* contraction. On the basis of this muscle

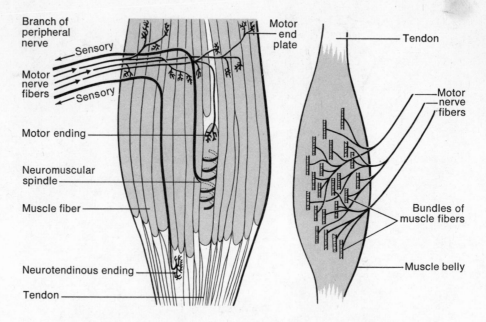

Figure 6.3 Schema of a Muscle and Its Nerve Supply*

action, there are two types of conditioning programs to improve strength: *static strength programs and dynamic strength programs.* In the former muscles are engaged in an activity in which no movement is involved; they contract isometrically against an immovable resistance. In dynamic strength programs muscles contract isotonically to exert a force required to move the resistance through the range of motion of the joint involved.

RELATIVE MERITS OF STRENGTH CONDITIONING PROGRAMS

Both isometric and isotonic contraction are effective in bringing about increases in the strength and tone of skeletal muscles when the overload principle is applied. However, physical and physiological changes can also be produced through strength conditioning programs that result not only in strength and tone gains but also in improvement of muscular endurance, muscle bulk, and power. You should become familiar with the physical and physiological changes that are related to the type of optimal exercise you wish to employ. You will find this information helpful in designing a strength conditioning program to meet your personal needs.

In recent years a great many studies have been done in the area of isotonic and isometric strength conditioning programs. In general, they indicate that both types of conditioning can effectively increase strength. Our concern here are the relative merits of static and dynamic strength programs in improving

*From E. Gardner, *Fundamentals of Neurology*, 4th edition, W.B. Saunders Co., Philadelphia: 1968. p. 147.

TABLE 6.1 Merits of Strength Conditioning Programs Based on Muscular Contraction or Exercise

Optimal Type of Muscular Contraction	Physical and Physiological Changes	Body Adaptations	Resulting Improvements
Isotonic and isometric	*Quality of muscle tissue facilitated* Recruitment of motor units Frequency of "firing" of motor units	Tension or force exerted per cross-section area of muscle increased	*Strength/power:* the ability to exert force to overcome a resistance is explosive force (strength and speed) *Muscular tone:* firmness of muscles and shape of body contours *Economy of effort:* capacity to do more work with less muscular effort or energy expenditure (use fewer muscle fibers to perform the task)
Isotonic and isometric	*Quantity of muscle tissue* The muscle cell membrane (sarcolemma), the sarcoplasm, and connective tissue surrounding muscles increased	Size of individual muscle cells (fibers) increased	*Muscle hypertrophy:* muscle bulk or size and shape of body contours
Isotonic	*Vascularization of muscle tissue* Tone, size, and number of blood vessels increased as well as gains in muscle hemoglobin (oxygen) and muscle glycogen (food)	Assimilation of nutritive (food) materials and oxygen and elimination of the waste products is increased	*Muscular endurance:* ability to persist and continue the activity and resist muscular fatigue in local muscle groups required to perform the task of activity (strength-tone and local circulation is increased)

other observable outcomes. Detailed discussion and explanations of these two methods can be found in the literature (2–4). A brief summary of the merits of these programs is presented in Table 6.1.

Rather obviously, changes do not take place to the same extent or at the same rate of improvement in all women. This is the principle of individuality. An important fact we should emphasize here concerns muscle size or bulk. Strength can increase without a corresponding proportional increase in size. Although it is true, *in general*, that strength is proportional to the cross-sectional area of muscle, strength can be improved with no increase in muscle size. This is reasonable if you consider that it is possible for you to exert great voluntary control over the amount of force used in your various physical activities. This control, the forces or strength you exert, which resides in the central nervous system, is the basis for an increase in strength without appreciable gains in muscle bulk. There is another fact you should consider if you are interested in developing muscle size and shape, body building and contouring. Your basic figure type, the amount of the mesomorphic component, will also determine the amount of gain possible in muscle bulk. Bluntly speaking, "Don't be afraid of strength." It is the essence for quality in the daily performance of activities, in performance of skilled movements in dance and sports, and in developing your figure potential.

SPECIFIC TECHNIQUES AND CONDITIONING EXERCISES

In general, conditioning programs involve exercises that are primarily selected to insure optimal development of the muscle groups in the arms, shoulders, trunk, hips, and legs. There are two basic approaches for employing isotonic exercise for dynamic strength conditioning programs:

> *Weight lifting*: Isotonic exercises with the resistance being the weight to be lifted—(dumbbell, barbell, weighted shoe or plate)
> *Calisthenics*: Isotonic exercises with the resistance being the body weight to be lifted, such as sit-ups, push-ups, pull-ups, wing-lifts, and kneebends.

The basic approach in employing isometric exercises in a static strength conditioning program is to contract a given muscle group maximally against an immovable resistance such as other muscles, a partner, or equipment (a rope, cable-spring, or furniture). Concrete examples for applying overload to improve strength, tone, and muscular endurance are given in Table 6.2. The program you choose should be based not only on personal needs but also on convenience in your life situation and personal satisfaction. You may wish to combine isotonic and isometric exercises and design your own program. Examples of basic exercises generally employed in each strength conditioning program are presented in Appendix A. You may select exercises from among those illustrated, or you may prefer experimenting with different body movements and creating exercises of your own. If you wish to examine or try out specific

TABLE 6.2 Techniques for Applying Overload to Gain Improvement

	Dynamic Strength Programs					Static Strength Programs
	Isotonic Exercises through Full Range of Motion					A Set Position: Isometric Exercises
	Weight Lifting			Progressive Calisthenics		
	Strength/Tone	Muscular Endurance and Tone	Muscular Bulk and Tone	Strength/Tone	Muscular Endurance and Tone	Strength/Tone
Resistance	Weight Lifted	Weight Lifted	Weight Lifted	Body Weight Lifted	Body Weight Lifted	Immovable resistance*
Rate of Work	Slow-Controlled	Slow-Controlled	Slow-Controlled	Slow-Controlled	Fast	Not Applicable
Intensity	Weight you can lift—4 repetitions	Weight you can lift—10 repetitions	Weight you can lift—10 repetitions	First Level of exercises: 10 repetitions.	First Level of exercises: Total number you can do in one minute	Maximal contraction held 6 seconds
Duration Total Repetitions	12	20	50	20	Repetitions as on percentile scale†	10
Number of Sets‡	None	None	3	None	None	None
Rest Interval	None	None	One minute between each set of 10 repetitions	None	None	None
Progression	After reaching 12 repetitions, increase weight 2½ lbs., proceed as before	After reaching 20 repetitions, increase weight 2½-5 lbs., proceed as before	After reaching 3 sets of 10 repetitions, increase weight 2½ lbs., proceed as before	After reaching 20 repetitions, proceed to next level of exercise, proceed as before	Proceed up the percentile scale each week according to number stated until you reach the top. Proceed to next exercise level and continue as before	Maximal contraction each time. For optimal development do at 3 different joint positions
How Often per Week?	4-5 times 2 minimal	4-5 times 2 minimal	4-5 times 2 minimal	4-5 times 2 minimal	4-5 times 2 minimal	4-5 times 2 minimal
How Long?	The answer to this question can be answered only by you. How long will depend upon how much strength, tone, muscular endurance, and muscle bulk you need to achieve your goals. As a rule of the thumb, optimal development for the average individual will require 10-12 weeks. The principle of intensity of the overload should also be considered: Rate of improvement will be faster the closer the intensity of the overload is to maximal. But too great an intensity for your present condition will result in excessive muscle soreness and stiffness. Proceed gradually and progressively work up to achieve your goal.					

*Another set of muscles, a partner, or equipment.   †See Chapter 17.   ‡Repeats of exercise after rest.

programs employing weight lifting or progressive calisthenics, suggested examples for personal action plans may be found in Part IV.

references and sources for additional reading

1. Guyton, A.C., *Function of the Human Body*. Philadelphia: W.B. Saunders Co., 1964, p. 226.
2. The Athletic Institute, *Exercise and Fitness*. New York: The Athletic Institute, 1960.
3. Karpovich, P.V., *Physiology of Muscular Activity*, 6th ed. Philadelphia: W.B. Saunders Co., 1965.
4. Berger, R.A., "Comparison of Static and Dynamic Strength Increases," *Research Quarterly*, Vol 33 (1962), 329.

Logan, G.A., and E.L. Wallis, *Figure Improvement and Body Conditioning Through Exercise*. Englewood Cliffs, N.J.: Prentice-Hall, Inc., 1964.

Rasch, P.J., *Weight Training*. Dubuque, Iowa: William C. Brown Company, Publishers, 1966.

Weight Training in Sports and Physical Education. Washington, D.C.: American Association for Health, Physical Education and Recreation, 1962.

techniques for
improving elastic tone:
flexibility or
range of motion

7 *Flexibility* can be defined as the range of possible movement in a joint or a series of joints involved in a movement (such as toe-touching). Flexibility, the range of possible joint motion, is specific to a given joint or combination of joints. Each individual has many joints in her body. Some of these may have more or less flexibility than others. The degree of motion or flexibility may vary because of bony structures, physical activity patterns, body type, and age.

SOME FACTS ABOUT BASIC SKELETAL STRUCTURES

The skeleton dominates the surface form of the body, and the shape of its joints determine all movement. The shapes of bones differ according to the functions they perform. They are heaviest where they support great weight, e.g., the leg and pelvic bones. They are flattened or have expanded surfaces for protection where they surround the three major cavities, the cranium, chest, and pelvis. Where motion is important, the bones are long with expanded articular surfaces at the extremities to strengthen the joints. Such bones are found in the limbs. Some bones, notably the shoulder blades and vertebrae, have prominent projections called "processes" that serve as levers for the muscles that attach to them. The numerous bones of the wrist and instep are closely and compactly grouped so that shocks received by the hand and foot can be transmitted to many surfaces and thereby lessened. Also, the numerous small bones make for greater mobility.

The joints, or articulations, are of three general types.

1. The *immovable* joints: cranial and facial bones.
2. The *slightly movable* joints: the joining bone surfaces are separated by an interposed pad of elastic fibrocartilage. Movement is effected only by compression of the pad at one or another side. This type of joint is found between the vertebrae, where the pad serves to cushion shock as well as to allow movement.
3. The *freely movable* joints: the bone surfaces are held in close proximity to one another, the movement being determined by the related shapes of the two surfaces. Each articulating surface is covered by a thin layer of articular cartilage. The whole joint is enclosed by a capsule that secretes a viscid lubricating fluid. Overlying the capsule are the connecting ligaments (fibrous nonelastic tissue), which strengthen the joint. Next are the tendons of muscles that cross the joint and serve to provide the force to move the bones and to strengthen the joint.

The freely movable joints are the concern here. There are many joints in the skeletal framework, but only a few types. Each type of joint has a capability for movement in certain directions based on the bony structure, i.e., the articulating bones forming the joint. Table 7.1 lists common types of joints and fundamental movements of major joints.

Examine the skeletal framework in Figure 7.1, identify the types of joints and fundamental movements possible at each of the major joints. These have served to classify muscles according to their function (rotators, abductors, adductors, flexors, extensors, supinators, and pronators). Range of motion is sometimes set by the bony structure (articulating surfaces, such as in extension of the elbow joint). In other joints, limitation of range of motion is imposed by: (1) the fascial sheath that covers muscle and surrounds muscle fibers and (2) the connective tissue that forms the capsule of the joint, the ligaments which bind bone to bone, and the tendon attachment of muscle to bone. The muscle and its fascial sheaths and tendons are the primary factors modifiable through physical activity. These are also the important factors that permit the range of motion required in sports and dance.

As human beings, we all are capable of these fundamental movements at the joints. But the range of motion at a joint or series of joints involved in a movement may vary; that is, some individuals have a greater range of motion at certain joints than others. The most common reasons for these variations are: (1) inherited body structures and (2) engaging in certain forms of physical activity. An individual of ectomorphic body type is apt to have greater range of motion because smaller joints, longer more slender muscle structure, and ligaments and capsular tissue that are more lax. The reverse would be true for a stockier body type with greater predominance of the mesomorphic component. But several investigators have found that there is *no* significant relationship between flexibility and various body measurements. Individuals with a longer upper body and arms and short legs have no advantage in touching the toes (1, 2).

TABLE 7.1 Major Joints

Type	Where Found	Directions	Fundamental Movements
Ball-and-socket	Hip Shoulder Trunk[3]	Forward-backward Sideward Around	Flexion[1] and extension[2] Abduction[4] and adduction[5] (hip, shoulder) Lateral flexion[6] (right and left—trunk) Rotation[7] in and out (hip and shoulder) Rotation (right and left—trunk)
Condyloid	Wrist Thumb Head-neck Fingers-hand Toes-hand	Forward-backward Sideward	Flexion and extension Abduction and adduction
Hinge	Elbow Knee Ankle Fingers Toes	Forward-backward	Flexion and extension
Pivot	Forearm Head-neck	Around	Rotation right and left (head) Rotation in and out (forearm) known as supination and pronation
Irregular	Foot (tarsals) Hand (carpals)	Gliding	Supination and pronation of the foot at mid-tarsal region Other very slight movements

[1] The angle of the joint diminishes, as in bending.
[2] The opposite of (or return from) flexion, as in straightening or extending.
[3] Although the spinal column is classified as a slightly movable joint, its movements resemble those of a ball-and-socket joint of the freely movable joints when examined as a whole.
[4] Movement away from the midline of the body.
[5] Movement toward the midline of the body.
[6] Bending sideways with the head or trunk.
[7] Movement of a body segment about its own longitudinal axis, as in turning or twisting. In outward rotation the body segment turns laterally, while in inward rotation it turns medially. Outward and inward rotation of the forearm are called *supination* and *pronation*, respectively. Inward rotation combined with adduction of the foot is also called pronation, while outward rotation and baduction of the foot is called supination.

Most important, however is that performing physical activities that demand greater range of motion for excellence tends to produce an increased range of motion in the joints used in this activity. This concept is supported by a study performed in our laboratory. Subjects were thirty women who specialized in five selected activities—basketball, modern dance, speed swimming, synchronized swimming, and gymnastics (3). In the study seven joint measurements were taken: (1) trunk flexion and extension; (2) hip flexion and extension; (3) shoulder flexion; (4) shoulder extension; (5) shoulder rotation; (6) leg abduction; and (7) ankle flexion and extension. The following results were found:

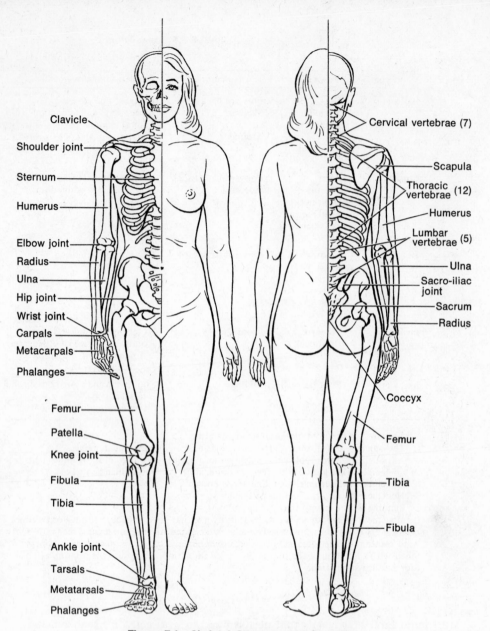

Clavicle

Shoulder joint

Sternum

Humerus

Elbow joint

Radius

Ulna

Hip joint

Wrist joint

Carpals

Metacarpals

Phalanges

Femur

Patella

Knee joint

Fibula

Tibia

Ankle joint

Tarsals

Metatarsals

Phalanges

Cervical vertebrae (7)

Scapula

Thoracic vertebrae (12)

Humerus

Lumbar vertebrae (5)

Ulna

Sacro-iliac joint

Sacrum

Radius

Coccyx

Femur

Tibia

Fibula

Figure 7.1   Skeletal Structure and Body Form

1. Modern dancers showed the highest overall flexibility, being high in six of the seven measurements.
2. Gymnasts were second, being high in four of seven.
3. Women basketball players and speed swimmers showed the lowest flexibility, with synchronized swimmers being slightly better by comparison.
4. All performers showed more flexibility in these joints than the average college women.

In considering the relationship of flexibility to physical activity, it would appear that active women tend to be more flexible than inactive women (4). There is a strong likelihood that performers in certain sports tend to show similar patterns in joint flexibility, which differ from the patterns of performers in other sports (5, 6). Flexibility would seem to be a specific factor related to specific forms of physical activity. Rather obviously, activities in daily life that require static positions in which muscles are held in shortened positions tend to produce a decreased range of motion. Muscles and their fascial sheaths and tendons adapt to the range of motion at which they are accustomed to being used. For example, sitting postures tend to produce limited range of motion at the knee, shoulder, and hip, and constant walking in high heels limits the range of motion at the ankle.

Flexibility is important to each and every person because graceful, efficient movement is unlikely without it. In addition, considerable evidence has been accumulating in recent years to indicate that maintenance of optimal joint mobility prevents, or to a large extent may remove, vague aches and pains that seemingly become more common with increasing age (7, 8, 9). This is particularly true for discomfort in the neck, shoulder, and back. Anatomical studies and work in medicine and rehabilitation (10) have provided us with "average" or "normal" degrees of motion at specific points (see the Laboratory Experiment at the end of this chapter).

RELATIVE MERITS OF FLEXIBILITY CONDITIONING PROGRAMS

Three factors are basic to understanding flexibility: elasticity, extensibility, and the stretch reflex. A muscle can stretch beyond its normal resting length and return to it again when the stretching force is removed. This is known as *elasticity*. In general, the maximum length a muscle can be stretched (*extensibility*) is approximately half again its resting length. If a muscle is forced beyond about 60% of its normal resting length, its fibers will tear or rupture. If the stretching force is great, it is possible to pull the tendon such as the Achilles tendon or the biceps tendon, from its attachment on a bone. The range over which a muscle works, its *amplitude* of action, is measured from a position of maximum contraction to maximum length. The average muscle fiber can shorten to about one-half its resting length; it can be stretched until it is approximately one half again as long as its resting length. A stretching force can be applied to muscles by movements in which one body segment is put in motion by active contraction of a muscle group. The momentum (weight of the body segment × speed) is then used to apply the stretching force to opposing muscle groups. Stretching exercises that invoke as little muscle activity as possible in the muscle groups to be lengthened appear to be most advantageous.

Whenever a muscle is stretched, the basic stretch, or myotatic, reflex response comes into play. For example, when the gastrocnemius muscle in the calf of the leg is stretched, the muscle spindles are stimulated and an impulse is generated. This impulse is conducted via sensory nerve fibers to a junction, in

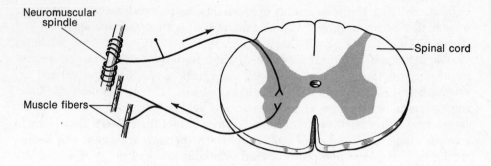

Figure 7.2   Schema of Stretch Reflex

the spinal cord, with a motor neuron that inverts the action of the muscle fibers of the gastrocnemius muscle. When the motor neuron is stimulated, impulses are conducted over its nerve fiber to the muscle fibers, which contract. This is the stretch reflex response; the amount of tension and rate vary directly with the amount and rate of the movement that causes the muscle to stretch. A jerky, fast bouncing or bobbing movement is therefore undesirable. On the other hand, a slow steady stretching movement appears to invoke an inverse stretch response. That is, this type of movement appears to inhibit reflex responses of the muscle, and a lengthening of the entire muscle group seems to take place.

Little research has been done on the relative merits of active (dynamic) or passive (static) stretch exercise programs for improving flexibility. Active stretch exercises have involved calisthenics in which muscles contract isotonically to put a body segment in motion by bobbing or bounding movements. The momentum of the body segment exerts force against the resistance of the opposing muscle groups that are to be stretched. Passive stretch exercises, on the other hand, involve holding a static position for a period of time. The position assumed places the muscles and the connective tissue in a position of greatest possible length. Many yoga exercises use this procedure (11). It has been shown that both types of stretching exercises are effective in bringing about gains in flexibility (12, 13). One researcher concluded that static flexibility programs have three distinct advantages: (1) less danger of exceeding extensibility limits, (2) less energy expended, and (3) less possibility of causing muscle soreness (14).

TECHNIQUES AND CONDITIONING EXERCISES

Techniques for applying overload to improve flexibility are illustrated in Table 7.2. Examples of basic exercises involving both static and dynamic programs are found in Appendix A. After assessing your needs, you can design a program to improve flexibility in the specific joints in which you need to improve range of motion. If you already have optimal range of motion in the major joints of your body, the problem is maintenance. Stretching the major

TABLE 7.2 Techniques for Applying Overload

	Static Flexibility Program for Specific Joint Motion	Dynamic Flexibility Program for Specific Joint Motion
Resistance	**Position-locks:** joints involved place muscle at greatest possible stretch	Momentum of body segment against muscles to be stretched
Rate of work	Not applicable	Slow, controlled
Intensity	Greatest possible muscle length held for 1 minute	Greatest possible muscle length
Duration total repetitions	3	30
number of sets	None	3 sets of 10
rest interval	30 seconds	30 seconds between each set
Progression	Greatest possible muscle length	Greatest possible muscle length
How often per week?	Once per day, 4-5 days per week	Once per day, 4-5 days per week
How long?	The answer is related to the goal you have set for yourself. Gains have been made in two weeks. Rate of improvement will be faster the closer the intensity is to your maximal limit (work in the "twilight zone of pain"). Pain should be gone immediately after maximum stretch has been released. If pain persists or soreness results the next day, intensity was too great. Proceed gradually and work up progressively.	

joints through the full range of motion once a day and holding for ten seconds should provide the basis for optimal maintenance. If you find that you are having difficulty with a specific joint or a series of joints, immediately institute a conditioning program. At the same time, examine your daily activity patterns that involve static positions and posture. Proper body alignment while sitting, standing, and working are important to the maintenance of optimal range of motion and prevention of vague aches and pains.

LABORATORY IN FLEXIBILITY

Assess your flexibility by comparing your range of motion at specific joints to the average ranges shown on the record sheet. Perform each of the motions illustrated here once; use a steady, controlled movement. By yourself or with a friend, decide whether you pass or fail and record this on the form provided. The results indicate if your present physical activities provide you with the exercise you need to maintain an optimal range of motion. Do any of your activities—certain sports or dance—require more than average flexibility? What steps will you take to improve or maintain your range of motion?

The Shoulder

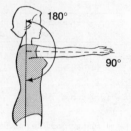

flexion

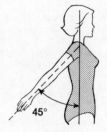

extension

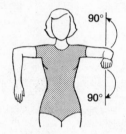

internal-external rotation

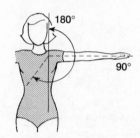

abduction-adduction

The Hip

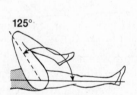

flexion (knee bent)

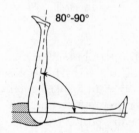

extension (knee straight)

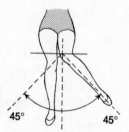

internal-external rotation

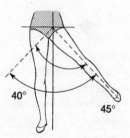

abduction-adduction

The Knee

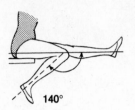

140°

flexion-extension

The Ankle

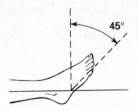

45°

plantar flexion

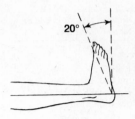

20°

dorsi flexion

The Foot

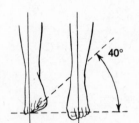

40°

supination

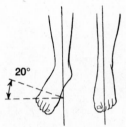

20°

pronation

The Elbow

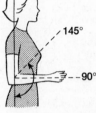

145°

90°

flexion-extension

The Forearm

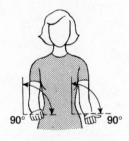

90°   90°

supination-pronation

The Wrist

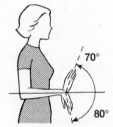

70°

80°

flexion-extension

The Trunk

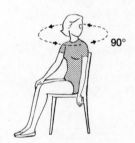

90°

rotation

The Head

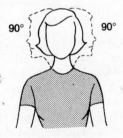

90°   90°

rotation (right-left)

Average or Normal Amplitude or Range of Motion	Pass	Fail

Shoulder
    Flexion (180°)
    Extension (180°)
    Internal-External Rotation (90°)
    Abduction-Adduction
Hip
    Flexion (knee bent) (125°)
    Flexion (knee extension) (80°)
    Adduction-Abduction (45°)
    Internal-External Rotation (45°)
Knee
    Extension-Flexion (140°)
Ankle
    Plantar Flexion (45°)
    Dorsi Flexion (20°)
Foot
    Supination (40°)
    Pronation (20°)
Elbow
    Flexion-Extension (145°)
Forearm
    Supination (90°)
    Pronation (90°)
Wrist
    Extension (70°)
    Flexion (80°)
Trunk
    Rotation (right, left) (90°)
    Hip-Trunk Flexion (touch toes)*
    Trunk Extension (12")†
Head
    Rotation (right, left) (90°)

*See Exercise 3 on p. 30 for a description of this motion.
† See the Profile Record on p. 32 for your score.

references and sources for additional reading

1. Broer, M.R., and N.R.G. Galles, "Importance of Relationship Between Various Body Measurements in Performance of Toe-Touch Test," *Research Quarterly*, Vol. 29 (1958), 253–63.
2. Mathews, D.K., V. Shaw, and J.B. Woods, "Hip Flexibility of Elementary School Boys as Related to Body Segments," *Research Quarterly*, Vol. 30 (1959), 297–302.
3. "Flexibility Characteristics of Women in Selected Dance and Sport Activities," Human Energy Research Laboratory, Michigan State University, Unpublished Research Material. East Lansing, Mich., 1966.
4. McCue, B.F., "Flexibility of College Women," *Research Quarterly*, Vol. 34 (1953), 316–20.
5. Leighton, J.R., "Flexibility Characteristics of Males Ten to Eighteen Years of Age," *Archives of Physical Medicine and Rehabilitation*, Vol. 37 (April 1956), 494–99.

6. ———, "Flexibility Characteristics of· Four Selected Skill Groups of College Athletes," *Archives of Physical Medicine and Rehabilitation*, Vol. 38 (January 1957), 24–28.

7. Goldthwaite, J.E., *et al. Essentials of Body Mechanics in Health and Disease.* Philadelphia: J.B. Lippincott Co., 1952, pp. 262–73.

8. Kendall, H.O., F.P. Kendall, and D.A. Boynton, *Posture and Pain.* Baltimore, Md.: The Williams & Wilkins Co., 1952, pp. 63–76.

9. Billig, H.E., Jr., and E. Loowendalhl, *Mobilization of the Human Body.* Stanford, Calif.: Stanford University Press, 1949.

10. Departments of the Army and the Air Force, *Joint Motion Measurement*, Technical Manual No. 8–640, Air Force Pamphlet No. 160–14–1. Washington, D.C.: Departments of the Army and the Air Force, 1956.

11. Rathbone, J.L., *Corrective Physical Education.* Philadelphia: W.B. Saunders Co., 1959, p. 242.

12. Logan, G., and G.H. Egstrom, "The Effects of Slow and Fast Stretching on the Sacrofemoral Angle," *Journal of the Association for Physical and Mental Rehabilitation*, Vol. 15 (1961), 85–89.

13. DeVries, H.A., "Evaluation of Static Stretching Procedures for Improvement of Flexibility," *Research Quarterly*, Vol. 33 (1962), 222–29.

14. ———. *Physiology of Exercise for Physical Education and Athletics.* Dubuque, Iowa: William C. Brown Company, Publishers, 1966, p. 365.

Cooper, J.M., and R.B. Glassow, *Kinesiology.* St. Louis, Mo.: The C.V. Mosby Co., 1963.

Scott, M.G., *Analysis of Human Motion.* New York: Appleton-Century-Crofts, 1963.

Wallis, E.L., and G.A. Logan, *Figure Improvement and Body Conditioning Through Exercise.* Englewood Cliffs, N.J.: Prentice-Hall, Inc., 1966.

techniques for improving organic tone: cardiovascular-respiratory endurance

8 *Definitions.* Endurance or postponement of fatigue is the ability to persist in performing specific physical activities. There are two kinds of endurance. *Muscular* endurance, which was previously discussed, is the ability to continue physical activity and resist fatigue in local muscle groups involved in specific movements such as sit-ups and push-ups. This kind of endurance depends on strength and improved local circulation (vascularization) in the muscle groups. But individuals with the same amount of strength and muscular endurance differ in their ability to exert effort before becoming winded. This type of endurance is spoken of as *cardiovascular-respiratory* endurance. It is illustrated by the development of the ability to run a mile, or swim, or ride a bike without undue breathlessness. This is primarily a matter of the strength of the heart and lungs. Cardiovascular-respiratory endurance is the ability to perform total body activity for long periods of time—let us say five or six minutes—without undue breathlessness or fatigue. To develop this kind of endurance, one needs to have an adequate amount of strength and endurance in the muscle groups concerned and, in addition, to develop a higher degree of heart and lung function.

SOME FACTS PERTAINING TO THE CIRCULATORY AND RESPIRATORY SYSTEMS

When activity changes from localized movement (as in calisthenics) to activity that involves total body movements (as in running) body adaptations change from local involvement of a small percentage of the body's musculature to involvement of a large percentage, with many muscle groups working. In local movements, muscular endurance, muscular strength, and flexibility may all be improved. But the central systems of energy supply are not extended to any large degree. In total body activity, the heart, lungs, blood vessels, and other organs undergo what is called organic adaptation. The condition of these organs as well as of the muscles determines your endurance.

The key is the capacity of your body to deliver oxygen to the working muscular tissues so that energy demands can be met. Life is activity. Any activity, whether beating of the heart, breathing, digesting, or moving the arm, requires energy. The body produces energy by burning (metabolizing) foodstuffs. Oxygen is the burning agent required for this vital process. When food and oxygen combine, energy is produced. The body can use the food it needs and store the excess food in the form of fat for later energy needs. The body cannot, however, store oxygen; it needs constant replenishment. In normal individuals, the supply of oxygen to the body tissues is sufficient to produce the energy required to perform ordinary activities. But as activities become more strenuous, energy demands become proportionally greater. Enough oxygen must go to active body tissues so that food and oxygen can combine to produce the energy needed. The capacity of the body to deliver an adequate oxygen supply to meet changing energy demands without undue fatigue depends on optimal functioning of the cardiovascular-respiratory systems. The heart and lungs are key organs.

the heart

The heart is the chief organ of the cardiovascular-respiratory system. It is the heart that propels the oxygen-laden blood from the lungs to the body tissues through the blood vessels and brings blood filled with carbon dioxide (the waste product) back into the lungs. The heart itself is a muscular organ and may be developed by exercise just like any other muscle. However, one does not exercise the heart itself. "The heart is exercised through the legs," say physical educators. In other words, total body activity is the form of exercise that will affect the heart. Such exercise will affect two basic areas: (1) the size, strength, and tone of heart muscular tissue and how well endowed it is with blood vessels for its own oxygen supply; and (2) the work load, the heart rate.

The heart needs oxygen for its own energy requirements. When the heart is exercised, it develops better circulation (vascularization) within its own muscular tissue, much as skeletal muscle does. The general circulation of the heart—the coronary circulation—improves. Dormant capillaries appear to open up in heart tissue, and existing blood vessels are enlarged. Such vascularization plays a large role in the health and efficiency of the heart. The health of the heart depends also on size, particularly interior volume. With exercise, the size of the heart itself increases through muscular development. This brings about a capacity not only to receive more blood but also to provide strength to pump more blood with each stroke. Each heartbeat pumps a greater amount of blood: this is spoken of as an increase in stroke volume. This

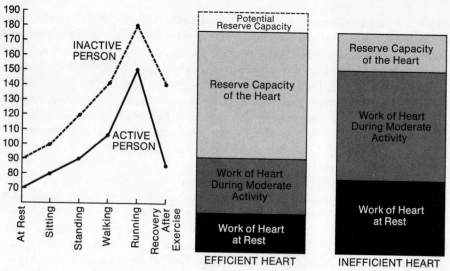

Figure 8.1 Heart Rate and Energy Reserves in Active and Inactive People

exercise response—the increase in the amount of blood pumped per heartbeat—is associated with a decrease in heart rate. As the heart is larger and stronger, it can beat more slowly because it pumps more blood with each stroke. In this respect, it is working more efficiently, doing more work with less effort to meet the energy demands of exercise. In turn, recovery after exercise is faster because the body is better able to maintain an equilibrium and has a greater reserve capacity to respond to additional demands.

It is also important to note that regular exercise reduces maximum heart rates. Healthy, efficient hearts are equipped with a protective mechanism that

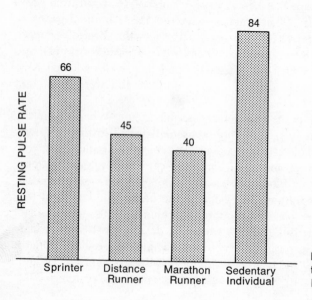

Figure 8.2 Relationship Between Kinds of Activity and Resting Pulse Rate

allows a relatively low maximum rate (about 190 beats or less per minute) in response to exhausting activity or uncontrollable emotional crises—that is, the person will respond without strain to such situations. On the other hand, a poorly conditioned heart may respond to such situations with a heart rate of 200 or more, which is dangerously high. In summary, then, a healthy, efficient heart responds better than one that is poorly conditioned. It does less work at rest, increases its workload less with moderate activity, has greater heart reserve and a built-in degree of protection in response to exhausting activity or emotional crisis, and recovers faster after activity (see Figure 8.1).

The lower your heart rate the more rest you give your heart. As Figure 8.2 indicates, athletes who participate in sport activities of long duration develop lower resting pulse rates. The comparison of the heart rates of active and inactive individuals in Table 8.1 clearly shows the importance of a lower pulse rate in everyday life. Imagine the effect of a lower heart rate in conserving energy throughout your life. Of even more importance are the

TABLE 8.1 Comparison of Heart Rates

	In a 24-Hour Period	
	Active, Fit Individual	Inactive, Unfit Individual
Resting heart rate	70 beats/minute	80 beats/ minute
1 hour equals	70 × 60 = 4,200 beats	80 × 60 = 4,800 beats
24 hours equals	100,800 beats	115,200 beats

implications in performing daily activities and the capacity to perform and enjoy pleasurable vigorous activities. During exercise, the heart beats harder and faster, but a healthy, efficient heart speeds up less, has greater resource capacity to meet all stresses, and can recover and return to its resting rate more quickly.

the lungs

The lungs and their relationship to the blood vascular system are vital for maintaining oxygen availability to meet energy needs. In an endurance-type exercise, the efficiency with which the lungs transmit oxygen to the blood is increased as much as 30%. This increase has been attributed to the condition inside the lungs and to the amount of air breathed in.

The first limiting factor on how much air the lungs can process is the condition inside the lungs. Air breathed in passes through a great number of passages of diminishing diameter until it reaches air sacs called "alveoli." There are many millions of alveoli, and it is here that oxygen is extracted and picked up by blood cells, and carbon dioxide (waste gas) is exchanged. Blood supply is a critical condition, as the better the blood supply around the alveoli, the better the chance of oxygen transfer and exchange of waste gases. Smoking, air pollution, and the breathing of abrasive substances (as in mining), as well as respiratory conditions such as emphysema, all affect the ability of the alveoli to exchange gases. They may destroy sections of the lung, build up mucus, or possibly constrict air passages. But there is recent evidence that exercise can improve lung function. Long continued programs of endurance-type activity affect the alveoli—actually may develop new partitions, thus increasing the total area from which the blood can absorb oxygen.

Another result of endurance-type exercise is an increase in the number of red blood cells, which carry oxygen and carbon dioxide, and in the amount of hemoglobin, the material within these cells which actually combines with oxygen and carries it to active body tissues. This means that much more oxygen can be carried from the lungs to active tissues, where it is in demand. These increases, along with tissue vascularization, bring about improvements in both muscular and cardiovascular-respiratory endurance.

The second factor limiting the amount of air the lungs can process is the actual ventilation of the lungs. The lungs, having no muscles of their own, depend for expansion and contraction on the respiratory muscles of the rib cage (the intercostals) and the diaphragm. As you inhale, the respiratory muscles contract and create a larger lung cavity, and the air, aided by atmospheric pressure, is pulled in. In exhaling, the muscles, aided by the elasticity of the lungs and the weight of the chest wall, force the air out. The actual capacity of the lungs depends upon the flexibility of the chest and the strength of the respiratory muscles. It has been shown that endurance exercise brings about an increase in ventilation of the lungs, causes deeper breathing and apparently improves the way the air gets to the walls of alveoli. Deeper breathing increases the flexibility of the chest and is partly due to strengthening of the respiratory muscles through exercise. When these muscles are in poor condition they tire readily, and the person breathes more shallowly.

RELATIVE MERITS OF ENDURANCE CONDITIONING PROGRAMS

Metabolic processes that supply the energy demands for most activities take place in the presence of an adequate oxygen supply. These activities are called aerobic exercises (with oxygen). The workload, the amount and rate of these activities is such that the demands do not surpass the body's capacity to produce energy. The means for processing and delivering needed oxygen is sufficient for the complete burning of foodstuffs and the production of energy. At such a rate of submaximal work, a steady state is reached and you literally "pay as you go" the oxygen needed to sustain this workload. On the other hand, some activities demand exorbitant amounts of oxygen in short periods of time. These demands surpass the body's capacity to supply oxygen, and you, literally, contract an "oxygen debt." The term oxygen debt was coined by A. V. Hill, a pioneer in exercise physiology (1). Such activity is termed "anaerobic

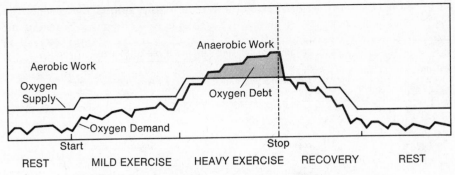

Figure 8.3 Relationship Between Oxygen Supply and Demand

activity," (without oxygen). It forces you to stop and recover and pay the oxygen debt. This is why the heart and respiration rates remain elevated after cessation of exercise. The extent to which both fail to return to resting rates and the length of the recovery period are proportional to the size of the oxygen debt incurred (see Figure 8.3).

aerobic exercise for endurance

Aerobic exercise is the key to cardiovascular-respiratory endurance. The primary objective is to increase oxygen consumption and, thus, increase endurance by conditioning the heart and lungs. Aerobic exercises must demand oxygen without producing an oxygen debt so that you can continually hold a steady pace over a period of time. There are two types of aerobic exercise. *Nonstop aerobic exercise* is continuous holding of a steady pace. There is no high and low heart rate; the heart rate is constantly maintained somewhere between 120 and 150. Examples of nonstop aerobic activities are running, swimming, and bicycling. *Stop and start aerobic exercise* is continuous in nature. The heart rate is pushed up to somewhere between 150 and 180 for short periods of time, then allowed to return to about 100 in an easy, coasting kind of activity. Such activities as handball, squash, badminton, and tennis are of this type: for example, you might start running hard, then coast, and so on. There is no rest, but rather continuous activity for a period of time. It is the continuous nature of the activity that conditions the heart and lungs. Some authorities state that desired changes can be produced in these organs within five minutes if the exercise is demanding enough to sustain the heart rate around 140 to 150 beats per minute for the entire time. Maximal time for the exercise is somewhere between 20 and 30 minutes.

anaerobic exercise for power

Anaerobic exercise is the key to power/strength where local muscular endurance is a factor. The primary objective is to increase the capacity to tolerate an oxygen debt. The exercise must demand so much oxygen in so short a time that energy demands surpass the body's capacity to produce it, which results in an

improving organic tone: cardiovascular-respiratory endurance **101**

TABLE 8.2   Relative Merits of Conditioning Programs Based on Type of Exercise

Physical and Physiological Changes	Body Adaptations—Optimal Type of Exercise	
	Aerobic Exercise Endurance: Distance Running	Anaerobic Exercise Power: Sprints
Heart		
Size	Increased	Slight increase
Stroke volume	Increased	Little change
Resting pulse rate	Marked decrease	Little change
Exercise pulse rate	Lower in steady state work	Little change
Pulse rate recovery	Marked increase	Little change
Circulation (coronary)	Increased	Slight increase
Lungs		
Ventilation capacity	Increased	Increased capacity
Circulation	Increased vascularization and blood flow	Unknown
Oxygen extraction	Increased capacity	Little change
Volume	Increased vital capacity	Little change
Oxygen utilization		
Efficiency (economy effort)	Increased	Little change
Maximal oxygen intake capacity	Increased	Little change
Oxygen debt capacity	Slight increase	Increased markedly
Steady state level	Marked increase	Little change
Recovery rate	Marked increase	Little change
Active muscle tissue		
Circulation	Marked increase in vascularization and blood flow	Unknown
Power/Strength	Little change	Marked increase

"oxygen debt." Anaerobic exercise is work at high intensity that drives the heart rate to about 180 for a short period of time; this is followed by short intervals of rest that bring the heart rate down to about 120 or 140. This cycle is repeated about 15 to 20 times in a progressive manner. Work periods last about 30 seconds, and the shortest intervals are about the same duration. It can readily be seen that sprint events in swimming and track and, in general, athletic events lasting less than one minute depend on muscular endurance and the ability to tolerate an oxygen debt. In fact, anaerobic training is used in competitive athletics. It increases endurance somewhat, but it is primarily for improving power. It is not the optimal way to condition the heart and lungs. The relative merits of aerobic and anaerobic exercises are shown in Table 8.2.

Aerobic exercise is the key to producing organic adaptations in the cardiovascular-respiratory system. Increased capacity for oxygen consumption provides benefits in the form of ability to sustain work without undue fatigue or exhaustion. In addition, a well-conditioned heart, healthy and efficient, provides built-in protection against emotional crises that could lead to deterioration and the possible onset of coronary heart disease. To maintain the heart and lungs in top flight condition, one must exercise regularly.

specific aerobic conditioning exercises

A conditioning program should be interesting and challenging, but it must also be feasible in the immediate environment. Some persons like to exercise at home, using small treadmills or exercise bicycles or running in place. Others like to get into the out-of-doors and run or bike. Still others live near a swimming pool, playing fields, or courts for tennis, squash, or badminton.

These activities are suggestions only. You may wish to use the principles and devise your own program using different forms of activity to provide variety. Each program should provide an overload to the cardiovascular-respiratory system so that the desired organic adaptations can be achieved. The decision is yours as well as the responsibility to carry it out.

references and sources for additional reading

1. Hill, A.V., C.N.H. Long, and H. Lupton, "Muscular Exercise, Lactic Acid and the Supply and Utilization of Oxygen: V. The Recovery Process After Exercise in Man." *Proceedings of the Royal Society*, 1924, pp. 96–97.

Barney, V.S., C.C. Hirst, and C.R. Jensen, *Conditioning Exercises*. St. Louis, Mo.: The C.V. Mosby Co., 1965.

Consolazio, C.F., R.E. Johnson and L.J. Pecora, *Physiological Measurements of Metabolic Functions in Man*. New York: McGraw-Hill Book Company, 1963.

Cooper, K.H., and K. Brown, *Aerobics*. New York: M. Evans & Co., Inc., 1968.

Johnson, W.R., ed., *Science and Medicine of Exercise and Sports*. New York: Harper & Row, Publishers, 1960.

Karpovich, P.V. *Physiology of Muscular Activity*. Philadelphia: W.B. Saunders Company, 1965.

Ricci, B., *Physiological Basis of Human Performance*. Philadelphia: Lea & Febiger, 1967.

Wallis, E.L., and G.A. Logan, *Figure Improvement and Body Conditioning Through Exercise*. Englewood Cliffs, N.J.: Prentice-Hall, Inc., 1964.

achieving
skilled performance in
physical activity

9 How many times have you thought yourself awkward? Do you think you have to be born a "motor genius" to achieve success in sports or with a sense of rhythm to dance? You will find there are all degrees of abilities in learning physical activities. Most important is that you recognize your strengths and limitations and learn to select activities that will make the most of what you have. Probably more people look like motor morons or lack rhythm because they have never used their capabilities rather than because of their limitations. The important thing is to learn how to select physical activities suited to your abilities and temperament. If you do this, you are likely to achieve success and an amount of skill that will give you joy and satisfaction.

To achieve success in physical activity you need:

1. A knowledge of self: your basic physical characteristics (body type, physical performance status); and your personal characteristics (temperament, desire, motivation, significance of the specific physical activity to you, as well as your aspiration level)
2. A knowledge of the physical activity: the physical requirements of the specific activity; the principles and patterns underlying all movement; the specificity of movement and the learning process.

The primary purpose of this chapter is to give you the basic knowledge you need to understand and analyze physical activity. An objective approach to analyzing physical activity and purposive movement patterns in work and play is based on two concepts: (1) all purposive movements have certain common elements, and (2) all purposive movements have specific characteristics.

COMMON MOVEMENT ELEMENTS

What are the common elements in all purposive movement patterns of your life? What elements are basic to all movement regardless of the use of the movement or the situation in which you use a specific form of movement to accomplish a particular goal? There are four elements common to all movement: (*1*) fundamental movement patterns; (*2*) bio-mechanical principles governing movement with respect to time, space, force, and flow of movement; (*3*) perception of feeling created by movement; and (*4*) the meaning or significance of the movement. You should develop your ability to think about and evaluate your own movement experience by conceiving your movement experiences in the four inter-related elements common to all movements.

fundamental movement patterns

First, each and every movement has structure. This structure is generally not a single isolated joint action but a pattern of movement or multijoint actions. For example a simple task like eating involves the changing relationship of the hand, elbow, shoulder, and trunk. All human activities are derived from basic patterns of movement. These basic patterns are adapted to a specific use as in dance or in bowling by refining and/or adding to the basic patterns. Most of you had personally experienced all of the basic patterns of movement by the time you were six years old. Since that time you have been refining your gross movement patterns by exploring time and space and your environment as well as by adding different combinations and sequences to your movements for the development of specific skills to be used in a specific situation to accomplish a particular task.

Purposive Movements in Activities of Work and Play with Basic Movement Patterns Involved

Force	Purposive movements	Basic Movement Patterns Involved
Resist a force	*To hold weight* Your body weight	Stand, hang, sit, lie, headstand, handstand
	Other weights	Holding objects Stunts: pyramids, angel balance
Impart force	*To move weight* Your body weight	Walk, run, jump, leap, hop, slide, gallop, climb, ride a bike, skate, swim, stoop, bend, extend, turn and twist
	Other weights	Throw, strike, kick, lift, stoop, pull, push, reach
Absorb force	*To receive weight* Your body weight	Fall, land
	Other weights	Catch

In your movement patterns in work, you are interested in conserving your energy, in expending it efficiently. In your movement patterns in sports, you are interested in developing maximum force and maintaining it over a period of time. All these basic skills of work and play involve imparting force, resisting force, or absorbing force. Instead of making a list of all the activities of work and play and the movements involved in each, we can classify them according to purposive movements.

bio-mechanical principles

Every movement involves interaction with environment—time, space, force, and flow. Because you live on this planet there are certain bio-mechanical principles governing all movements. Your body, as a living machine, creates its own energy and expends it in every action of your life. This expenditure of energy may be efficient; the results you achieve may be equal to the energy you use to produce them. Or, the expenditure of energy may be inefficient; you may have had to put in twice as much energy to achieve the results you wanted. The important question, then, is how to make your body operate efficiently. Like a machine, your body at rest or in motion will function most efficiently when its operations obey the basic principles that govern human motion and balance. If you break these principles, your body begins to function inefficiently.

There are three essential principles that govern all effective movement.

> *Equilibrium*
> Ways to maintain greatest stability
> Ways to maintain maneuverability
> Ways to recover from movements
>
> *Motion*
> Types of motion
> Ways to determine type of motion
>
> *Force*
> Ways to produce effective force
> Ways to direct the application of force
> Ways to absorb or dissipate force

Each of these principles with their important factors is discussed in detail below.

Equilibrium. Important factors for maintaining balance. Your balance is important in everything you do, not just in preventing a fall or regaining your balance. Your balance is important in order for you to build your maximum force and for controlling the direction of your movements. You know that your skeleton is not a rigid structure, but is made of many movable segments. You are constantly balancing those segments. The only time you are free of this constant struggle of balance is when you lie down. Your life, however, is made up of movement, both mental and physical. You may sometime find yourself in positions in which balance is difficult to achieve, but you should understand how to increase and decrease your stability. Without stability you would have difficulty in controlling your accuracy of movements, and in building force.

The important principles for equilibrium are outlined below.

1. The body is balanced when its center of weight is over the supporting base.
2. The nearer to the center of the base of support the line of gravity falls, the greater the stability.
3. The larger the base of support, the more stable the body.
   a. The base should be enlarged in the direction of the moving force or the opposing force or the receiving force.
   b. If the base is enlarged to hip width, too great a strain is placed on joints, causing them to lose maneuverability or quickness of motion to move or to give when receiving a force.
4. The lower the center of weight, the more stable the body. The distance depends on the purpose of the activity and the condition of the muscles.
5. External weights added to the body become part of the total body weight and affect the location of the center of weight, displacing it in the direction of the added weights.
6. Whenever one body part moves away from the line of gravity in one direction, the center of weight shifts in that direction. If the shift puts the center of weight beyond the base, another body part must move in the opposite direction to bring the center of weight back over the base; if this is not done, balance is lost.

You know the ideal way of holding your body weight. It is to pile up your body segments with the line of gravity passing through the center of each segment and falling to the floor in the center of your base of support.

If you want to increase your balance:

1. Keep your center of weight directly over your base of support.
2. Keep your base of support large in the direction in which you are going to receive the force. *Do not overextend*, however, because you won't be able to move quickly.
3. Keep your center of gravity close to your base of support. Keep your hips low. In coming down from a jump, lower your center of gravity and you will find it easier to maintain your balance.
4. Counterbalance your movements with the opposite arm or leg or other body parts.
5. Keep your eyes on one spot.

Motion. Important principles for producing a type of motion. Movement is a change of place or position. Movement involves direction and speed. There are three types of movement:

1. Rotation or angular: movement in a circle. The body and/or any of its parts move around an axis . . . all parts move in an arc about an axis such as in a somersault or in throwing or striking events.
2. Rectilinear: movement in a straight line.

a. The body or its parts move in the same direction at a uniform rate of speed, such as in skating, skiing, driving a car.

b. Most body movements are a combination of rotational and rectilinear movements, e.g., angular movement of legs in walking, whole body moving ahead in straight line in swimming, pull or push thrust in fencing.

3. Projectile motion: movement of body or an object as a whole in a curved path. Motion of the object is brought about at first by a combination of rotatory and rectilinear movements, then, due to gravity and air resistance, the projectile falls earthward, e.g., all projectiles . . . flight of arrow, throw of ball, person broad jumping.

If force is applied through the center of weight of an object that is free to move, the movement will be in a straight line. If force is applied away from the center of weight of an object, the movement will be a rotation. The farther away from the center of weight of the object you apply the force, the greater will be the amount of rotation or spin on the object.

The type of rotation that occurs when you apply force other than through the center of weight of the object is depicted in the spin of the balls in the following illustration.

Spin of Balls: Size, shape, weight, construction, air and wind resistance, and gravity all affect the way a ball travels through space.

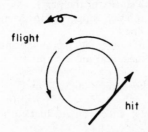

The Curve: A rapidly spinning ball (one hit other than through the center of weight) creates greater friction on one side than on the other side. It seeks the line of least resistance. The result is a curve.

Curve to Left: hook in golf, slice in tennis, outcurve in pitching, hit inside of ball.

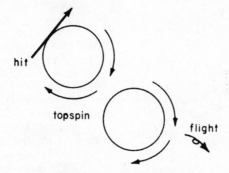

Topspin: ball spins toward ground, hit up and over center of gravity, comes to ground fast.

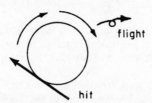

Curve to Right: slice in golf, and tennis, incurve in softball, hit outside of ball.

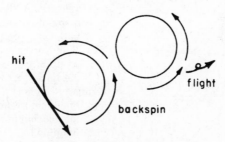

Backspin: chop in tennis, undercut in golf, ball spins upward, hit down and under the center of gravity, tends to rise before falling.

Force. Important principles for production, direction in which your force is applied, and the absorption of your forces:

1. Building or production of force
   a. Muscular strength and tone
      (1) More force is available from strong muscles than from weak muscles.
      (2) All muscles in the body are not equal in their potential of strength; for example, the larger muscles of the hips, thighs, and legs are stronger than those of the arms.
      (3) Muscles moving the body weight or other weights must have a firm base of action . . . stabilizing is accomplished by muscles of the pelvic girdle for leg action and by muscles of the chest and upper back and shoulders for arm action.
      (4) Muscles extended or lengthened before contraction exert more force . . . tension.
      (5) Larger muscles should be used to overcome the initial inertia of body weight or objects.
      (6) Total effective force is the sum of all forces produced by the muscle groups applied in the same direction and sequence.
   b. Sequential movement—the more sequential the motion, the more force is obtainable.
      (1) Flow of motion from one body part to another . . . flow of momentum (mass times velocity of the part).
      (2) Transfer of weight, trunk rotation, upper arm, lower arm, hand, fingers . . . in throwing.
      (3) Transfer of weight, upper leg, lower leg, foot in kicking.
      (4) Pushing-pulling . . . hip, knee, and ankle, arms for grasping or holding weight.
      (5) Stooping-lifting . . . hips, knee, and ankle, arms for grasping or holding weight.
      (6) Walking-climbing . . . hips, knees, ankle, foot, arms for counterbalance.
      (7) Force is the change in momentum of one body part to another per unit of time. The greatest momentum occurs at the moment of impact or release, each body part having a greater momentum than the preceding part.
   c. Timing.
      (1) Body forces are added successively; each force should be brought in when the one before it has reached its peak velocity. Adding a force too soon or too late inhibits the momentum and prevents the force from flowing to the next part, e.g., throwing, striking, walking.
      (2) Body forces are added simultaneously in many tasks—such as pulling, pushing, lifting, carrying—to overcome initial inertia and move the object.
   d. Range of motion . . . distance over which force is applied.
      (1) Speed and range of motion are linked together in developing maximum force in throwing and striking, running and jumping.
      (2) The greater the distance and, therefore, the time over which a force is developed, the greater will be the force.
         (a) The greater the number of body levers or body parts

involved in a movement, the greater the distance and, therefore, time to develop force.

(b) The greater the range of motion at each joint for the specific levers brought in, the greater the distance and, therefore, time to develop force. Range depends on muscle strength to move.

(c) The greater the length of each lever, the greater the distance and, therefore, time to develop force. The same principle can be applied to the length of the total lever involved (body is total lever).

(3) The faster the muscles contract, the greater the speed or velocity at the end of the moving lever, the greater the force imparted at the moment of impact, release, takeoff.

(4) The slower the muscles contract, the less energy is required, e.g., in lifting, pulling, pushing.

(5) The greater the distance over which force is applied, the more work takes place. It requires less work to move an object on a level than to lift or lower an object. Work = load × distance moved.

e. Nature or quality of the movement . . . muscular contractions involved in the movement.

(1) Sustained contractions involve contraction of the prime movers and the antagonistic muscles at the same time. Since the prime movers have the greater force, movement, which may be *fast or slow and sustained*, occurs in their direction. [Pull, push, lift, carry, thrust in fencing, climb stairs, stoop, lift, canoe, motion of arms in swimming.]

If both sets of muscles contract with equal force, no motion results. Unbalanced forces must exist if motion is to occur.

(2) Ballistic movements involve vigorous contraction of the prime movers, with the antagonistic muscles relaxing completely. Momentum of the distal levers (extremities) completes the movement. The movement may be *rapid or slow and ballistic* [Leg kick in swimming, leg action in running and walking, arm action in throwing and striking.]

2. Direction over which force is applied.

a. Movement upward . . . apply force through the center of weight of the body, a line from the ball of the foot through the center directly upward. If you move the line forward, you have lost part of the force because it will be used to send you upward and forward.

b. Movement forward . . . apply force through the center of weight in the direction you want to go, a line from the ball of the foot through the center of weight which is over the forward foot or ahead of the forward foot, e.g., walking. In running, since the body leans more, force should be applied from the foot through the center of weight, which is outside of the base of support.

c. Lifting and lowering of body weight . . . the center of weight should be directly over the center of the base of the support line from the center of weight to the base of support.

d. Point of contact with object . . . rotating objects, spinning balls, moving furniture . . . apply force away from center of weight . . . the farther away, the less the energy.

e. Move object in straight line . . . apply force through the center of weight in the direction in which you desire to go, e.g., power driving in golf, moving furniture.

    f. Angle of impact and angle of release . . . your goal should be the greatest distance, your direction of force should be 45 degrees.

    g. Force applied in a direction other than the one in which you desire to go, or to move the object, is lost, and the motion becomes ineffective.

    h. Balance . . . dynamic equilibrium . . . balance in motion.

        (1) Landing from jump . . . widen the base of support to hip width, lower the center of weight over the base.

        (2) In the follow-through after impact or release of ball . . . widen the base of support in the direction in which you are applying force. Follow the same directions when you are receiving a force, e.g., a ball.

        (3) Maintaining balance . . . an adequate supporting surface and a firm base are important factors in facilitating the maintenance of balance.

The angle at which a ball hits any object will affect the angle at which the ball rebounds. For maximum distance the ball should be released at a 45 degree angle. The kind of surface will affect the height of the rebound of the ball. The accompanying illustrations and descriptions show how force affects balls in relation to their spin or rotation and in relation to the angles of their impact and rebound

Angles of Impact—Angle of Rebound and Striking Surfaces.

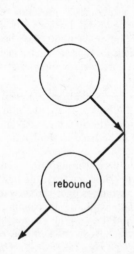

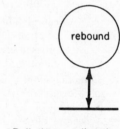

Ball thrown directly down rebounds straight up.

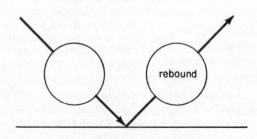

Hard Surface: rebound is higher.
Hard Abraded Surface: higher rebound, skidding prevented, more spin.
Firmness of Grip and Implement: firm grip on racket, tense strings, faster rebound.

Ball thrown at ground or ball hitting racket or ground at an angle leaves at that angle.

3. Absorption or dissipation of body forces (momentum), or the momentum of other objects.
   a. The more gradual the reduction of momentum or force, the less likelihood for injury or rebound to occur (give at the hip, knee, and ankle in landing from jump; give at the shoulder, elbow, hands and transfer weight in the reverse direction of the on-coming force in catching a ball or object).
   b. Use as large an area as possible to absorb the force (sliding into a base . . . using as large and as soft a body area as possible in falling or tripping). An exception is a fall into water when one should use as small a body area as possible.
   c. One of the purposes of follow-through in sports is to prevent injury by absorbing the momentum generated by the body. Use as large a distance as possible for the number of joints involved and the movement potential at each joint. Momentum of the arm is absorbed easily over a greater distance and then the strength of the opposing or antagonistic muscles contract and check the motion.

PERCEPTION OF MOVEMENT

Each and every movement involves more than moving the body or its parts in space. Each movement involves feeling and thinking, which enable you to become aware of or to perceive the movement—to bring it to a conscious level. You perceive the movement pattern in eating; you are aware of the structures involved, the muscle tension or force employed, the sequence of your move-ments, the direction in which you are moving, and so forth. Have you not had the experience of "feeling" when you hit a golf ball correctly or when you walked downstairs with ease and grace? Earlier we discussed kinesthetic perception in relation to its physiological bases. Here we will describe it in more detail.

kinesthetic perception

Your sense of force and direction is called "the kinesthetic sense." Probably this is the most important factor in the control of body movements. It provides you with awareness and perception of different movements in time, space, direction, and of the flow of movement. If you closed your eyes and someone asked you to raise your arm in front of you to shoulder level, you could do it. Vision is not necessary for this knowledge. You can *feel* where you are and what you are doing.

Earlier it was stated that your kinesthetic sense was important to you for becoming aware of balanced body lines—postural postions. Now, you find that this is important to you in controlling all body movements. How does it work? You are continuously being sent messages—nerve impulses to make you aware of your body or any of its parts. There are small sensory organs in and around joint spaces, muscle tendons, and the muscles themselves. Any change of position of the joint or tension in the muscle fires these sensory organs, and nerve impulses are sent to the spinal cord and to the brain, letting you know about it so that you can make the necessary adjustments. Nerve impulses then go to the muscles—the motor system—for adjustment to take place.

How fast you are moving: the speed at which you should contract your muscles to bring your arm in at the right time. Moving your hand too fast would cause you to knock over a glass of water for which you were reaching.

How much force you need: the number of muscle fibers and the sequence in which they should be brought in. Holding a glass with too much force would cause you to break it.

The direction in which you are moving: you know whether to move your hand forward or backward to reach for a glass.

The position of the body or its parts in space: you are aware of your pelvic position and of the position of any other body part.

The muscle or kinesthetic sense varies widely in different persons. Such differences may help to account for your aptitude for certain motor activities, especially activities requiring a great deal of control, accuracy, and fast reactions.

The smoothness, accuracy, and efficiency of your movements involve a continuous stream of nerve impulses passing to your muscles from the brain and spinal cord and another stream of sensory impulses from the sense organs located in the tendons, muscles, and joints to the spinal cord and brain. By such a constant feedback system, the instructions to your muscles can be constantly modified and adapted to meet different situations. Simply, this means that your muscles are under the control of the "will." You can change to your liking any movement pattern, for example, the way you walk or talk. You have the capacity to learn and relearn or change if you desire. However, remember, if you desire to change the way you walk, it will take concentrated thought on your part to change such an old established habit. But it can be done if you desire, if you practice, and if you remember.

In summary kinesthetic perception is an important "muscle sense" that enables you to become aware of or to perceive a movement pattern:

1. You perceive movement because movement is a sensory-motor experience.
    a. Position in space or change of position.
    b. Pattern of movement . . . different body parts or levers to use to accomplish a specific goal.
    c. Force to use . . . muscle groups or number of levers to use.
    d. Nature or quality of movement . . . sustained or ballistic.
2. Some of us have greater perception than others; perception can be developed through movement experiences involving feeling and thinking, not mere doing.
    a. Once a movement pattern is learned, we have the "feel" of this pattern.

b. Then we can delegate control to a lower motor center than the conscious level.

Rhythmic patterns. The relationship of time and force is the rhythmic organization—the flow of your movements. Your rhythmic patterns

Eight Simple Ways of Moving

Even rhythm ⸺⸺⸺ ⸺⸺⸺
Equal amount of time for each part

Walk: Alternate transference of weight from one foot to the other. There is a period of time when both feet are on the ground at the same time.

Run: Alternate transference of weight from one foot to the other directly. There is a period of time when both feet are off the ground at the same time. The tempo is faster than a walk.

Leap: Alternate transference of weight from one foot to the other accentuated by a lift of the body from the floor. It is slower than the run and may be made for height or for horizontal distance. There is a period of time when both feet are off the ground at the same time.

Jump: Transference of weight from one or both feet and landing on both feet at the same time. May be made for height or for horizontal distance.

Hop: Transference of weight from one foot back to the same foot.

Uneven rhythm ⸺⸺⸺⸺⸺⸺ ⸺⸺
Two parts with one part longer than the other
(Some people believe that these steps are just combinations of those above.)

Gallop: Rhythm is long, short. Step forward or backward and then close, with the original foot always leading. Transfer your weight to forward foot and slide rear foot to heel of forward foot. Shift weight to back foot and step forward again with the same foot.

Slide: Rhythm is long, short. Step to the right side on right foot and then bring left foot up to side of right foot. Shift weight to left foot and repeat.

Skip: Rhythm is long, short. Step and hop on the same foot, and then alternate on left and then on right.

What about forms of locomotion and music? Let's see what happens when you use an even number of beats or counts to a measure (4/4) and then an uneven number of counts to a measure (3/4) and run, jump, hop, leap, walk, gallop, skip, and slide.
Let's examine some of the rhythmical patterns in your sport activities.

Activity	Rhythmical Pattern (Time Intervals)					
Bowling						
Arm pattern		Swing Back			Swing Through	
Foot pattern	Step	Step	Step		Step	
Swimming						
Arm pattern		Pull			Pull	
Foot pattern	Kick	Kick	Kick	Kick	Kick	Kick
Tennis (forehand stroke)						
Arm pattern		Open, Hold			Swing	
Foot pattern		Pivot			Step	
Others?						

can be improved through practice. You can increase your sensitivity or awareness through conscious experience in the analysis of the rhythmic structure of
movement. Why should you be aware of the different rhythmical organizations
of your movements? The reason is simple. Your learning is facilitated when
you understand the rhythmical organization—timing, accent, and force. All
your movements have a rhythmical pattern. You must find the pattern to
accomplish your goal. Movement that flows rhythmically with perfect timing
is efficient and highly coordinated. Equally important, your perception of the
rhythmic flow of your movement will enable you to have greater appreciation
of the rhythmical motion in others.

THIS	First hour	Second hour	Third hour	Fourth hour
	10 min. rest	10 min. rest	10 min. rest	15 min. rest

Rest often if you have 4 hours housework to do

NOT THIS	First hour	Second hour	Third hour	Fourth hour
				45 min. rest

Take time to study the rhythm of your movements in your work and play; to
examine the rhythmic patterns you use to move yourself through space in performing your daily living activities. The descriptions of eight ways of moving
(p. 115), daily working patterns (above), and sports activities (pp. 118–19)
will stimulate your perception of movement patterns.

THE SIGNIFICANCE OF A MOVEMENT
WITHIN A SITUATION

Every movement has its own meaning or significance to you and to others
in the situation in which it occurs. For example, the pattern you use in eating
has a particular meaning and significance. Do you eat with your head down
and elbows on the table? If so, what impression of yourself do you give to

others? What is this a symbol of? Of course, this depends on the meaning given to your movements by a group. Each culture establishes the symbolic meaning of movements—of the games, sports, and dances that make up part of that culture. Some movements are judged as masculine or feminine. Each culture sets certain expectancies for achievement in different movements or organized activities for men and women, and girls and boys. Each small subculture within the culture provides local or provincial approval or disapproval of different forms of physical activities. You, as an individual within a particular cultural milieu, also attribute a significance, a symbolic meaning, to your own movements. This is revealed in the activities you select, the extent of participation, and the level of aspiration for you within the culture. This significance permeates your actions in work and play. It determines how you act toward others. Are your body movements and gestures patient or impatient, aggressive or submissive, tolerant or intolerant? How do you act or react to different situations? Do you stand up straight and face the situation? Are your movements decisive or indecisive? Can you recognize and identify your bodily movements, gestures, attitudes? How do you communicate your *self* to others? Can you recognize the interplay of your movements—the physical manifestation of moods, of leading or following, of mutual responding, of giving and taking?

In summary, each and every movement has its own meaning:

1. Symbolic of self: the way in which you perceive yourself and the world you live in as depicted by your postures and movements, and the games, sports, or dances you participate in.
2. Interaction with others: the way you react to others—exuberant or inhibited; aggressive or submissive; nervous in front of an audience; tense before a game.
3. Communication: art form of dance—the way movements are done; the sequence, pattern, quality, or nature of movements portray your way of life, your thoughts, ideas, and concepts of the individual self, others, and the world.

SPECIFICITY OF MOVEMENT

We said earlier that there are elements common to all movements. If this is true, how would you differentiate between different kinds of movements? What makes a dance movement, a bowling movement, a tennis movement, an archery movement? Although all movements have elements in common, differences do exist. Such differences enable you to distinguish activities from one another. The basis for distinguishing one kind of movement from another is twofold: (1) the situation in which the movement is executed, and (2) the use of the movement performed. For instance, walking to answer the phone at work is considered a working movement, but walking to a rhythm pattern on the dance floor is considered a dance movement. The situation in which you perform the movement determines whether it is dance, sport, athletic, work, corrective or therapeutic.

specific movement characteristics

Although two activities may be similar in that like movements are involved, the use of the movement and the situation in which it is performed are specific for that movement event. Each purposive movement has specific characteristics of time, space, force, flow, and pattern. Each purposive movement has specific sensory or perception characteristics created by the movement event. For instance, examine these arm patterns for selected sport activities shown below. Notice the similarity of patterns in all the activities. The bio-mechanical principles for the building, summation, and dissipation of force are common to all these events; yet in each, specific characteristics are evident in pattern, time, space, force, and flow of movement. Each event has specific physical requirements—characteristic of that activity and varying in the amount needed for skilled performance. Examine the Sport Rating Chart in Appendix A to understand the specificity in each kind of activity.

UNDERARM ACTIVITIES

Building Force		Summation of Your Forces	Dissipation of Your Forces
Backswing	Forward Swing	Accent	Follow-through

SIDEARM ACTIVITIES

Building Force		Summation of Your Forces	Dissipation of Your Forces
Backswing	Forward Swing	Accent	Follow-through

Building Force		Summation of Your Forces	Dissipation of Your Forces
Backswing	Forward Swing	Accent	Follow-through

learning conditions

Training for a skilled movement for one event is specific for that event. The state of training for one skill makes very little contribution to performances in another movement event in a different situation and use. This is because each skilled movement has specific characteristics. The process of training involves the neuromuscular refinements of the specific characteristics, the organic adjustments necessary for performance, and the mind set for evaluating the sensorisomatic experience for accomplishing the skill for a particular situation. You need to understand the elements common to all movements, apply these to the specific movement event, and practice the specific characteristics of the movement in the situation in which you desire to use it.

The actual process you go through in learning a motor skill is outlined below:

1. *Remember*:
   vision
   kinesthetic sense
   hearing
   verbalization
   past experience

   Watch someone show you how a skill should be done and/or tell you how it should be done so that you know what you are supposed to do (total rhythmic pattern). Try to remember if you have done anything like it before and remember how you did it. Perceive the time intervals for different portions of the movement, the force of different portions of the movement, and the accent.

2. *You try it*:

   Develop a "sense of feel" for the rhythmic pattern you want to use, see yourself in motion, and feel yourself performing the rhythmic pattern, the time, force, and accent.

3. *You look again*:

   You see it done again and now you perceive more of the total movement and its parts. You become more aware of the timing of each part involved in the movement, the varying of force, and the accent.

4. *You try it again*:   You see and feel yourself doing it and you remember more. You listen to directions for correcting common mistakes and change your pattern if necessary.

5. *You practice*:   Continually try to be effective in the movement you want to learn. Listen to directions. Practice with "feeling" and thinking, not just doing.

6. *You do it*:   Perform the whole pattern of movement in an actual situation for specific use.

What should you know about practicing? If you practice the wrong way, that is the pattern you will use. What do you need to know to practice intelligently? In order to achieve maximum results from your work and play, you must know how to practice intelligently.

1. You should understand the basic principles governing all body movement--postural patterns of the body for graceful efficient motion in work and play. *Think through the activity.*

2. You should understand the movement classification of your skill and how to apply the basic principles to the skill you want to learn. Understanding enhances your learning.

3. You should be able to analyze your movements so you know when and why they are right or wrong. This is the basis for education and re-education.

4. Then you need to know what to do to correct wrong movements. Practice or time spent with no understanding of whether you are doing the movement correctly or incorrectly will hinder, not help, your learning process. You may develop the wrong pattern.

5. You should always practice with concentration on what you are doing and how you are doing it.

6. Early stages of learning sometimes involve retrogression. You may get poorer before you get better. This is true if you must unlearn certain patterns before you can develop the correct ones.

7. Shorter practice sessions with longer rest periods between are generally more beneficial than long practice periods with short rest intervals. This is true in the early learning stages, for practicing too long may inhibit rather than improve your performance.

8. In the early learning stages you may have some rapid periods of improvement. This is generally followed by periods of leveling off.

9. You may reach a plateau in your learning. This may result from factors such as:
   a. The skill is too complex for you. Your teacher should break it down into simpler movements.
   b. You have practiced too long and too consistently.
   c. You are tired and fatigued. This interferes with your learning.
   d. You have reached your level of achievement.

10. Readiness for learning will determine how effectively you learn. Your past experiences, personal attitude, present skill level, present physical condition and, possibly, your body type will all affect your progress in learning.

11. Your physical attributes and your learning potential must be

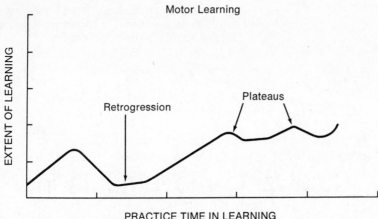

Motor Learning

Adapted from Van Huss, et al., *Physical Activity in Modern Living* (Englewood Cliffs, N.J.: Prentice-Hall, Inc., 1960).

accepted for what they are, but your skill level, interest, motivation, and present condition are changeable through new experiences with practice and thought.

12. Some activities are easier to learn than others. This varies with the complexity of the activity and from one individual to another.

13. For best learning to occur you need to operate at a level of maximum challenge. Your level of maximum challenge is affected by your attitude, objectives, and goals in learning.

Once you have learned a skill, concentration lessens, and you can use your conscious thought (higher motor) to follow the strategy of your play or your work, and delegate the movement to lower motor centers.

references and sources for additional reading

Broer, M., *Efficiency of Human Movement*. Philadelphia: W.B. Saunders Co., 1960.

Bunn, J.W., *Scientific Principles of Coaching*. Englewood Cliffs, N.J.: Prentice-Hall, Inc., 1955.

Cooper, J.M., and R.B. Glassow, *Kinesiology*. St. Louis, Mo.: The C.V. Mosby Co., 1963.

Howland, I.S., *Body Alignment in Fundamental Motor Skills*. Jericho, N.Y.: Exposition Press, Inc., 1953.

Metheny, E., *Body Dynamics*. New York: McGraw-Hill Book Company, 1952.

———, *Connotations of Movement in Sports and Dance*. Dubuque, Iowa: William C. Brown Company, Publishers, 1965.

———, *Movement and Meaning*. New York: McGraw-Hill Book Company, 1968.

Scott, M.G., *Analysis of Human Motion*. New York: Appleton-Century-Crofts, 1963.

Slusher, H.S. *Man, Sport and Existence*. Philadelphia: Lea & Febiger, 1967.

Williams, M., and H.R. Lissner, *Biomechanics of Human Motion*. Philadelphia: W.B. Saunders Co., 1960.

analyzing movements in
work and play

10 An objective approach to the study of your movement characteristics is based on the premise that motor performance is comprised of two discrete components: purposive movement patterns and bio-mechanical principles underlying all effective performance in activities of work and play.

The reasons for this approach are as follows. *1.* It may help you to become aware of similar types of movement involved in all activities. *2.* It may help you to become aware of the underlying principles governing effective performance in all activities. *3.* It may help you to judge and kinesthetically discern how to adjust to use specific characteristics of each motor skill.

Before you begin to study your own movement characteristics in the basic skills of work and play, examine carefully the analysis that follows. The purposive movements with basic movement patterns primarily with the underlying principles involved in *work* are presented first; those involved in *play* are presented next.

To help you understand the bio-mechanical principles primarily involved in each movement pattern they have been separated into four major groupings and applied to each of the purposive movements—holding the body weight or other objects, moving the body weight or other objects.

1. *Equilibrium or Stability*
    Center of weight
    Base of support
    Relation of center of weight to base of support
2. *Force*
    Sequential movement
    Timing

Range of motion
Speed or rate of movement
3. *Force Direction*
Line of direction over which force is applied
Angle of impact, takeoff, release, or point of contact
4. *Nature of the Movement*
Sustained . . . fast or slow or postural tonus
Ballistic . . . rapid or slow
Collapse

The first group of activities analyzed involves purposive movement in work; the second group, purposive movement in play.

A SUMMARY; BASIC SKILLS

What are your movement characteristics in purposive movement patterns, work skills, sport and dance skills? All of these skills are involved in (1) resisting a force, (2) absorbing a force, and (3) imparting a force. Such skills may require a great mobility, a great stability, or a combination of both—maneuverability with stability. In the work skills you are interested in conserving energy and expending it efficiently. In sport skills you are interested in achieving maximum energy (body force) with prevention of injury. In dance skills you are interested in the flow of energy in different rhythmical patterns.

A skill is learned. It is developed through conscious thought with practice. The learning of a skill may be easy for some and very difficult for others. The degree of skill or level of performance will vary for different activities in each of us, just as it varies among all of us. The most important thing is the development of your potential. Each of us desires to be competent. This desire for competence may have nothing to do with competition per se. You may enjoy swimming without wanting to compete. This desire for competency in your movements is found in the work skills, e.g., walking in heels, sewing a dress, making a cake. All of us do not have the inclination and natural endowment to achieve mastery in every activity, but each of us should make the most of our potential. Your movement involves moving your mass (weight) or the mass of some other object through space with respect to time. Your movements are done to accomplish certain goals. You want to thread a needle, type, play a piano, swing a tennis racket, learn a new dance step, or catch a bus.

Work Skills.   What is your skill or performance level in fundamental movement patterns involved in your daily activities? What stimulates others to remark: "Her movements are so free and easy," "Her movements are so graceful, no matter what she is doing," "She is so efficient in the way she works"? As all these patterns involve imparting force, resisting a force, or absorbing a force, they can be classified. Look at the chart following. Think of the way you move in your work skills.

Are you aware of your body? Can you perceive, "feel," your movements? Can you analyze your movements? Do you understand the basic factors

Force	Purpose	What are Your Movement Characteristics?
Impart Force	*To Move through Space* Your body weight:	walking in flats or heels stooping to pick up a pencil getting in and out of a car climbing stairs
	Other weights:	lifting a baby from the floor pushing a chair pulling a door
Resist Force	*To Hold Weights* Your body weight:	standing in flats or heels combing your hair sitting in class sitting at rest lying down to read
	Other weights:	holding books holding a baby holding a suitcase reaching for a hat on top shelf
Absorb Force	*To Receive a Weight* Your body weight:	tripping on a step stumbling and falling in heels
	Other weights:	catching a hat box catching a suitcase

involved in imparting, resisting, and absorbing a force? Do you know how to improve your performance, to adapt your movements to achieve a desired purpose? How would you evaluate your performance?

 Play Skills. What is your performance level in the fundamental patterns involved in sports and dance? What stimulates others to remark: "She does it with such ease," "It looks so easy when she does it," "Her movements

Force	Purpose	What are Your Movement Characteristics?
Impart Force	*To Move through Space* Your body weight:	running, jumping, hopping, skipping, leaping, galloping, climbing, skating, swimming, dancing
	Other weights:	throwing a ball, striking a ball, kicking a ball, pulling a bow, paddling
Resist Force	*To Hold a Weight:* Your body weight: Other weights:	headstands, handstands, float angel balance stunt pyramids
Absorb Force	*To Receive a Weight* Your body weight:	landing from a jump falling on ice sliding to home plate
	Other weights:	catching a ball with your hands trapping a ball with your feet

have such power and grace," "She moves beautifully"? Here again, the patterns can be classified because they are all involved in imparting, resisting, and absorbing a force. Look at the chart that follows; think of the way you move in your play skills.

WORK

Holding Your Body Weight

Why do it this way? Because you look better—grace and poise. Because you use less energy—efficiency. Because you protect yourself—no undue strains. Because you use your muscles properly—shape your figure.

Do You Know How?

To Sit for Work

Stability	*Force*	*Force Direction*	*(Nature of Movement)*
Keep trunk erect and over base of support—your thighs. Knees bent at right angles and feet flat on floor.	Muscles use less force when body parts are balanced. Rhythm: not too long in one position without change of total body and the parts directly involved in the movement.	Keep trunk balanced over base of support—your thighs—for working so muscles can maintain balance.	Postural Tonus

To Rest

Or Do You Do This?

Hips perched on edge; settled in middle; chair too low or too high; feet twisted around chair.	Sit too long in one position; cross legs at calf.	Bend at back and waist; sit on spine.	Muscles stretched for too long a period of time.

Do You Know How?

To be seated

Stability	Force	Force Direction	Nature of Movement
Walk toward chair. Turn so you feel the calf of your leg on the chair. Place one foot ahead of the other and maintain balanced standing posture.	Bend knees and bend slightly forward from hips.	Keep hips tucked under and lower yourself directly downward.	Slow, controlled motion.

To arise from a chair

| Place one foot back under the chair with body weight slightly forward. | Put weight on back foot. Shift weight to forward foot as you extend your hips and knees. | Keep hips tucked under. Lift directly upward through your center of gravity. | Same |

To climb stairs

| Place one foot on step above. Balance weight over forward foot. | Extend hips and knees forward. Lift body upward and forward as other leg is placed in position. | Same | Same |

Do You Know How?

To get in and out of a car

Stability	Force	Force Direction	Nature of Movement
Place one hand (right) on the door handle or window. Place left foot on floor just inside car door.	Bend knees and turn your body forward to face door.	Transfer your weight to foot inside the car. Slide into seat. Face ahead, draw in leg, and close the door.	Slow, controlled. Sustained muscular contractions.

(To get out, reverse the entire sequence or pattern of movement.)

Or Do You Do This?

Unstable position. Feet too close together, or feet apart but not in the right direction for what you want to do.	Lift or lower your body weight with your back muscles rather than the strongest muscles (hips and legs). Or use your arm muscles to push yourself up and lower yourself.	Hips not tucked under throughout the movement. Center of gravity out of line with force and direction in which you want to go.	Wrong kind of motion. Too fast, too slow. Collapse.

Do You Know How?

To stoop and reach

Stability	Force	Force Direction	Nature of Movement
Stand close to object, body balanced. Place one foot ahead of the other, weight on both feet.	Bend hips and knees, keeping back straight. Lower body only as far as necessary to reach object easily.	Keep hips tucked under and over your base of support. Lower your weight directly downward.	Slow, controlled. Sustained muscular contractions.

To lift, carry, reach

The object must be balanced with your weight. Hold it over your base of support and close to your line of gravity.	Use hands to grasp object. Straighten hips and knees, not too quickly, not too slowly. Use hands to grasp and hold, not to lift.	Lift object directly upward, keeping it as close to your line of gravity as possible.	Same

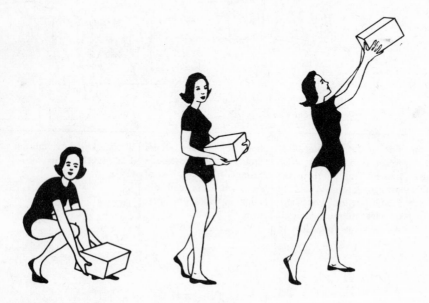

Have you ever stood outside a classroom building and watched the way various friends, acquaintances, and strangers walk as they pass by? Did you notice any attractive, graceful walks, or was it a revelation to observe what ungainly gaits most people have? Any gait using as little unnecessary movement and as little lifting up and down as possible makes for efficiency and grace.

Do You Know How?

Balance

Total body line balanced slightly forward. Extend from ball of foot, big toe, knee, hip, trunk, and head. Arms counterbalance leg swing; eyes look ahead.

Force

Hip leads, prepares new base of support. You move yourself forward by extending hip, knee, ankle, and toes (using the strongest muscles).

Or Do You Do This?

Total body line too far forward. Head and shoulders lead with hips pushed out behind.

Total body line too far back. Chest and abdomen lead with head and hips held backward.

Walking (continued)

Do You Know How?

Transfer of Weight	Stride	Speed	Foot Placement	Push-Off	Nature of Movement (shoulders, arms, elbows, hips, legs)
First strike the ground with center of heel, then transfer weight to outer half of foot, ball of foot, and finally push off from big toe. Three point walk.	Optimum for your leg length and clothes.	Optimum for your purpose.	Parallel.	Direction, forward and upward; knees balanced and easy; hips balanced.	Free and easy swing.

Force Direction: Apply force directly upward and slightly forward through the center of gravity in the direction in which you want to go.

Or Do You Do This?

Transfer of Weight	Stride	Speed	Foot Placement	Push-Off	Nature of Movement
Heel strikes ground and you transfer your weight to the outer border of foot. Roll out.	Too long.	Too slow.	Toed-in.	Direction, up and down, too much force applied directly upward and not forward; knees back; hips moving sidewards, sway at each step (rumba walk).	Loose, floppy, uncontrolled motion.
Heel strikes ground and you transfer your weight to inner border of foot and off big toe joint. Roll in.	Too short.	Too fast.	Toed-out.	Direction, flatfooted; knees bent too much; hips twisting too much (shake walk).	Too tight, tense, held; force too vigorous.

Moving or Projecting Your Body Weight Through Space

Do You Know How?

To run

Balance	*Force*	*Force Direction*	*Nature of Movement*
Center of gravity ahead of base of support, counter–balanced with arm swing.	Sequence pattern (extension of hips, knees, ankles, and toes). Acceleration; timing.	All movements directed through the center of weight and in the direction in which you want to go. Center of gravity slightly ahead of base of support.	Free and easy; sustained, slow or fast.

To run fast

Base of support, one foot only. Center of gravity moving ahead of base of support. Hip rotation counterbalanced with arm swings.	Extension of hip, knees, ankle, and final push-off from toes. Timing: begin with short, fast steps and then try to lengthen your stride. Acceleration: keep moving as fast as possible.	Body inclined forward, toes directed straight ahead. Arms swing directly forward and backward in opposition. Leg drive straight ahead and back. Land lightly on ball of foot. Center of gravity ahead of base of support.	Free and easy swing of leg from hip and arms from shoulder when you hit your stride.

Or Do You?

Lack arm swing.	Not enough knee extension. Land flat-footed, no push with toes. Too short stride. Slowing down and speeding up.	Body inclined too far back. Too much up and down movement at center of gravity. Arm and leg swing outward and not straight ahead. Toeing out.	Not free and easy.

Which Do You Do?

Do You Know How?

To jump and land (vertical form)

Balance	Force	Force Direction	Nature of Movement
Two-foot takeoff, feet a-part. Center of gravity lowered by bending knees. Hips tucked under.	Arms swing back behind body as body bends forward; knees and hips bend. Extend hip, knees, and ankles and push off with toes as arms swing forward and upward and back extends. Reach and stretch. Land with give at toes, ankles, knees, and hips. Accelerate as fast as you can, with timing to have summation of forces.	Toes straight ahead. Body weight centered over base of support. Eyes directed upward. Arms swing directly upward. Landing, keep weight centered over base of support. Arms may come out in front to aid in maintaining balance.	Sustained and fast in legs and in foot and arm swing.

Or Do You?

Feet too far apart or too close together. Hips out in back.	Not fast enough; not enough extension in joints. Failure to use toes in push-off. Timing: not summated. Landing: failure to give at joints, thus not absorbing shock.	Weight too far forward or back for projecting directly upward. Landing: weight too far back, land on heels. Not using arms for counterbalance.	

Which Do You Do?

Do You Know How?

To swim

Balance	Force	Force Direction	Nature of Movement
Center of bouyancy rather than center of weight. (If you lack buoyancy you sink because you are heavier than water. Your problem is not sinking but breathing.)	Arms and leg pattern different for each form. Push-pull with arms. Kick with legs. Timing factors affect; length of arm stroke; how you enter water; and effective part of stroke where arm is drawn directly backward. Depth and speed of kick.	Body moves in opposite direction from that in which you apply force. Push down, you go up; push back, you go forward; push forward, you go back. Keep body parallel to surface, head at water level, buttocks below surface. Eliminate all excess movement up, down, and sideward (rolling in).	Legs and feet, whiplike action; arms, sustained pulling; recovery, relaxed; reach, sustained and relaxed.

Or Do You?

| Center of bouyancy too low in water. | Force derived from arms rather than legs. Arm stroke too long and leg kick too deep. Or arm stroke too short, leg kick too shallow. | Too much turning head and body sideward. Head up too high and feet too low. Apply force downward and upward rather than forward and backward. | |

Which Do You Do?

Do You Know How?

To throw (striking arm patterns: overarm, underarm, sidearm,

Balance	Force (increased by)	Force Direction (accuracy)	Nature of Movement
Knees bent and easy. Hips tucked under. Feet apart and pointing in the direction in which you are going to apply force. You may step forward with sliding foot as you begin to rotate your body.	Transfer weight to forward foot, twist trunk, rotate arm forward. As upper arm approaches forward shoulder, the lower arm extends, quickly followed by release of ball from wrist and fingers. Ball leaves hand as forearm passes vertical position. Arm extended when starting from shoulder. Timing: bring in each part of sequence at peak of preceding part. Usually backswing is slower than forward swing. Also, the greater the arc or distance, the greater the force. Acceleration: moving forward at increasing speed or rate of movement of each body part.	All movement through center of weight of body and directly in line with target. Grip: apply force to center of weight of ball. Keep eye on target. Stability maintained and in line of direction of target. Follow-through adds nothing to force, but protects body from sudden stop, positions body for next movement, and helps keep force moving in proper direction. Angle of release: maximum distance, 45°; short distance, 90°.	Free and easy whiplike action of elbow, wrist, and fingers; enough tension to hold ball.

To play tennis

Transfer your weight back, twist trunk back, rotate arm back, wrist back.	Transfer weight forward, twist trunk forward, allowing shoulder and elbow to follow and rotate inward. Back foot may be brought forward. Balanced for next action.	Maximum force. At release or impact, weight on forward foot, arm extending out from shoulder. Point of contact ahead of body. Angle of impact or release. Firm grip on racket.	Free and easy whiplike action of elbow, forearm, and wrist.

LABORATORY: ANALYZING YOUR MOVEMENTS

Experiment 1: Analyze Basic Movement Patterns in Play

Directions: First: List specific sport and dance activities that you particularly enjoy in the first column. *Second:* What are the basic movement patterns primarily involved in these activities? Write these in the second column. *Third:* Give the physical characteristics required for efficient, graceful performance, such as: (1) speedy actions and reactions; (2) steady persevering; (3) creative-imaginative movements; (4) all-out explosive actions and reactions. You may find better descriptions; if so, use them.

Purposive Movement Classification	List Specific Activities	Basic Movement Patterns Involved	Physical Requirements	Temperament Aspects
1. Holding body weight				
2. Moving your weight				
3. Moving your body weight and other weight				

Take two of the above activities and analyze their rhythmical pattern. Select one sport and one dance.

Sport

Dance

Experiment 2: Analyze Throwing-Striking Patterns

Directions: Select one activity using overarm, underarm, or sidearm patterns. Have your partner check the word or phrase that best describes your movements in this activity for each of the positions listed in the chart below. Rate your total performance—form, then complete the questions below.

How do you build your force?

1. *Ready position*						
Weight	Slightly forward		On heels		On toes	
Knees	Easy		Back		Too flexed	
Hips	Tucked under		Out back		Too high	
Stride	Optimum		Extended		Narrow	
Arms	Ready, easy		Relaxed		Tensed	
Grip	Right		Wrong		Tensed	
Eyes	On the target		Elsewhere		Closed	
2. *Back swing*						
Order	Sequential		Arms only		Weight only	
Knees-Hips	Easy		Back		Crouched	
Swing	Free and easy		Lifted		Pulled	
Time of swing	Optimum		Too late		Too soon	
Speed of swing	Optimum		Too slow		Too fast	
Height of swing	Optimum		Too high		Too low	
Eyes	On the target		Elsewhere		Closed	
3. *Forward swing*						
Order	Sequential		Arms only		Weight only	
Knees-Hips	Easy		Back		Crouched	
Swing	Ballistic		Lifted		Pushed	
Swing time	Optimum		Too late		Too soon	
Acceleration	Optimum		Too slow		Constant speed	

Accent—summation of your forces.

Contact—Release						
Weight	Forward		Middle of stance		On back foot	
Knees	Easy		Back		Bent	
Hips	Tucked		Locked		High	
Arm position	Extended, easy		Locked		Bent	
Arm	Right direction		To the left		To the right	
Grip	Firm		Too relaxed		Too rigid	
Angle	Optimum		Too large		Too small	
Contact point	Optimum		Loss of balance		Too crouched	
Eyes	On the target		Elsewhere		Closed	

How do you dissipate your forces?

Follow—through						
Weight	Balanced		Loss of balance		Wrong direction	
Motion	Optimum		Stop too late		Stop too soon	
Eyes	On the target		Elsewhere		Closed	

Your Rating: Work your rating scale out with the rest of the class before you rate yourself.

1. Physical form: High—3, Medium—2, Low—1.
2. Distance you throw: High—3, Medium—2, Low—1.
3. Your performance accuracy: High—3, Medium—2, Low—1.

What is your most important problem in improving your total performance?

What do you need to do to improve your performance level, and how do you plan to do this?

action plans
for designing
personal programs

specific

conditioning programs

BASIC BEGINNING WEIGHT LIFTING PROGRAM

11   The general benefits that may be derived from a progressive weight lifting exercise program are: (*1*) firming up flabby muscles for reapportioning of body contours; (*2*) improving general physical condition (strength, tone, and muscular endurance of essential muscle groups); (*3*) developing strength and muscular endurance for more successful participation in sports or dance.

Specific benefits may be accomplished through this program because weight-lifting exercises can be prescribed for localized muscle groups (to strengthen weak areas); can develop muscle bulk for building and shaping specific body regions; can prevent injuries in specific activities that require additional strength; and can condition for specific sport activities (to improve physical performance).

There are certain procedures that should be followed in a weight training program. These include the following.

1. Each exercise should be performed through a complete range of motion.
2. Each exercise should be performed with the body in proper balanced alignment for the position required for the exercise.
3. Each exercise should be performed with a weight that you can handle with comparative ease. The general rule is that you begin with a weight you can lift five or six times with a dumbbell and ten times for barbell and weighted shoes.
4. Each exercise should be performed in a steady rhythm. Do not jerk the weight. Controlled movement is the proper form for all exercises.
5. Each exercise should be performed so that you inhale as you lift the weight and exhale as you lower it. Holding your breath as you

Basic Beginning Weight Lifting Program

Objective: To Improve General Physical Condition of Essential Muscle Groups

Regular Exercises	Beginning Level of Overload		Progression	Principal Muscles and Body Regions Affected
	lbs.	repetitions		
Dumbbells				
1. Dumbbell curl	2½	5	Increase by 1 repetition a week until you reach 10. Then increase weight by 2½ to 5 lbs.	Biceps and brachialis of front of the upper arm
2. Triceps extension	2½	5		Triceps of back of the upper arm
3. Straight arm pull-over	2½	5		Latissimus dorsi of the back
4. Supine arm lift	2½	5		Deltoid of the shoulder (front) Pectoralis major of the chest
5. Lateral raises	2½	5		Deltoids of the shoulder (top) Trapezius of the upper back
6. Side bends	5	5		Oblique abdominal muscles at side of waist
Barbell				
7. Trunk flexion	15	10	Increase by 2 repetitions a week until you reach 20. Then increase weight by 2½ to 10 lbs.	Erector spinal muscle group of the back Gluteus maximus of the hip
8. Heel raisers with half squat	15	10		Quadriceps of the front of the thigh Gastrocnemius of the calf
Weighted shoe (metal)				
9. Prone – single leg extension	5	10		Gluteus maximus of the hip Hamstrings of the back of the thigh
10. Standing – single leg flexion	5	10		Lower abdominal muscles of the back Quadriceps of the thigh
11. Standing – single leg side lift	5	10		Gluteus medius of the hip
12. Sitting – single leg extension	5	10		Quadriceps of the front of the thigh
13. Inclined board sit-up	—	5		Upper abdominal muscles of the trunk

140

lift compresses the chest and produces a high intrathoracic pressure which prevents venous return of the blood to the heart. This partially shuts off circulation to the brain and you may become dizzy or feel faint. This is known as the "Valsalva phenomenon."

6. For best results, it is recommended that you exercise three days per week.

7. One last point should be made. Always check before lifting a barbell to make certain that the collars holding the weights on the bar are fitted tightly to the bar.

An example of a basic program is shown opposite; description of the exercises used in the program and a weight training record form follow.

To achieve desired results it is important to keep a record of your progress. An example of an exercise record for weight training is given on p. 145. If you are interested in firming up flabby muscles for reapportioning certain body proportions, record your initial measurements for each body area you wish to improve. Directions for taking measurements were described in Chapter 2. Every two weeks retake your measurements and evaluate the outcome. Have you reached your desired goals? If so, it is time for decision making. You can continue this program once per week to maintain your current level, or you can increase the sport activities in your daily life. If you use the sport approach, you should check your measurements once a month to evaluate your status and your need to return to the weight training program. Similar procedures are used if you are interested in improving strength and muscular endurance for successful participation in a sport. Record your initial percentile score on tests of strength and muscular endurance for essential muscle groups (See Profile, page 32 in Chapter 2). Every four weeks retest yourself and record the results. When you feel you have reached your desired goal, you can continue this program once per week during the sport season to keep in top condition.

Exercise 1: Dumbbell Curl
Feet parallel, palms forward. Bend elbows and bring dumbell to shoulders. Alternate arms.

Exercise 2: Triceps Extension
Supine on floor with knees and elbows bent and dumbbells held at shoulder joint. Extend one arm upward and lower slowly. Repeat with the other arm.

Exercise 3: Straight Arm Pull-Over
Supine on floor with knees bent, arms extended above shoulders. Bring dumbbells to shoulders alternately.

Exercise 4: Supine Arm Lift
Supine on floor with knees bent and arms extended to the side at shoulder level. Bring arms upward and above the chest. Lower slowly. May proceed alternately.

Exercise 5: Lateral Raises
Feet parallel, arms at sides. Lift arms sidewards to shoulders and then above the head. Lower slowly to the sides.

Exercise 6: Side Bends
Stand, dumbbell held in left hand at the side of the body. Bend trunk at the waist to the right as far as possible, then to the left as far as possible. Repeat with the dumbbell in other hand. (May use barbell.)

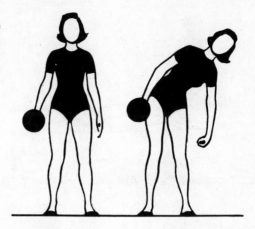

Exercise 7: Trunk Flexion
Stand, barbell held at back of neck with both hands. Bend forward at the hips with back straight and knees stiff. Return to standing position slowly. (May use barbell.)

Exercise 8: Heel Raises with Half Squat
Stand with heels raised slightly from the floor and barbell held at shoulder level. Slowly bend knees, then extend and assume starting position.

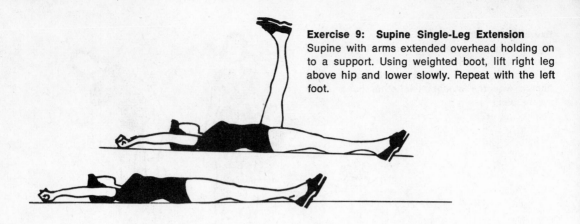

Exercise 9: Supine Single-Leg Extension
Supine with arms extended overhead holding on to a support. Using weighted boot, lift right leg above hip and lower slowly. Repeat with the left foot.

Exercise 10 (left):
Standing Single-Leg Back Extension
Standing, holding on to a support, using weighted boot. Extend leg back, lower slowly. Repeat with other leg. (May do while lying down.)

Exercise 11 (right):
Standing Single-Leg Side Lift
Standing, holding on to a support, using weighted boot. Extend leg to the side, lower slowly. Repeat with other leg. (May do while lying down.)

Exercise 12: Sitting Single-Leg Extension
Sitting on bench with legs bent at right angles to thighs, using weighted boots. Extend leg and lower slowly. Repeat with other leg. (May sit on floor.)

Exercise 13:   Inclined Sit-Up

Supine on inclined plane with feet supported by
a strap. Curl up as far as possible. Curl back to
starting position by lowering your body weight
back to position slowly.

Weight Training Program Record

Directions: First, decide on your purpose: this is basic to selecting specific exercises that will affect
specific body areas. Each exercise requires the work of certain muscle groups that are related to specific
regions of the body. Decide which areas of your body you wish to work on to improve body proportions
or your strength and muscular endurance for specific sports.

Second, record your measurements of those body regions you wish to change (part C).

Third, keep a weekly record of your exercise program, and every two weeks retake your measurements
and retest your strength and endurance to evaluate your progress.

A. Exercise Record

Name of Exercise	Body Region (muscle group) Affected	Purpose	lbs. and repetitions for each week						Initial lbs	Maximum lbs
			1	2	3	4	5	6		
1.										
2.										
3.										
4.										
5.										
6.										

continued

B. Improvement Chart: Strength and Muscular Endurance*

date of test						
Strength: grip						
Muscular Endurance: sit-ups						
push-ups						
dorsal curls						
arm hang						

*See the Profile on p. 32. Record your average percentiles.

C. Improvement Chart: Body Proportions

date of measurement						
Waist						
Chest						
Hips						
Thighs						
Calf						

A BASIC CIRCUIT EXERCISE PROGRAM

The benefits that may be derived from a carefully developed program of circuit training include: (1) the development of cardio-respiratory and circulatory endurance; (2) the development of muscular strength and muscular endurance, power, agility and speed; (3) the firming of flabby muscles for the improvement of body contours; (4) the improvement of general physical condition. Specific benefits may be gained by choosing exercises capable of alleviating particular problems in your figure or physical fitness.

The Circuit. The gym or playing field where training will take place is divided into 8 to 12 areas which are numbered consecutively. These positions are called *stations*. Each girl decides on the exercises she will perform at these stations individually, according to her goals and needs. The aim of circuit training is to develop not only muscular strength and tone but also cardio-vascular endurance. Exercises should insure active functioning of the arm and shoulder, trunk, buttock, hip and leg muscles, and should be of sufficient difficulty to raise the heart rate and maintain it at a level above 125–135 beats per minute. One complete circuit around all the stations is called a *lap*; a short circuit is usually accomplished in ten minutes. It is usual to perform three laps of a short circuit in about twenty minutes. After a period of training to get used to the stress, a longer circuit may be developed.

Basic Circuit Training Program

Station Number	Activity	Circuit Number 1	2	3	Benefits
		repetitions			
1	Squat jumps	8	10	12	Leg strength and muscular endurance
2	Straddle bench jumps	14	18	22	Leg strength and muscular endurance
3	Sit-ups	10	15	20	Abdominal muscle strength and tone
4	Step-ups	15	20	25	Leg strength, tone and respiratory cardiovascular-endurance
5	Push-ups	4	8	12	Arm and shoulder girdle strength, tone, and endurance
6	Trunk extension	6	8	10	Lower back muscle strength
7	Run in place	55	60	65	Cardiovascular-respiratory endurance
8	Star jumps	10	14	18	Leg strength, tone, and muscular endurance

The repetitions listed above are only a guide for a beginning program. They should be adapted to your own skill level. If you have difficulty doing the number shown at first, reduce the number. If your present level of fitness is high, increase the repetitions.

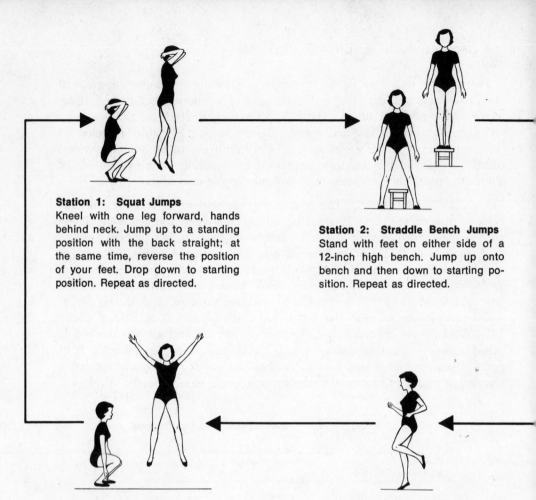

Station 1: Squat Jumps
Kneel with one leg forward, hands behind neck. Jump up to a standing position with the back straight; at the same time, reverse the position of your feet. Drop down to starting position. Repeat as directed.

Station 2: Straddle Bench Jumps
Stand with feet on either side of a 12-inch high bench. Jump up onto bench and then down to starting position. Repeat as directed.

Station 8: Star Jumps
Crouch as low as you can with your feet flat on the floor and your arms crossed in front of you between your knees. Push hard off the floor with your legs, flinging your arms and legs wide apart to form a star figure. Land on the floor with your legs together and drop back to starting position. Repeat as directed.

Station 7: Run in Place
Start in standing position. Begin running, lifting your knees as high as possible and using your arms for balance. Repeat as directed.

Training Dose. This is the specified number of repetitions to be made in a given amount of time at each station. First see how many repetitions of each exercise you can perform. Multiply this number by one-half (0.05): this figure is your training dose. For instance, if you can perform 10 push-ups, your starting training dose at the push-up station would be 5.

Target Time. You perform three complete laps of all your exercise stations without stopping to rest, doing the training dose of each exercise. The total time you take to perform the three laps is recorded. With

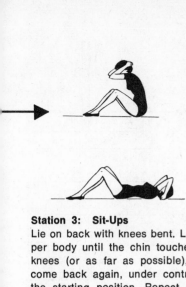

Station 3: Sit-Ups

Lie on back with knees bent. Lift upper body until the chin touches the knees (or as far as possible), then come back again, under control, to the starting position. Repeat as directed.

Station 4: Step-Ups

Stand facing 12-inch high bench. Step up with right foot, then left. Step down with right foot, then left, Repeat as directed.

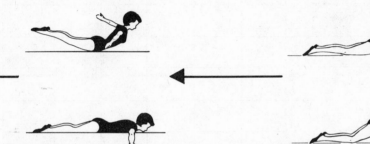

Station 6: Trunk Extension

Lie on your stomach with hands behind neck. If possible, support your ankles beneath a heavy object (but don't worry if none is available). Lift your upper body off floor as far as possible and then lower yourself to floor under control. Repeat as directed.

Station 5: Push-Ups

Hands on floor, shoulder width apart, arms straight, supporting the upper body; knees and toes rest on floor. By bending your arms allow body to drop, under control, toward the floor until your chest rests lightly against it. Keep your back straight. Then raise yourself to the starting position. Repeat as directed.

improvement you will be able to reduce this time. It is a good stimulus for improvement to aim for a one-quarter reduction in time. Once you are able to reach this target time, re-establish new training doses for yourself as well as a new target time.

You may use the overload principle by:

1. Testing and retesting after you reach your goal, and establishing new maximal repetitions for each exercise
2. Decreasing the target time
3. Increasing the number of exercises in each lap.

Circuit Training Program Record

A. Training Record

Name of Exercise	Body Regions Affected	Purposes	Training Dose and Best Time for Each Week					
			1	2	3	4	5	6
1.								
2.								
3.								
4.								
5.								
6.								
7.								
8.								
9.								
10.								
11.								
12.								

B. Improvement Chart

Date of Test						
Muscular Endurance						
Organic Tone						
Flexibility						

150 action plans for designing personal programs

A PROGRESSIVE CALISTHENICS PROGRAM

The benefits of calisthenics are: (*1*) increased strength, tone, and muscular endurance; (*2*) increased flexibility; (*3*) increased cardiovascular-respiratory endurance; and (*4*) improved general physical condition.

In the following paragraphs we present a *progressive* calisthenic exercise program. There are three graded levels arranged gradually, progressively, for sound building. Each level is composed of seven basic exercises. As you move from one level to the next level, there are slight changes in the way each exercise is performed. These changes are graded increases which call for increased effort on your part. The plan calls for doing the seven basic exercises in the same order for the prescribed time or number at each level. The order is important to follow for it allows you to warm up and get set for greater effort within each exercise workout. The basic exercises with order for their performance and prescribed time or number to be performed at each level are presented below.

Your objective at each level will be to reach the point where you can do all the exercises without undue effort or strain. If you feel sore and stiff or unduly breathless, ease up and slow down your rate of progression. The important objective is to keep exercising regularly and to progress at your own pace until you reach your desired goals.

Progressive Calisthenics Program

Exercise Number	Name of Exercise	Prescribed Time/ Number of Repetitions	Purposes
1	Toe touch	20 repetitions	*Warmup exercises* To stretch and limber up the body and speed up the heart and lungs to prepare for greater effort
2	Sit-ups	1 min.	*Conditioning exercises*
3	Back-ups	1 min.	To tone up abdominals, back, arm and
4	Push-ups	1 min.	other major muscles and improve muscular endurance
5	Running in place	3 min.	*Heart and lung exercises* To stimulate and strengthen circulatory and respiratory systems and improve muscular endurance and tone of leg muscles
6	Pelvic control	10 repetitions	*Postural exercises* To tone up major muscles for improving body alignment
7	Relaxation techniques	3 min.	*Relaxation exercises* To release neuromuscular tensions in various body regions

Procedures. Perform each exercise as described on the following pages. Speed or number of repetitions within a set time limit is not recommended for the flexibility exercise (number 1); *this is performed to a four-count rhythm, twenty times a minute.* Here the overload is the amount of stretch you can achieve. The aim of exercises 2–5 is to provide overload by repeating the exercise as many times as possible within a set time. The pelvic control exercise (number 6) for posture is performed with slow controlled movements to increase kinesthetic perception or body awareness and at the same time improve muscular tone of major muscles controlling these body areas; *this is performed ten times.* Progressive relaxation techniques (number 7) can be used at the end of each exercise bout; this is performed for 3 minutes.

At Level 1, your objective will be to gradually work up to the top step. When you can do the seven basic exercises easily and comfortably at this level, you will be ready to proceed in the same fashion with the more difficult exercises at succeeding levels. The goal is to perform each exercise correctly within the prescribed time limit or the set number of repetitions. Only this way can you be insured of maximum benefit. The exercises should not be a race against time. Start slowly and move forward gradually. Stay at each step one or two weeks before proceeding upward. If at first you cannot complete the exercise, stop and rest briefly, and then take up where you left off and complete the count. You will find each succeeding workout less difficult than the first.

Determining Your Starting Level. You begin the program at Level 1. Your starting level for toe touch, pelvic control, and relaxation exercises (1, 6, and 7) are predetermined as prescribed above. To determine your starting level for exercises 2–5 perform these exercises in the prescribed time. How many repetitions of each were you able to do? This number will indicate your starting level. Circle the number of each exercise on the Level 1 Chart (opposite). If you can't find the exact number of repetitions under the exercise, circle the number closest to your own number or performance level. This is your starting level. Perform each of these exercises (2–5) according to the number of repetitions that indicates your performance level. Move upward on the Level 1 Chart to the next step only after you have completed *all* required repetitions at your starting level. For most girls this should be about a two week period at the starting level. Each exercise should be done easily and comfortably without undue stress before moving to next step in Level 1. It is recommended that you exercise a minimum of 2–3 times per week.

Upon completion of the top step in Level 1, you are ready to progress to the next level. Begin the exercises for Level 2 at the lowest step. Continue upwards in each exercise through the steps. Continue in the same way through Level 3.

Choosing your goals. When you begin this program, there is no need to pick the level you want to achieve. The level you can reach depends upon your age, your body build, your potential physical capacity, and your motivation. Decide upon what you want to achieve through this exercise program. As you progress through the levels, you should be continually evaluating your own general physical condition, your health-physical fitness.

(*Continued p. 161*)

Progressive Steps (number of repetitions)

Steps	Exercise 2	3	4	5	Steps	Exercise 2	3	4	5	Steps	Exercise 2	3	4	5
10	49	63	42	380	10	50	68	34	350	10	20	53	20	280
9	33	57	27	326	9	39	62	29	312	9	19	41	16	247
8	31	52	21	306	8	36	54	24	298	8	16	37	12	233
7	29	47	18	300	7	33	46	21	270	7	15	34	10	228
6	28	42	15	270	6	31	43	19	253	6	11	32	9	217
5	26	42	14	255	5	30	41	18	244	5	10	30	8	204
4	25	40	12	251	4	28	39	16	229	4	9	25	7	198
3	23	32	10	232	3	27	36	14	212	3	7	23	6	194
2	21	28	8	213	2	24	34	12	200	2	5	21	5	181
1	20	27	6	204	1	22	31	9	193	1	4	16	4	150
Level 1					Level 2					Level 3				

LEVEL 1

Exercise 1

Feet astride, arms overhead. Touch floor or bend as far forward as possible. Bounce once; hold. Stretch upward and bend backward with one leg back, alternating legs each time you do the exercise. Keep knees straight.

Exercise 2

Lie on back with feet 6 inches apart, hands on thighs. Curl head toward chest just far enough to see heels. Keep legs straight, head and shoulders just clear of floor. Lower slowly to starting position.

Exercise 3

Lie on stomach with arms overhead. Raise head, left arm, and right leg off floor. Thigh must clear floor. Keep knees straight. Lower slowly. Repeat with opposite arm and leg.

Exercise 4

Lie on stomach with hands under shoulders, palms flat on floor. Touch chin to floor in front of hands. Touch forehead to floor behind hands. Straighten arms, supporting body weight on hands and knees. Lower body in straight line to floor. *Three definite movements.*

Exercise 5
Run in place. Count a step each time left foot
touches floor. Lift feet 4 inches from floor. Every
50 steps do 10 scissor jumps. Repeat sequence.

Exercise 6
Lie on back with knees bent and feet on floor.
Arch back. Flatten back using abdominal and
buttock muscles. Hold back close to floor and
extend both legs out straight. Bend one knee
and bring one foot back to position, then other
foot. Repeat.

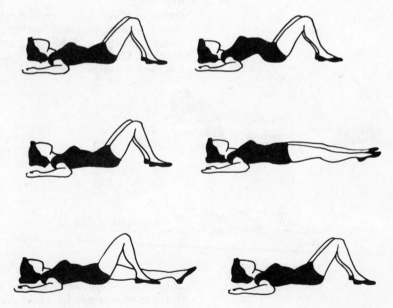

Exercise 7
Contraction and release techniques for relaxation. Practice 3 minutes. (See Chapter 15.)

LEVEL 2

Exercise 1
Feet astride, arms overhead. Touch floor 3 inches outside left foot, between feet (bounce once), and then outside right foot. Stretch upward and bend backward with one leg back, alternating legs each time you do exercise. Keep knees straight at all times.

Exercise 2
Lie on back with legs straight, feet together, and arms overhead on floor. Feet may be hooked under a chair or held. Swing up and touch toes or ankles. Curl back with hands sliding up thighs and trunk to overhead position.

Exercise 3
Lie on stomach with hands clasped behind lower back. Lift head, shoulders, chest and both thighs as high as possible off floor. Lower. Repeat.

Exercise 4

Rest weight on hands placed under shoulders, palms flat on floor, arms straight. Lower body in straight line to floor, touching chin first to floor. Lift body to starting position.

Exercise 5

Run in place. Count a step each time left foot touches floor. Lift feet 4 inches from floor. Every 50 steps do 10 astride jumps. Repeat sequence.

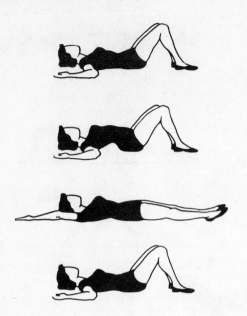

Exercise 6

Lie on back with knees bent, feet on floor. Arch back, then flatten back using abdominal and buttock muscles. Hold back close to floor. Extend both legs out straight and slide both arms on floor overhead. Bend one knee and bring foot back to starting position, then other foot. Slide arms to side.

Exercise 7

Contraction and release techniques for relaxation. Practice 3 minutes. (See chapter 15.)

LEVEL 3

Exercise 1

Feet astride, arms overhead. Touch floor 3 inches outside left foot, between feet (bounce once), and outside right foot. Stretch upward, bend backward; circle to right and stretch sideward, bend to left and stretch sideward. Return to original position. Keep knees straight at all times.

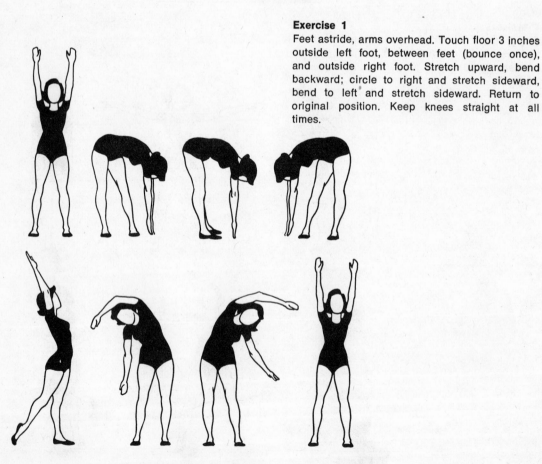

Exercise 2

Lie on back with legs straight, feet together, arms on floor overhead. Swing up and raise legs in bent position with feet together. At the same time twist and touch both hands to the floor on right side as knees twist to left side. This is one complete movement. Keep feet off floor as you swing up and return to starting position. Alternate twist each time.

Exercise 3

Lie on stomach with arms out sidewards, palms on floor. Lift head, shoulders, arms, chest, and both thighs as high as possible off floor. Keep legs straight, chin tucked up against neck.

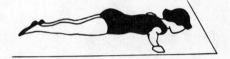

Exercise 4

Rest weight on hands placed under shoulders, palms flat on floor, arms straight. Lower body in straight line; touch chin, chest, and thighs to floor. Lift head and upper back off floor, then straighten arms and lift rest of body to front leaning rest position. Two definite movements to come up.

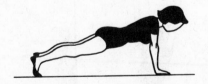

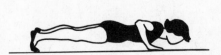
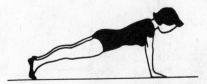

Exercise 5
Run in place. Count a step each time left foot touches floor. Lift feet 4 inches off floor. Every 50 steps do 10 knee bends with jump so that heels are off floor.

Exercise 6
Stand with heels, buttocks, upper back, and head touching wall, feet together, arms on wall at shoulder level, and elbows bent at a 90° angle. Arch back, then flatten back using abdominal and buttock muscles. Keeping back in this position slide arms on wall upward as far as possible. Return arms to starting position and relax. Back close to wall so that hand cannot get between wall and back.

Exercise 7
Contraction and release techniques for relaxation. Practice 3 minutes. (See chapter 15.)

Progressive Calisthenics Program Record

Directions: Record your progress for each exercise by marking the number of repetitions for each class period.

Exercise	1	2	3	4	5	6	7	8	9	10	11	12	13	14	15	15 Day Total
1																
2																
3																
4																
5																
6																
Level																

Exercise	16	17	18	19	20	21	22	23	24	25	26	27	28	29	30	30 Day Total
1																
2																
3																
4																
5																
6																
Level																

Name of Exercises: 1._____;   2._____;   3._____;   4._____;

5. _____;   6._____.

When you feel you have achieved desired ends, this is the point, the level, where you stop. Now, the problem is to maintain your physical well-being at this level of performance. You have two choices: work out at this level once per week to maintain physical condition, or put more regular activity through sports and daily living activities into your life. Remember there will be no dramatic overnight changes.

A CARDIOVASCULAR-RESPIRATORY ENDURANCE PROGRAM

A program designed specifically for improving endurance will bring about five important physiological organic adaptations: (1) a lower resting heart rate; (2) lower heart rate for submaximal workload; (3) greater maximal stroke volume; (4) capacity for withstanding a greater oxygen debt; (5) faster recovery to baseline values (normal heart and respiration rate) after completion of the work. The exact physiological benefits to you may vary, but there is little doubt that you will feel better, mentally and emotionally. A woman who is physically fit usually has a good outlook on life, with the self-confidence and self-esteem to do well in whatever her talents and ambitions lead her to try.

running program

Running is perhaps the best possible conditioning exercise for cardiovascular-respiratory fitness and endurance. It not only strengthens the heart-lung complex, but also gives tone to most of the muscle groups of the body.

Before commencing a program, give yourself a pretest over a distance that can be spaced out previously measured by the odometer of your car, or on your college track facilities. The aim is to move as far as possible in 10 minutes. It is permissible to walk, jog or run, but *don't stop moving*. This will give you an idea of your endurance capacity at the beginning of training. It may allow you to eliminate some of the early weeks of work at the easy levels and get an advanced start (perhaps at the level of the second or the fourth week). After the program is completed and you have attained your goals, you can maintain your endurance by following the program presented in Figure 11.1.

swimming program

In training for endurance, swimming is the next best activity after running. Most of the large muscle groups are used, and their tone is increased. It is perhaps a little less convenient to condition through swimming; it is difficult to get as many opportunities to swim as to run. Nevertheless, swimming is an excellent cardiovascular-respiratory endurance conditioner.

Before beginning the program, you should have a pretest to see whether you are able to begin at a higher level than that indicated for the first week. Use the crawl stroke, as other strokes (except the butterfly) are not as strenuous. Following either of the suggestions for swimming in Figure 11.1 will help you maintain the endurance you've built up.

Running Program

Week	For Distance and Time		In Place	
	Intensity (distance)	Duration	Frequency	Intensity (time)
	miles	min.	steps/min.	min.
1	0.50	5.00	70	5.00
2	0.50	4.30	70	6.30
3	1.00	10.00	70	7.30
4	1.00	9.45	70	8.30
5	1.00	9.30	70	10.00
6	1.50	15.00	70	11.00
7	1.50	14.45	70	12.00
8	1.50	14.30	70	13.00
9	2.00	20.00	70	14.00
10	2.00	19.45	70	15.00
11	2.25	23.00		
12	2.25	22.30		
13	2.50	25.00		

Repetitions: 5 times a week. *Rest intervals:* During the early stages, walk for a while if you feel like resting, but do not stop moving.

bicycling program

It is best to use a bicycle that has no gears, as then there will be no temptation to use an easy gear. If gears are fitted, keep to high gear (the hardest). The terrain chosen should be varied with hills, downgrades, and flat sections. You may also choose to take advantage of the scenic aspects of the countryside through which you'll be riding.

Once again, give yourself a pretest to find which weekly level you should begin with. Then progress to meet your goals. In the early stages, you can take rests if you wish; sit on the bike and relax for a few moments, but don't get off the bicycle. You should follow the program five times a week. To maintain condition after all goals have been reached, see the bicycling target goal in Figure 11.1.

sports programs

It is possible to develop cardiovascular-respiratory endurance through participation in vigorous sports, if you play five times a week. Such sports that may be enjoyed in the appropriate seasons, or all year round, include skiing (a full day's effort *outside*, not in the lodge), skating, tennis, squash racquets, badminton, field hockey, and basketball. As you play, of course, you will develop your skill and the sports will become more interesting and enjoyable. Tennis is a case in point here. It is difficult to be active and play a vigorous games unless you have developed the basic skills. Golf is a good game for developing endurance through walking. The provision here, though, is: You must walk; riding a cart doesn't exercise your heart and lungs. At this

Swimming Program

Weeks	Intensity (distance)	Duration
	yards	min.
1	50	1.30
2	100	3.00
3	150	4.30
4	200	6.00
5	250	7.00
6	300	8.00
7	350	9.00
8	400	10.00
9	500	12.00
10	600	14.00
11	700	17.00
12	800	20.00
13	850	23.00

Repetitions: 5 times a week.

Bicycling Program

Week	Intensity (distance)	Duration
	miles	min.
1	1	5.30
2	1	5.00
3	1	4.30
4	1.5	7.00
5	1.5	6.30
6	1.5	6.15
7	2	10.00
8	2	9.30
9	2	9.00
10	2.5	13.00
11	2.5	12.45
12	2.5	12.30
13	3	14.00

Repetitions: 5 times a week.

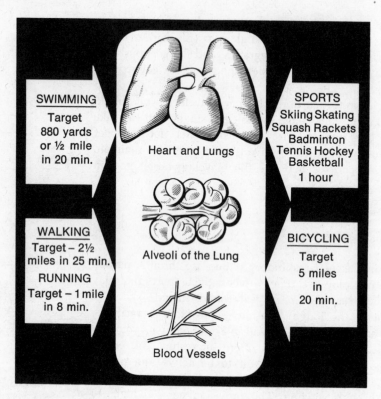

SWIMMING
Target
880 yards
or ½ mile
in 20 min.

WALKING
Target – 2½
miles in 25 min.

RUNNING
Target – 1 mile
in 8 min.

Heart and Lungs

Alveoli of the Lung

Blood Vessels

SPORTS
Skiing Skating
Squash Rackets
Badminton
Tennis Hockey
Basketball
1 hour

BICYCLING
Target
5 miles
in
20 min.

Figure 11.1 Endurance Program: target goals for maintenance (3 to 5 times a week)

Cardiovascular Respiratory Endurance Program Record

Date	Exercise	Intensity (Distance)	Duration	Goal (Plan by Week)

fairly low level of work, you must participate for a considerable period. Work up to a minimum of 18 holes. A sports rating chart my be found on p. 278.

INTERVAL TRAINING PROGRAM FOR POWER EVENTS

Interval training prepares a student for competitive athletics such as track, swimming, and power-strength events by: (1) developing her tolerance of oxygen debt; (2) improving her muscular strength and speed; and (3) improving her muscular endurance. The principle used in this type of training is *overload*, with overstress for a distance shorter than that which is to be performed in competition. In addition, rest periods are of short duration so that the body does not have sufficient time to recover between exercise bouts.

procedure 1: conditioning for the 100-yard sprint

A sprinter can run 100 yards in 13.4 seconds; she wants to reduce this time to 13.2 seconds.

For practice she will run half (or even a quarter) the distance, usually at half her target speed. Her rest interval will be one and one-half times her beginning speed goal. (This may be increased up to two and one-half her speed goal if a shorter rest is insufficient.) Her start interval will be the speed goal plus the rest interval.

Training Distance: 100-yard Sprint

Progression Steps	Tentative Goal	Speed Goal	Rest Interval	Start Interval	Repetitions
			sec.		
1	13.2	6.6	9.9	16.5	Build to 12
2	13.2	6.6	6.6	13.2	8
3	13.2	6.6	3.3	9.9	4
4	13.2	6.6	.0	6.6	2
5	12.8	6.4	9.6	16.0	12
6	12.8	6.4	6.4	12.8	8
7	12.8	6.4	3.2	9.6	4
8	12.8	6.4	.0	6.4	2

You may vary this program with over-distance runs every 2 to 4 days: (a) Run six 3-minute runs for distance, calling out each minute. Rest 1 minute between trials and record the total distance. (b) Run 440 yards, and jog for 440 yards. Repeat the cycle for 20 minutes.

procedure 2: conditioning for the 100-yard Australian crawl

A swimmer who can Australian crawl 100 yards in 1.15 minute wants to reach a target time of 1.10 minute.

For practice she will swim 50 yards at half her target time, resting for the same amount of time (half the target speed) unless this is too severe. Her start interval will be the speed goal plus the rest interval.

Training Distance: 100-yard Australian Crawl

Progression Steps	Tentative Goal	Speed Goal	Rest Interval	Start Interval	Repetitions
			min.		
1	1.10	0.35	0.35	1.10	Build to 12
2	1.10	0.35	0.20	0.55	8
3	1.10	0.35	0.10	0.45	4
4	1.10	0.35	0.00	0.35	2

You may vary this program with over-distance swims every 2 to 4 days. Using the crawl stroke, swim 220 yards with four repetitions. Take a 1-minute rest between trials.

Interval Training Program Record

Interval Training for:

Training Distance:

Progression Steps	Tentative Goal	Speed Goal	Rest Interval	Start Interval	Repetitions

references and sources for additional reading

1. Leighton, J. R., *Progressive Weight Training*. New York: The Ronald Press Company, 1961.
2. Massey, B., *Kinesiology of Weight Lifting*. Dubuque, Iowa: William C. Brown Company, Publishers, 1959.

A.A.H.P.E.R., *Youth Fitness Test Manual*. Washington, D.C.: American Association for Health, Physical Education, and Recreation, 1965.

Barney, V. S., C. C. Hirst, and C. R. Jensen, *Conditioning Exercises*. St. Louis, Mo.: The C.V. Mosby Co., 1965.

Cooper, K. H., and K. Brown, *Aerobics*. New York: M. Evans & Co., Inc., 1968.

Howell, M. L., and W. R. Morford, *Fitness Training Methods*. Toronto, Canada: Canadian Association for Health, Physical Education, and Recreation, 1965.

President's Council on Physical Fitness, *Adult Physical Fitness*. Washington, D.C.: Government Printing Office, 1963.

Rasch, P. J., *Weight Training*. Dubuque, Iowa: William C. Brown Company, Publishers, 1966.

R.C.A.F., *Exercise Plans for Physical Fitness*. New York: Pocket Books, 1962.

Ricci, B., *Physical and Physiological Conditioning for Men*. Dubuque, Iowa: William C. Brown Company, Publishers, 1966.

Sills, D., L. E. Morehouse, and T. L. DeLorme, *Weight Training in Sports and Physical Education*. Washington, D.C. American Association for Health, Physical Education, and Recreation, 1962.

Sorani, R., *Circuit Training*. Dubuque, Iowa: William C. Brown Company, Publishers, 1966.

Steinhaus, A. H., *How to Keep Fit and Like It*. Chicago: The Dartnell Corporation, 1963.

Time-Life Special Reports, *The Healthy Life*. New York: Time-Life Books, Div. of Time Inc., 1966.

Wallis, E. L., and G. A. Logan, *Figure Improvement and Body Conditioning Through Exercise*. Englewood Cliffs, N. J.: Prentice-Hall, Inc., 1964.

exercise and weight control

THE PURPOSES

12 The specific physical-physiological benefits of a weight reduction program are twofold: (1) loss of excessive body fat, and (2) improvement of the figure through the development of general muscle tone.

Motivation and knowledge are essential for effective weight control programs, whether for reduction or maintenance of best body weight. Weight reduction and maintenance are not simple tasks today. Success in dieting seems to be greater in individuals who are slightly or moderately overweight, who became overweight as adults, who are well-adjusted emotionally, and who accept weight reduction as a realistic, attainable goal (1, 2). Anyone who is markedly overweight should be examined by a physician to rule out organic or functional disease as a causal factor. All pharmacological or psychological approaches to weight reduction should be under the direct supervision of a physician. Any logical approach through dietary control and the use of exercise will be based essentially on direct action to modify food intake and energy expenditure. In general, the principles underlying weight reduction and the prevention of excessive body fatness are similar.

THE PRINCIPLES

Five essential principles should be examined in detail when designing a personal weight control program.

1. *Exercise is an important factor in developing a realistic weight control program. An additional expenditure of energy can make a significant contribution to creating an energy or calorie deficit and can result in weight loss or weight maintenance.* Calories (or food energy) are essential for everyone. How

many calories you need depends chiefly on age, body size, and daily energy outgo or physical activity habits. *Age.* Because of the physiological changes occurring with age, fewer calories are needed as you grow older. For each decade beyond 30, it has been estimated that 5% fewer calories are needed to maintain a stable weight. *Gross body size.* Height, weight, and body build affect the number calories you need. In general, the caloric cost of physical activity tends to be proportional to gross body size—the larger, heavier person uses more calories in physical activity. *Caloric cost of exercise.* The energy outgo, or caloric cost, of various physical activities depends not only on gross body size but also on the amount of effort demanded by a specific activity. In general, the more muscles involved in the activity, the larger the muscles, the faster the movements, and the longer the duration, the greater the caloric cost of the activity. An additional expenditure of energy can contribute significantly to creating an energy or calorie deficit, and result in weight loss.

You have probably heard that exercise takes a long time to burn up a pound of fat. In round figures, one pound of body fat contains 3,500 stored-up calories. In order to burn (lose) one pound of body fat, you have to do 5,000 push-ups, walk to the top of the Washington Monument 45 times, play hockey for 4 hours, or ride a horse for 40 hours. This seems to be a tremendous program. But is it really when done on a regular, progressive basis? Think of it in terms of six months or a year. Just one-half hour a day of some kind of exercise you like will result in a loss of 15 pounds over a 12-month period— and that is *without dieting.* You expend up to 585 calories in cycling, up to 550 in walking fast, up to 685 in skating, up to 750 in dancing, up to 685 in swimming, and up to 800 in tennis, basketball, and hockey. These rates are for approximately one-half hour a day of these activities. It should be obvious now that regular daily activity is important.

The most effective type of weight reduction plan will combine some degree of regular increased energy expenditure with some degree of caloric restriction; it will not rely on either of these components alone. Most studies show that overweight individuals are less active than their normal weight counterparts and actually have a relatively low caloric intake. For these individuals in particular, physical activity in small increments on a regular basis is extremely important in any weight reduction plan.

2. *Exercise prescription should be on an individual basis suitable to the mode of living and the personal choice of physical activity. Stepped-up activity in one's daily routine and/or supplementary activities in one's leisure can provide the approach for a definite exercise plan.* Certainly it is obvious that strenuous activity of an irregular nature is no better than "crash diets." Both approaches have the same lasting effects—NIL! Just as with dietary control, increased physical activity must become a regular part of one's changed pattern of living if it is to have a permanent effect on weight status. Therefore, understanding how to reorganize one's life to include regular physical activity is a sound measure for preventing excessive fatness and is most practical for weight reduction. *Stepped-up physical activity*: You need to look for opportunities to move, to become active in your day-by-day routine. Walk when possible. Walk extra distances. Walk up a flight of stairs rather than using an

elevator. Don't take action out of your life; *put* it back in where possible. Each action is energy spent, which is cumulative in its effect. Bend, stoop, lift, carry, stretch, and wiggle, using the proper form to prevent aches and pains. *Supplementary activities*: You might wish to undertake a regular planned program of exercise each day. If so, a circuit training or endurance training program may be just "your cup of tea." Of course, alternative activities that are more personally satisfying for you can be devised. A home, neighborhood, or dorm conditioning program can help maintain good physical condition and muscle tone as well as burn up calories. Or you may wish to participate in vigorous recreational sports and games. Remember it is the continuous nature of these activities that is important. Examine the energy cost of various activities. Find one in which you have skill and which is personally satisfying to you and yet vigorous enough for your purpose. Plan your recreation time accordingly.

3. *Diet prescription should be on an individual basis adapted to the individual's rate of energy expenditure. Weight may be lost on any level of calories below the number required to maintain the weight of the individual.* No one food is fattening. Too often people pay more attention to the type of food they consume than to the amount. A sound knowledge of the caloric value of foods will guide the individual who wants to lose weight and will arm her against the misleading claims of manufacturers of so-called miracle diet foods. The caloric value of common foods is provided in Appendix B.

It is important to reiterate that *weight loss depends on negative caloric balance.* It is the caloric deficit that governs weight loss: Caloric intake must be less than caloric outgo of energy expenditure—simply stated, the caloric discount!

A pound of body fat is considered approximately equivalent to 3,500 calories. A deficit of 500 calories usually results in a weight loss at the rate of 1 pound per week; a 1,000-calorie deficit will result in a weight loss of approximately 2 pounds a week. Some individuals may find that water retention follows weight loss, particularly middle-aged and older individuals. Thus, there may not be an immediate weight decline as designed in the program. In general, there will be plateaus followed by abrupt weight losses. For individuals not under medical supervision, a weight loss of more than 2 pounds a week should be considered excessive. A daily intake of less than 1,000 calories is not tolerated well by the body over a long period of time. The individual should be evaluated by her physician before undertaking such a stringent reducing diet.

4. *The choice of a food and eating pattern should be on an individual basis. The individual's differences in hunger and satiety patterns will lead to the most suitable plan. Some individuals will be more successful if they eat fewer—but larger—meals. Others will be more successful if they eat a number of small meals and snacks.* By trial and error you can discover your own sensations of hunger and satiety, and plan accordingly. Many individuals, however, are deficient in self-perception and are likely to eat too much or too little. Individuals who do not feel hungry until they start eating and then have difficulty stopping are obviously not candidates for numerous

Recommended Daily Dietary Allowances

The allowance levels are intended to cover individual variations among most normal persons as they live in the United States under usual environmental stresses. The recommended allowances can be attained with a variety of common foods, providing other nutrients for which human requirements have been less well defined.

Family members	lbs.	Height	Calories	Protein*	Calcium*	Iron†	Vitamin A I.U.	Thiamine†	Riboflavin†	Niacin‡	Ascorbic acid†	Vitamin D I.U.
Men:												
18-35	154	5'9"	2,900	70	0.8	10	5,000	1.2	1.7	19	70	
35-55	154	5'9"	2,600	70	0.8	10	5,000	1.0	1.6	17	70	
55-75	154	5'9"	2,200	70	0.8	10	5,000	0.9	1.3	15	70	
Women:												
18-35	128	5'4"	2,100	58	0.8	15	5,000	0.8	1.3	14	70	
35-55	128	5'4"	1,900	58	0.8	15	5,000	0.8	1.2	13	70	
55-75	128	5'4"	1,600	58	0.8	10	5,000	0.8	1.2	13	70	
Pregnant (2nd and 3rd trimester)			+ 200	+20	+0.5	+ 5	+1,000	+0.2	+0.3	+ 3	+30	400
Lactating			+1,000	+40	+0.5	+ 5	+3,000	+0.4	+0.6	+ 7	+30	400
Children:												
1-3	29	2'10"	1,300	32	0.8	8	2,000	0.5	0.8	9	40	400
3-6	40	3'6"	1,600	40	0.8	10	2,500	0.6	1.0	11	50	400
6-9	53	4'1"	2,100	52	0.8	12	3,500	0.8	1.3	14	60	400
Girls:												
9-12	72	4'7"	2,200	55	1.1	15	4,500	0.9	1.3	15	80	400
12-15	103	5'2"	2,500	62	1.3	15	5,000	1.0	1.5	17	80	400
15-18	117	5'4"	2,300	58	1.3	15	5,000	0.9	1.3	15	70	400

Source: National Research Council. Revised 1963.
*Grams
†Milligrams
‡Niacin equivalents include dietary sources of the preformed vitamin and the precursor, tryptophan. 60 milligrams tryptophan equals 1 milligram niacin.

small meals. On the other hand, those who get hungry on any kind of caloric restriction might be more successful on five small meals a day than on two or three large ones. In general, the choice of food and eating patterns for overweight individuals are as varied as for those of normal weight or those who are underweight. There is one striking difference, however. Overweight individuals tend to do their overeating late in the day and at night. So, caution—watch evening eating with particular care.

Many kinds and combinations of food can lead to a balanced diet. A diet should be built around familiar foods if it is to have lasting effects. It should be nutritionally sound and one with which you do not feel hungry. Fad diets sometimes have a short-term effect, but they have very little lasting worth. There is no evidence to favor the practice of eating slowly. Yet, on psychological grounds, it does make common sense; for some it takes time for the satiety mechanism to work. Clearly, the development of a diet prescription for weight loss requires more than a knowledge of nutrients and caloric values. The diet should conform to the individual's cultural patterns and usual eating habits. The new pattern of eating with some modification must become the established pattern of food intake if one is to maintain her best weight.

5. *Diets for weight maintenance or weight reduction should be nutritionally sound. That is, dietary plans for weight reduction are considered modifications of the normal nutritious diet with a reduction or adjustment in calories which should facilitate the loss of stored fat without damaging body structure or health-fitness.* A plan—A Daily Food Guide—that can serve as the basis for a weight program follows. The pattern of choices is based on what is known about the need for protein, vitamins, minerals, and other nutrients. Foods rich in proteins, key minerals, vitamins, and other essentials are grouped into four main classes according to their major contributions of nutrients. The number of servings it takes to add up to a good diet is listed. Also, the exact recommended daily dietary allowances designed for maintenance of good nutrition is presented for your reference.

A Daily Food Guide: Recommended Allowances

Meat Group: 2 or more servings. Beef, veal, pork, lamb, poultry, fish, eggs; alternates: dry beans, dry peas, nuts

Milk Group: for everyone. Children, 3–4 cups; teenagers, 4 or more cups; adults, 2 or more cups.

Bread and Cereal Group: 4 or more servings. Whole grain, enriched, or restored

Vegetable and Fruit Group: 4 or more servings. Include (a) a citrus fruit or other vegetable for vitamin C, (b) a dark green or deep-yellow vegetable for vitamin A—at least every other day, and (c) other vegetables and fruits, including potatoes

plus other foods as needed to complete meals and to provide additional food energy

From *Food for Fitness*, Leaflet No. 424, U.S. Government Printing Office, 1958.

exercise and weight control **173**

ENERGY EXPENDITURES IN VARIOUS PHYSICAL ACTIVITIES

calculating energy

The energy or caloric cost of performing different types of physical activities has been measured. Energy expenditure is determined by measuring the amount of oxygen consumed during a specific activity and computing the equivalent number of calories required. The caloric equivalent of a liter of oxygen varies from 4.68 to 5.04 calories, depending on the type of foodstuff being oxidized—carbohydrate, fat or protein. This procedure has been used as the basis for grading rates of work involved in physical activities—from the least to most costly activity.

Energy Cost of Daily Activity

Classification	Movements	Calories Per Day for Women
Sedentary	Working but mostly sitting	1,600-1,800
Light	Working but mostly sitting and standing	1,900-2,200
Moderate	Working mostly standing and walking	2,300-2,500
Very Active (heavy)	Working mostly walking or standing requiring moderate strength	2,600-3,000
Vigorous (unduly heavy)	Working mostly walking or standing requiring vigorous muscular activity	3,000 +

Energy is also required in the process of establishing internal equilibrium—regaining metabolic balance or homeostasis. Calories are required in the recovery process as well as in the physical activity itself. Therefore we add to the caloric cost of an activity the energy cost of recovery after the cessation of the activity.

variables affecting caloric cost of activity

The caloric cost of physical activity depends upon some additional variables. You are probably already aware of some of these. Such variables affecting caloric cost of performing an activity are:

1. skill or competence level in the specific activity
2. present status of physical condition or fitness level
3. gross body size (height, weight, body build)
4. environmental conditions (temperature, humidity, and altitude).

Sample Sheet for Calculating Energy Spent during a Typical Day

Activities	Hours Spent in Each Activity	Energy
At Work as a Student		
Sitting activities: Studying, listening, watching, eating	6 hours	Sedentary
Standing activities: Laboratory, waiting, talking, watching, dressing	1 hour	Sedentary
Walking activities: To and from classes, domestic activities in room	2½ hours	Light
Other activities: Cosmetic work	½ hour	Light
At Leisure		
Sitting activities: Listening, watching, playing instrument, knitting	3 hours	Sedentary
Walking activities: On a date, to the store, just walking	1 hour	Light
Other activities: Bicycling, bowling	1 hour	Moderate
At Rest or Sleep		
Daytime dozing	1 hour	Rest & Sleep
Sleep	8 hours	
Grand total	24 hours	Moderately active overall rating

Computation of Energy Expenditure

Energy Rating	Hours Spent	X	Average Caloric Cost	X	Body Weight	=	Total
Rest & Sleep	9		0.50		120		540
Sedentary	10		0.80		120		960
Light	4		1.50		120		720
Moderate	1		2.50		120		300
Active	0		—		—		—
Very Active	0		—		—		—
Vigorous	0		—		—		—
					Grand total		2,520

TABLE 12.1 Approximate Energy Expenditure in Various Physical Activities in Work and Leisure

Type of Physical Activity	Number of Pounds Bodyweight								Per Pound	Gross Energy Cost*	Energy Rating	Heart Rate/min.
	100	110	115	120	130	140	150	160				
1. Lying and resting											Rest-Sleep	Resting levels
Sleeping	43	47	49	52	56	60	65	69	0.43			
Awake (resting-lying)	50	55	58	60	65	70	75	80	0.50	0.50		
Resting-sitting	65	72	75	78	85	91	98	104	0.65			
2. Sitting											Sedentary	
Reading-studying	69	76	79	83	90	97	104	110	0.69			
Hand sewing-knitting	72	79	83	86	94	101	108	115	0.72	0.80		
Typing rapidly	91	100	105	109	118	127	137	146	0.91			
3. Standing												Slight increase above resting levels
Standing (relaxed)	69	76	79	83	90	97	104	110	0.69			
Standing (tense-rigid)	74	81	85	89	96	104	111	118	0.74			
Dressing and undressing	77	85	89	92	99	109	116	123	0.77			
Ironing	93	102	107	112	121	130	140	149	0.93	0.90		
Dishwashing or dusting	93	102	107	112	121	130	140	149	0.93			
Singing	79	87	91	95	103	111	119	126	0.79			
4. Walking and other											Light	75-100
Slowly (2.6 mph)	130	143	150	156	169	182	195	208	1.30			
Clerking (filing-store)	195	215	224	234	254	273	293	312	1.95	1.50		
Light domestic work	236	260	271	283	307	330	354	378	2.36			
5. Recreational and other												
Bicycling (5½ mph), walking (3½ - 4½ mph), canoeing (2½ mph), golf, lawn mowing, bowling, fencing, rowboating, gardening, calisthenics.										2.50	M†	106-125
Swimming (¼ mph), badminton, tennis, squash, volleyball, roller skating, horseback, riding, basketball, table tennis, walking (5½ mph).										3.50	A	125-150
Skin diving, ice skating, water skiing, hockey, lacrosse, scuba diving, ice skating, square-folk dancing, modern dance, running.										4.50	VA	150-175
Mountain climbing, sprinting, bicycling (13 mph) long distances.										5.00+	Vig.	175+

These values represent data from a summary by R. Passmore and J. V. Durnin, "Human Energy Expenditure," *Physiological Review,* Vol. 35 (May 1955) 801; and by C. F. Consolazio, R. E. Johonson, and L. J. Pecora, *Physiological Measurements of Metabolic Functions in Man* (New York: McGraw-Hill Book Company, 1963). Actual measured values used where available; other values represent a "best guess."

*cal./hour/lb. of body weight
†M, moderate; A, active; VA, very active; Vig., vigorous

In addition, the foregoing variables are related to the factors of age and sex. Because of this, the approximate energy expenditures listed above are guides and should not be considered rigid or absolute values.

LABORATORY:
DESIGNING A WEIGHT CONTROL PROGRAM

If you are a candidate for a weight control program (either reduction or maintenance of your current weight), the importance of being informed about the caloric value of food and the caloric cost of exercise is obvious. Furthermore, you must be able to accurately estimate your daily food intake as well as your daily energy expenditure. This knowledge is essential if you are to design a logical, personal weight control plan. Your daily caloric intake and output in physical activity will result in your gaining, losing, or maintaining your weight. By understanding and controlling these variables you will be able to attain and keep your best weight.

The following experiments are designed to help you put these principles into practice:

1. 3-day Food Record for fitness. Does your average diet provide all the nutrients you need to feel and look fit?
2. 3-day Diet Record and Caloric Estimates. Use this to calculate your average intake.
3. 3-day Activity Record and estimate of caloric output. How much energy do you ordinarily expend?
4. Evaluation of your Energy Needs. Are your caloric input and output equal? Will your present habits enable you to maintain or achieve your ideal weight?
5. Personal Progress Chart and Record. Chart your current status and your goals; don't let overweight, underweight, bad proportions, or excessive fatness "sneak up" on you!

Experiment 1: 3-Day Food Record for Fitness

Directions: Write the number of servings in the proper space after each meal. If you ate none of a particular food group, write "zero." Add the number of servings at the end of three days, divide by the recommended number, and multiply by 100 to get per cent score. If the score is less than 100 per cent, you are not eating enough of a food group.

Four Basic Food Groups	Recommended Minimum Daily Servings	1st Day	2nd Day	3rd Day	Divide by	Your Score	Multiply by 100 for Per Cent
1. Milk Group	4				12		
2. Meat Group	4				6		
3. Vegetable-Fruit Group							
Dark-green or deep-yellow vegetables	1				3		
Citrus fruit	1				3		
Others	2				6		
4. Breads and Cereals Group							
Whole grained and enriched	4				12		

Experiment 2: 3-Day Diet Record and Caloric Estimates

Meal	Day 1 food and amount	calories*	Day 2 food and amount	calories	Day 3 food and amount	calories
Breakfast						
Snacks						
Lunch						
Snacks						
Dinner						
Partying						
Snacks						
	totals					

*See Appendix B for tables of caloric values.

Formula: $\dfrac{\text{Average caloric}}{\text{intake (3 days)}} = \dfrac{\text{sum of totals}}{3}$

Your 3-day average $= \dfrac{\text{(totals)}}{3} =$

Experiment 3: 3-Day Activity Record

Time Period	Day 1 activity	time spent	Day 2 activity	time spent	Day 3 activity	time spent
Getting up until noon meal						
Noon meal to evening meal						
Evening meal until bedtime						
Sleep						
totals						

Experiment 3 continued: 3-Day Estimate of Caloric Output

Directions: On the chart that follows write down the number of hours you spent in each of the various types of activities during the 3 days you just recorded. To find how many calories you expended, multiply the estimated calories per pound per hour (column 1) by the number of hours you spent in each activity. Find the total calories per pound for each day, and multiply this by your weight to get your average daily caloric output.

Type of Activity	Estimated calories per lb. per hr.	Day 1 hours	Day 1 calories per lb.	Day 2 hours	Day 2 calories per lb.	Day 3 hours	Day 3 calories per lb.
Sleeping and rest							
Sitting reading, writing, eating, sewing, knitting, studying, typing, classes, playing cards, watching TV or movies, visiting. . .							
Standing: grooming, waiting in line, dishwashing, doing laundry, cooking, clerking in a store. . .							
Walking: going to and from classes, domestic work (cleaning, active baby-sitting). . .							
Bicycling							
Sports and games (list individual activities; refer to output estimates)							
totals							

(a) To calculate your daily caloric output, multiply total hours per day times total calories per pound for that day, and multiply this times your weight.

_____ X _____ = _____ X _____ = *(daily output)*

(b) To find your average caloric output add that value for each day calculated in *(a)* and divide by 3.

_____ + _____ + _____ = _____ = *(average daily output)*
                                              3

180.

Experiment 4: Evaluation of Energy Needs

1. Are your caloric intake and output equal?
   caloric intake _____
   caloric output _____
   difference (+ or –) _____

2. If a pound of fat consists of approximately 3,500 calories, how long will it take you to gain or lose (cross one out) one pound? _____ days.
   At this rate, what will your weight change be in one year? _____ lbs.

3. Approximately how many calories do you need each day to maintain your present weight? _____ calories.

4. Do you need to reduce or increase your caloric intake, or are you now at your ideal weight?

5. Write your personal perscription for personal activity in a weight control program (either reduction or maintenance of your present weight, whichever is best for you.)

Stepped-up Physical Activity at Work or in Transit

Daily activities (be specific)	Time you will spend	Estimated energy output (cal./lb./hr.)

Supplementary Leisure-Time Activities

Daily activities (be specific)	Time you will spend	Estimated energy output (cal./lb./hr.)

Experiment 5: Weight Control Program Record

Directions: If you are overweight, enter your weight on the top line at the left of the graph. On the next line write your weight minus 2 or 3 pounds. Continue subtracting 2 or 3 pounds and entering the weight on each line down the chart until you have reached your ideal weight.

If you are underweight, write your weight on the bottom line at the left of the graph. Enter your weight plus 2 or 3 pounds on the line above, and continue adding 2 or 3 pounds per line until you reach your ideal weight.

Weigh yourself once a week at the same time of day. Put a dot on the chart opposite your weight for each week. By connecting these dots with a line you will chart progress in weight gain or loss.

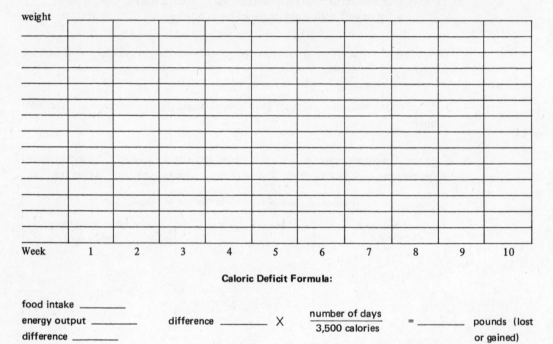

weight

| Week | 1 | 2 | 3 | 4 | 5 | 6 | 7 | 8 | 9 | 10 |

Caloric Deficit Formula:

food intake _____

energy output _____ difference _____ X $\dfrac{\text{number of days}}{3,500 \text{ calories}}$ = _____ pounds (lost

difference _____ or gained)

references and sources for additional reading

1. *Weight Control Source Book*. Chicago, Ill.: National Dairy Council, 111 North Canal Street.
2. *Obesity and Health*. U.S. Department of Health, Education and Welfare, National Center for Chronic Disease Control.
3. *Recommended Dietary Allowances*. 6th Rev. Ed. Food and Nutrition Board, National Academy of Sciences, National Research Council, Pub. 1146. Washington, D.C., 1964.

Directions: Record your findings for weight, body proportion, and fatness which were measured and recorded in Chapter 2. For diet, record average caloric intake (exercise 1 in this chapter) and per cent for each food group (exercise 2 in this chapter). Record all measurements once per week.

	date:									

Weight
  actual
  difference
    (+ or –) from
    ideal weight										

Body proportions
  bust
  waist
  abdomen
  hips
  thigh
  calf										

Fatness triceps										
Diet average caloric intake										

Food groups
  milk
  meat
  vegetable-fruit
  bread-cereals										

exercise

and figure control

13 One important concept of body image to be considered is that of the "ideal" measurements that make a perfect shape. If there were such a creature as an ideal woman, physically speaking, with whom we could compare our measurements, we might get an exact standard.

body proportions

At one time the dimensions of the Venus de Milo were considered perfect female measurements. Fashions have a tremendous influence on establishing the so-called ideal figure. The siren of the twenties was waistless, hipless, and flat-chested. Later fashion accentuated the small waist, full hips and bosom. Such changes result in an alteration in the concept of the ideal pin-up girl. Look at the differences in proportions of the "ideal women" (*opposite*). Instead of comparing yourself to an ideal standard, ask yourself, "Are my measurements desirable in terms of my basic figure type?" Or, "Am I making the most of what I have?"

fat distribution

A comment is in order about the problem of unusual fat depositions in otherwise nonobese individuals. This is without doubt one of the most common and one of the most difficult problems to deal with and, perhaps, accept. To a large extent, the distribution of body fat is controlled genetically and hormonally.

MISS U.S.A., 1960	AVERAGE AMERI-CAN WOMEN	AVERAGE RUS-SIAN WOMAN	VENUS DE MILO
Weight 129			
Height ......5'7"			
Bust ....36"	Bust ....33"	Bust ....38"	Bust ....43"
Waist ......23"	Waist ......26"	Waist ......29"	Waist ......38"
Hips ......37"	Hips ......37"	Hips ......43"	Hips ......44"

Fat deposition patterns cannot be changed. You may have fat distributed evenly over your body; you may find fat concentrated around the middle section of your body; or you may find a disproportionate fat distribution from your waist down. This pattern of fat distribution may be particularly distressing to young women who are concerned with their appearance. A lack of understanding of your inherited endowment may lead to unwarranted anxieties, excessive dieting, impaired health, and a poor self-image. Self-perception and self-acceptance should be the important considerations.

spot reducing

You already know that to lose fat you must use it as food energy or fuel. Exercise can and does increase the caloric output. If you reduce your caloric intake or keep it constant and increase your caloric outgo, you will reduce the fat in your body. But, as has been stated above, you have inherited patterns of fat distribution. No one exercise and no one diet will affect the amount of fat in a specific fat deposit in your body. Three other important facts should be considered at this time.

1. You may lose 2 pounds by staying in a steam bath for an hour or by wearing so-called sweat garments while exercising; you may lose 5–6 pounds or more during a strenuous physical activity played over a period of time especially on a hot day; but this is a temporary weight or water loss, which is quickly regained when you drink and eat.

2. Massage by hand or with mechanical devices will not reduce local deposits of fat. Fat is not broken down nor absorbed away like magic nor moved to another part of the body. Fat must be burned, oxidized. Massage in and of itself does not tone the muscles or build strength. Massage, however, has real value—it can aid in restoring elasticity to sagging skin when used along with diet and exercise, rest and sleep; it can help in relieving aches and pain in specific muscle groups undergoing muscle spasm; it can make you feel better if you personally enjoy massage.
3. Vibratory machines will not reduce fat deposits. These machines do have some value in aiding circulation and the release of muscle tension. But the value in developing muscle tone, reducing, or preventing fat from accumulating is *nil* (1).

So, of what value is exercise in a spot-reducing program? You can streamline body contours—take off inches—and build a shapely figure based on your figure type through prescribed exercises by:

1. selecting specific exercises to improve muscle tone and strength, thereby preventing sag, droop, and unsightly bulges in specific body regions
2. improving postural lines, thereby preventing unsightly bulges that affect body poise.

What kinds of exercises should you use to tone or firm the muscles, to take off inches and streamline body contours? Select exercises that use specific muscles in the body region concerned. Examples of these are presented in Appendix A. Based on your personal need, select appropriate exercises and design your exercise program. Aids for designing such a program will be found at the end of this chapter.

EXERCISE AND POSTURAL CONTROL

body lines

A second important concept of body image to be considered is that of balanced body lines or posture. The body is composed of many movable segments and should not be considered as one solid, rigid structure. The five important body segments that need to be considered in attaining balanced body or postural lines are shown opposite.

When these segments are supported upon one another in the best possible balance, you have good posture and good appearance with minimum expenditure of energy and minimum strain on joints and ligaments.

What is the postion of best balance? Suppose you have a stack of building blocks. Imagine yourself placing these blocks upon each other to represent the figure of the human body. You would find that there is only one position in which the greatest degree of stability in the upright position is possible. You will arrive at this position by resting each block directly and securely over the

center of its supporting block or base of support. Your wooden figure will then have the position of best balance in the upright position.

The force of gravity pulling toward the center of the earth holds these blocks together. This pulling force is constantly acting upon all material mass in our universe. Every object has mass. You can measure the force of gravity acting upon an object by its weight. If your weight is 120 pounds, the pulling force of gravity upon your body mass is 120 pounds of 1 G (or one unit of gravitational force times your body weight).

The force of gravity acts on all parts of your body. It may, however, be considered as concentrating its pull on the mass center of your entire body or on the mass center of each of your body segments. This mass center—the imaginary balancing point of the total body or the balancing point of each of the body segments—is called the center of gravity. An imaginary line dropped vertically down from the center of gravity is called the line of gravity.

The location of your center of gravity in the upright position will depend upon your figure type and your weight distribution. It probably lies about two inches above the hip joint, midway through the body from front to back and halfway through the body from side to side. The center of gravity is not a stationary point. It is constantly being altered by the shifting of the body's weight or parts during work and play.

When all parts of your body are in a position of best balance, the force of gravity pulls you together; the force exerted by your muscles to balance the body parts is at a minimum, and the internal stresses on bone, ligaments, and tendons are minimal. When something does go wrong, it is usually the result of poor balance or a shift of balance in the region of the pelvis. The pelvis is the keystone segment of the body, the point where all motion originates and where the balance that affects the rest of the body segments is maintained or lost.

Since people differ in weight, shape, and physical capacities, you should be able to recognize *individual differences* in the ease of balancing the body in the upright position. There is some clinical evidence to support the contention that

Mesomorphic characteristics
Lower center of gravity
Strong, short muscles
Strong, short ligaments
Tight, strong fascia
Less movable segments (joints)

Ectomorphic characteristics
Higher center of gravity
Long, slender muscles
Long, slender ligaments
Lax, weak fascia
Great movability of body segments (joints) allows center of gravity to be shifted off balance.

the tall, thin individual may be most susceptible to postural problems, while the husky, well-knit individual is least susceptible. This may be due to certain inherited capacities that affect the ease with which one balances the body in the upright position. Perhaps this will be more apparent when you examine these two body types—the mesomorphic and the ectomorphic (above).

Keep in mind also that it is impossible to set up rigid standards for good or poor posture because no two persons can conform to exactly the same postural position. There is as much difference between their habitual postures as between the expressions on their faces. Both are reflections of the individual's heredity, culture, and personality. To assess the expressive component of posture, two experiments have been included at the end of this chapter. Regardless, however, of the individual's figure type, environment, and personality, her posture is *good* when it obeys the laws of balance, as previously described, and *poor* when it does not.

techniques and exercises for total body alignment

These techniques are designed for one primary purpose—to improve your muscle sense or kinesthetic perception of the balanced position of the total body. The goal is to consciously achieve a balanced position so that when you assume any other position, you will be uncomfortable. A description of a balanced position when standing seems in order at this time.

> Your *weight* will fall ahead of your outer ankle bone and be distributed toward the outside of each foot.
> Your *feet* will be parallel and slightly apart.
> Your *knees* will be free and easy, neither bent nor thrust back
> Your *hips* will be under you, neither leading nor thrust back.
> Your *abdomen* will be up and in, neither relaxed nor protruding.

Your *chest* will be held up and easy, neither sagging nor too high and leading.

Your *shoulders* will be free and easy, neither forward, back, nor elevated.

Your *shoulder blades* will be drawn down and flat on your back

Your *arms* will hang naturally and relaxed at your sides, neither held rigidly nor too relaxed.

Your *trunk* will be within normal limits of curves, neither too straight and flat, nor too rounded and hollow; and you will stretch your back straight upward toward the crown of your head.

Your *head* and *chin* will be easy and centered over your trunk with the chin held at right angles to front of your neck.

Specific techniques to aid you in attaining balanced alignment are presented below.

Try to find your position of balance by feeling it, seeing it, and holding it for a few seconds. Relax. Then see if you can find this position again. Repeat.

1. See it. Work in front of a mirror and try to visualize the balanced position of your body segments—the total body line running through the center of weight of each body segment and falling slightly in front of the outer ankle bone. Feel it.

2. When you find this position, become aware of the position of the body parts—the sense of weight on the feet, the free and easy position of the knees, the balance of the pelvis, the position of the trunk and the chest, the free and easy balance of the shoulders, and the feeling of the head and chin.

3. If you have difficulty in finding the balance of your body parts, test yourself against a wall or door. Stand with the back against the wall or door, heels, hips, and head touching. Stretch tall and easily, keep waistline in, shoulders balanced and easy, arms relaxed at the side, head straight, chin horizontal, and chest held in midposition. The space between your lower back and the wall should be at a minimum, just enough to feel the pressure on your finger tips if you tried to slide your hand through.

4. If you are still having difficulty developing the balanced feeling, try this exercise:

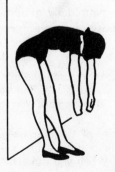

Stand with the hips supported against the wall, feet several inches from the wall, body bent forward at the waist. Gradually bring the body to an extended position by first pressing the lumbar region of the spine to the wall and then attempting to touch each segment of the spinal column to the wall.

One good exercise that brings about the feeling of the balanced position and, at the same time, assists in developing the muscles necessary to maintain this balanced position follows.

Stand with the back against a wall, heels about 3 or 4 inches from the wall, feet straight ahead and 2 inches apart, knees easy. Place the hands up beside the head with elbows touching the wall, and bent at 90 degrees. Tilt the pelvis to flatten the lower back against the wall by pulling up and in with the lower abdominal muscles. Hold head straight and chin level. Stretch tall in this positon. Tighten muscles on inner side of feet, rolling weight slightly toward outer borders of the feet and rotate legs slightly outward with kneecaps facing straight ahead by tightening the buttocks muscles. Hold this position about 3 counts. Relax. Repeat exercise 3 times, 3 times per day. You may occasionally stretch the arms up over head, keeping them in contact with the wall.

If this exercise is difficult for you, try it on the floor. Then try it sitting on a stool, with the knees bent at right angles and feet flat on the floor. Then proceed to standing position.

Once you achieve the sense of balance in the standing position with concentration, your next step is to practice. Relax. Balance. Relax. Repeat this procedure about 5 times, 3 times per day. Continue as long as necessary so that during the day, without a mirror, you can check yourself. If you are off balance, you should balance yourself and continue with your daily activities.

To become more consciously aware of your balanced position in the upright position, utilize the following procedures:

1. Balance yourself in front of a mirror. Walk away from the mirror and then return. Are you in a balanced position? If not, find your balanced position and repeat the exercise. Repeat until you can come back and be in a balanced position.

2. After you can do this, increase the difficulty of the exercise—not only walk, but stoop, lift, carry objects, climb stairs, and change the height of your heels. *Practice. Practice.* When you can achieve

the balanced position with concentration then you are ready for the next step.

3. You may find that special attention must be given to controlling the middle segment of the body, namely, the pelvis. This segment is probably the most important segment for balance at rest and in motion. It supports the trunk, head, chest, and shoulders and is the connecting line between the upper segment of the body and the lower, such as the legs and feet. If the pelvis is out of position, the upper segment of the body cannot be held in balance, nor can the lower segment. Try it and see. Assume the fatigue slump position and now, without changing the forward position of the pelvis, try to balance your head, shoulders, chest, trunk, knees, and body line. You can't without first bringing the pelvis into balance. Similarly, assume the hollow back position and follow the same procedure as above.

Sets of muscles cooperate to hold the pelvis under the body where it belongs. The abdominal muscles lift the front brim of the pelvis; while at the same time, the gluteal or buttocks muscles anchor the rear of the pelvis down. Here is a progression of pelvic control exercises, which involve the combined action of the abdominal and gluteal muscles.

1. Lie down on your back, knees bent, and feet on the floor close to your buttocks, with hands up beside the head.
Pull up and in with the lower abdominal muscles. Be sure the upper abdominal muscles are relaxed and your breathing is regular. Relax. Repeat 3 times.
Next, pull up and in with your lower abdominal muscles and pinch your buttocks together. Hold. Relax. Repeat 3 times.
Remember: Breathing is regular at all times. You may increase the difficulty of the exercises by gradually extending the knees until they are straight. Repeat the same exercises.

2. Lie on your back, bend knees, and place feet flat on the floor. With hands at the sides of the head, flatten lower back to floor. Hold the back flat and slide heels down along the floor. Keep back flat and return knees to bent position, one at a time.
NOTE: If you are unable to do these exercises, it may be because of tightness in the low back muscles, or because you have not yet developed awareness of your pelvis in space.

Now that you understand the basic principles and can achieve balanced positions in various activities with concentration, you are ready for the next step: *remembering your balanced position in your daily living activities.* You must become consciously aware of balance in all your activities. Check yourself frequently. Soon you will find, upon checking, that you are in balance. Then the balanced position has become a habit, and you will probably maintain this position as your usual posture. Any other position will feel unnatural or awkward to you.

You may find that just being aware of balanced posture does not solve your problem because you lack the strength, endurance, flexibility, and relaxation to maintain the position of balance freely and easily. You may need supplemental exercises. You can pick out the exercises you need if you know where you need to develop these qualities. The following information will help.

postural control and general health-physical fitness

To achieve a position of best balance or optimal body lines for your basic figure type, you need to have a sufficient amount of organic tone, elastic tone, muscle tone, in specific body regions. Through self-assessment you should be able to evaluate your present status in these essentials, particularly as reflected in your posture.

Muscle Tone (*strength and endurance*). Muscles must be constantly balancing all of the body segments (standing still or in motion), or you would collapse in a heap on the floor. Because the body is flexible (has a range of movement at a joint), the job of staying erect against gravity makes far greater demands on certain muscle groups than upon others. Those muscles that hold the body upright are called "antigravity muscles." When the pull of these muscles is evenly balanced, the body stands erect.

The important question is whether or not the muscles directly responsible for balancing the body parts in the upright posture against the force of gravity

Antigravity or Postural Muscles

1. Inner border of the leg and foot (anterior tibialis, posterior tibialis—long toe flexors)

2. Calf (gastroenemius-soleus)

3. Front of thigh (quadriceps femoris)

4. Buttocks (gluteus maximus)

5. Back (spinal extensors)

6. Front (abdominals)

7. Shoulder blades (shoulder adductors—trapezius and rhomboids)

receive enough use in the daily activities of the modern woman. Of course, you climb stairs, walk, and occasionally run. These activities may provide enough exercise for the antigravity muscles of the lower and upper leg, but what about the muscle groups of the trunk, abdomen, shoulders, and feet?

Muscles may also be weakened by prolonged stretching. Muscles that are permitted to pull too hard may move a body segment off balance. If this body segment is permitted to be carried in this position for a period of time, the muscles controlling it (pulling it) will become short and tight. The opposite muscle group will be stretched. Muscles under prolonged stretch become weak and lack tone. This results in unattractive body lines and unshapely body contours.

Elastic Tone (*range of motion or flexibility of major body segments*). You should have sufficient joint mobility to give you the freedom and ease needed to maintain balanced body lines. Too much or too little mobility is definitely unwanted. Either extreme from the optimum range of your basic figure type may be detrimental to your balanced alignment and the efficiency of your movements.

Organic Tone (*cardiovascular-respiratory endurance*). You should have optimal functioning of the heart, lungs, and blood vessels to give you zest and spring or vitality. Without this, fatigue and tiredness, or what is called "the fatigue slump," is the result.

habitual movement patterns

You probably sit hour after hour each day, and if your chair is too high or too low, you are likely to be sitting out of balance with the desk or working surface. Probably, you stand and move in that same postural pattern. Clothing may produce the wrong kind of internal stresses, and your bones, muscles, ligaments, and fascia will respond to the pressures. Occupational positions held with the muscles out of balance and stresses upon the joints will produce positions of imbalance, which you will carry with you whether at rest or in motion, at play, or working around the house.

You may have learned to sit, stand, and move by imitating someone with poor balance characteristics. These may include carrying books on one hip, sitting on one leg, standing with the weight thrust over one hip, or slumping to be the same height as friends. Remember, *old dogs* can be taught *new tricks*, if they desire to learn.

LABORATORY: DESIGNING A FIGURE CONTROL PROGRAM

Record your measurements in experiment 1. Then, with a friend's help, evaluate your performance of simple, daily activities such as walking, sitting, and climbing stairs. Refer to Chapter 10 for descriptions of proper movement patterns. By defining correct performance and evaluating your level of grace and efficiency you should gain insight into your own movement habits. These experiments thus constitute a summary of the chapter.

If you find you wish to improve your postural patterns, experiments 1–3 will serve as guidelines for building a personal program into your daily life. Use experiment 4 to record your self-prescription and evaluate your progress. You should now be more conscious of form in all activities and be in a better position to check yourself once in a while every day. Experiment 5, which deals with the expressional or attitudinal components of posture, is included to stimulate class discussion and experimentation.

Experiment 1:   Figure Control Program Record*

Posture Measure (see p. 27)

Side View	date				Front View	date			

Proportions (see p. 25)

	date			
Chest				
Waist				
Abdomen				
Hips				
Thigh				
Calf				
Arm				

General Health-Physical Fitness (see p. 32)

	date			
Strength				
Flexibility				
Muscular endurance				
Cardio-vascular respiration				
Ability to relax at will**				

*To test your level in these areas, turn back to the Profile Record in Chapter 2. Record your posture rating for body segments; measurements for proportions; and average percentiles for health-physical fitness.

**Ways of measuring your ability to relax are presented in Chapter 15.

Experiment 2: Record of Your Walking Patterns

Directions: First, study the material presented in Chapter 10. Then have a partner evaluate your walking performance, in flats and heels, checking each body segment described under the four principles below. Circle the words that best describe your movements (using one color for flats, another for heels). Then rate your performance on the scale below and answer the questions that follow.

Unbalanced		Balanced	Unbalanced

1. Stability

Body Line Backward		Balanced Slightly Forward	Forward

2. Force

Sequence	Chest lead	Hip lead	Head and shoulder lead
Transfer of weight	Ankles	Three-point walk	Ankles roll out
Stride	Too short	Balanced	Too long
Arm swing	Too short	Balanced	Too long
Speed	Too fast	Balanced	Too slow

3. Direction

Feet	Toe-out	Parallel	Toe-in
Push-off	Flatfoot	Forward-upward	Upward
Knees	Back	Balanced-easy	Bent
Hips	Rumba	Balanced	Twist

4. Nature of movement

Body	Loose, sloppy	Free and easy	Tight, tense
Shoulders and arms	Loose, sloppy	Free and easy	Tight, tense
Elbows	Flapping	Free and easy	Bent
Legs	Loose, sloppy	Free and easy	Tight, tense

1. On a scale of 3 (high) to 1 (low), how would you rate your performance in flats?_____ In heels? _____

2. What is the most important difference in walking in heels?

3. What do you most need to improve in your movements in flat heels?

4. How do you plan to do this?

Experiment 3: Record of Movement Patterns in Work

Directions: First, review the definition of efficient, graceful performance of each pattern. Then, under the scale for rating each pattern write in the movement characteristics you would look for in a correct performance. Lastly, have your partner rate you: circle 3 points for an excellent performance (correct in all details); 2 points for a performance with slight to moderate deviation from correct form; and 1 point for a performance that deviates markedly from correct form.

Walking   3   2   1   Sitting   3   2   1

Pushing-pulling   3   2   1   Reaching-holding   3   2   1

Stooping-lifting   3   2   1   Climbing stairs   3   2   1

Summary of Your Movement Characteristics in Work

$$\text{Your rating} = \frac{\text{sum of your total points}}{6} = \underline{\hspace{2cm}}.$$

Your performance: High   Medium   Low.   Frequency of: always   sometimes   seldom
                 3   2   1   3   2   1

Experiment 4: Exercise Record for Figure Control Program

Exercises

Prescription	Purpose	Weekly Progression			
Posture Control 1. 2. 3.					
General Health- Physical Fitness 1. 2. 3.					
Proportion 1. 2. 3.					

Changes in Daily Living Habits

Do you need to improve your:	Your Plan

1. Relaxation
2. Sleep and rest
3. Diet and nutrition
4. Postural patterns in:
    lifting-stooping
    pulling-pushing
    climbing stairs
    reaching-holding
    walking	

Experiment 5: Appraising the Attitudinal Component of Posture
Perception and Symbolic Meaning of Your Movement Characteristics

PART I, Human Behavior and Movement Characteristics

Directions: This device is a way of helping you to understand about yourself and other people. It tells nothing more than what you want it to say. It will have value only if you do your best to get an accurate description of yourself and other people as you see them.

First: Working with a partner or a group, make a list of trait words depicting different human behavior and personality characteristics, such as aggressive, pompous, studious, fearful, fashionable, competitive, stubborn, broad-minded, sarcastic, nervous, generous, cheerful, facetious. From this list, select the ten trait words which your partner or the group believe to be most common.

Second: List the direct opposites of these ten words.

Third: Using this list of trait words and their opposites, portray these qualities through bodily attitudes and movements. Try to perceive the movement as to range of motion (large-small), the force of the movement (strong-weak), the accent of the movement (where does it fall?), and the flow of the movement (tense-relaxed, smooth-jerky). Do the same for bodily attitudes.

Word Traits	Perception of Movements and Bodily Attitudes
1.	
2.	
3.	
4.	
5.	
6.	
7.	
8.	
9.	
10.	

Opposites	
1.	
2.	
3.	
4.	
5.	
6.	
7.	
8.	
9.	
10.	

PART II, Perception of Self and Others

Directions: First: Using the list of trait words which you have just selected, rate yourself by your answers to three questions: 1. How often are you this sort of person? 2. How do you feel about being this way? 3. How much of the time would you like this trait to be characteristic of you?

Second: Using the following rating scale, record the number in the appropriate column.

Column I (Question 1)

1—Seldom like me
2—About half the time like me
3—Most of the time like me

Column II (Question 2)

1—Dislike being as I am
2—Neither dislike or like being as I am
3—Like very much being as I am

Column III (Question 3)

1—Seldom would like this to be me
2—About half the time would like this to be me
3—Most of the time would like this to be me

Self		Others	
Word Trait I II III	Opposite I II III	Word Trait I II III	Opposite I II III
1.	1.	1.	1.
2.	2.	2.	2.
3.	3.	3.	3.
4.	4.	4.	4.
5.	5.	5.	5.
6.	6.	6.	6.
7.	7.	7.	7.
8.	8.	8.	8.
9.	9.	9.	9.
10.	10.	10.	10.

PART III, Cultural Meaning of Movement and Bodily Postures

Directions: Describe such movements and/or bodily postures that have symbolic meaning reflecting the people of the United States. Also, give some provincial aspects of movements. Then see if you know some characteristic movements of other countries.

United States		Other Countries	
Movement/Posture	Symbolic Meaning	Movement/Posture	Symbolic Meaning

references and sources for additional reading

1. Hemland, V., and A. Steinhaus, "Do Mechanical Vibrators Take Off or Redistribute Fat?" *Journal for the Association of Physical and Mental Rehabilitation*, Vol. 11 (May-June 1957), 342.

Kraus, H., *Therapeutic Exercise*, 2nd ed., Springfield, Ill.: Charles C Thomas, Publisher, 1963.

Lowman, C.L., and C.H. Young, *Postural Fitness*. Philadelphia: Lea & Febiger, 1960.

Metheny, E., *Body Dynamics*, New York: McGraw-Hill Book Company, 1952.

———, *Movement and Meaning*, New York: McGraw-Hill Book Company, 1968.

Wells, K.F., *Posture Exercise Handbook*, New York: The Ronald Press Company, 1963.

Williams, M., and C. Worthingham, *Therapeutic Exercise for Body Alignment and Function*. Philadelphia: W.B. Saunders Co., 1957.

exercise and

relaxation

14 There are two basic techniques for relaxation: stretching exercises and progressive relaxation. Stretching exercises are prescribed to release tension in specific target areas of the body that seemingly develop residual tension. Techniques employing progressive relaxation are divided into three exercise series: (*1*) modified Jacobson, (*2*) slow controlled movements, and (*3*) passive or breathing concentration.

STRETCHING EXERCISES

There are two kinds of stretching exercises. The *first* will bring about a pulling, stretching sensation. These exercises should be done to count. Start out doing them to 4 counts and then gradually increase the number. Extend first in one direction and then flex or bend in the other. This kind of exercise is very applicable in releasing tensions and chasing fatigue produced from set postures of work while typing, sewing, driving, or writing.

The *second* kind of exercise will bring about a feeling of free-flowing, swinging, pendulum movements. These exercises are done to a set rhythmical pattern, first in one direction and then in the other. This type of exercise is very applicable in developing sensations of free and easy poise and graceful movements. It can be used to release undue muscular tensions before athletic events. The athlete wants to be sure a joint is free to move in all directions and that undue tensions and stimulation of the game won't tie her up. She may swing her tennis racket in all directions with big circular motions or move the arms in big circles or the legs in all directions, jumping easily up and down and sideward. These two basic kinds of movements are used to release tension in different body regions through the exercises which follow.

Before you begin any special exercises you will find it worthwhile to stretch.

You may lie and stretch or sit and stretch. S-T-R-E-T-C-H your arms overhead. R-E-A-C-H. P-U-L-L. Feel the tension as you reach upward? Let it go. Try the same thing on a diagonal pattern, stretching one arm and the opposite leg. Push down with your foot and stretch or pull up with your arm. Reverse the movement. Repeat the process several times. This is a good method for releasing tensions throughout your body as well as an aid in recognizing the feel of tensions as they build up and let go.

your back

Seal Lift. Lie face down on the floor with the soles of your feet toward the sky. Place your hands at the side of your body opposite your chest. First, lift your head and stretch your neck upward and lift your chest off the floor. Arch your back and push with your hands until your elbows are straight. Slowly return to the starting position. Repeat 2 or 3 times. You might try a modification of this sitting in a chair.

Folding-Unfolding Your Back. Sit on heels, arms relaxed at sides. Relax trunk forward, chest leading, and slowly curl up in a ball with your head under, back rounded. Return to starting position by gradually straightening spine; begin at lower back, with upper back, shoulders, chest, and finally the head assuming its starting position. Do this exercise with arms extended along the floor and pull the arms back into position last.

Swinging Pendulum. Stand with back to wall, hips supported by wall. Let trunk fall forward and downward in a relaxed, easy manner, arms hanging loosely, head relaxed. Sway body from side to side, keeping arms, shoulders, and head relaxed. Come slowly back to starting position by bringing your lower back, upper back, shoulders, and then head into place. Repeat a couple of times.

your shoulders, neck, and head

Shoulder Roll and Lift. Seated cross-legged, move shoulders up. Relax them and let them fall back into position. Move shoulders forward and then roll back and relax into position. Repeat several times. Try this in your chair to relax shoulder and upper back tension.

Shoulder and Head Drop. Sit, clasp hands behind your buttocks. Slowly push your hands downward toward the floor, roll your shoulders back, and pull down with your shoulder blades. Pull your head backwards. Release the tension. Roll shoulders forward, bring shoulder blades up, and let head drop down. Repeat 2 or 3 times. You may try this exercise in a standing or lying position.

Neck and Head Drop. Sit with head up and chin at a right angle to your neck. Feel the weight of your head pulling back, back, back. Let it fall. Slowly lift head forward to starting position. Let it fall slowly forward as far as possible. Keep your shoulders in contact with your chair. Pull your head back into position and then let it drop to the right. Repeat to the left. Continue these movements 2 or 3 times.

your hips and pelvis

Swinging Pendulum.   Stand in a balanced position with one hand on a support in the beginning. Slowly start swinging your leg forward and backward. Gradually increase your swing. At the top of your forward and backward swing, sense the weight of your leg and let it swing you back and forward. Be sure you maintain balanced alignment throughout. Repeat the procedure with your other leg.

Rolling Your Pelvis.   Lie on your back, arms overhead. Roll to the left, keeping shoulders on the floor by lifting right hip until you reach the point where you let go and the rest of your body follows, without exerting any tension (energy). Then lift the left shoulder and allow it to pull you over to complete the roll. Repeat several times in the same direction then reverse directions.

Hip Lift.   Lie on the floor with your knees bent halfway and your feet on the floor. Keep your arms at your side. Slowly raise your hips off the floor until you are resting your weight on your feet and your upper back and shoulders. Return slowly to your starting position. Repeat this several times.

your feet

Toe Curling.   Sit or lie on floor. With your legs straight, curl your toes under slowly. Release. Bring toes back as far as they will come. Relax them completely. Begin your curling movements again. Repeat 5 or 6 times. In between times, you can try toe spreading.

Foot Lift.   Sit or lie on floor. With legs straight, bring your foot back toward your shinbone as far as possible. Slowly return it as far as possible in the opposite direction. Repeat the movement 5 or 6 times. You may add toe curl to the downward movement and toe extending on the movement toward your shinbone.

PROGRESSIVE RELAXATION

These techniques involve learning and practicing the art of relaxing neuromuscular tensions at will. If you are able to relax your tensions voluntarily when you become tense, you are lucky. If you cannot relax, learning the art of relaxing and practicing at least 5 or 10 minutes a day will pay you dividends. The speed at which you learn to relax at will depends upon your mental concentration and your perception or awareness of localized neuromuscular tensions.

Three basic techniques are employed for progressive relaxation: (1) modified Jacobson or tension approach; (2) slow controlled movements, and (3) a passive approach. Examine each technique. Experiment with them. Find one that appeals to you or combine them and design a program to meet your personal needs.

series I: modified Jacobson

Lesson 1. Lie down on your back, arms away from the body and legs apart. Close the eyes and lie as still and relaxed as you can. Clench the fists tightly. Do you feel the muscles become tense? Hold for a moment; now let it go slowly, more, more, do not force it, let it go still more. Now try it again. (The fingers should not become straight nor should there be jerky or extra motions.)

Lesson 2. Lie down, eyes closed, arms away from the body, legs apart. Bend the feet downward. Hold; let them go slowly, more, more. As the legs relax, let the arms relax also. Continue to let the legs go more and more. Repeat action.

Lesson 3. Under physical or emotional strain, you know that the breathing becomes more rapid and often uneven. Lie down, eyes closed, arms away from body, legs apart. Take a deeper breath than normal, exhale slowly until the chest sinks as far as it will go without effort. Do not force air out. Take another deeper breath, exhale slowly, again inhale and exhale. Slowly extend your exhalation phase.

Lesson 4. Lie down, eyes closed, wrinkle the forehead, hold it. Do you feel the tensions? Now let it go slowly, more and more; continue to let it go. (Repeat the same thing slowly, more, more.) Let the rest of the body go at the same time. Continue, letting the muscles do more of nothing.

Lesson 5. Lie down with the eyes closed, look to the right, hold them. Feel the tension? Let the eyes slowly return to their normal position. Move the eyes to the left, hold them. Now let them go slowly. Repeat the same procedure. Continue to look nowhere in particular. Just let the eyes go; do not hold them. (Students whose eyes move considerably when closed should obtain additional help.)

Lesson 6. Hold your lips tightly together. Do not clench your teeth or make other unnecessary motions with the muscles of the face. Pucker up the lips, hold them. Now let them go slowly, more slowly, more, more; continue letting them go. (Repeat action.) Clench the teeth; slowly let the jaw relax and drop. Let it go more. (Repeat action.)

Lesson 7. Many of us complain of a tired back caused by improper posture in sitting. Lie down, let the body go, arch the back so that the weight is on the head and the buttocks. Notice the feeling of tension along the spine. Hold it. Now let it go slowly, half way. You can still feel some tension. Now let it go more, more, more. (After a few seconds, repeat the technique.)

Lesson 8. Usually the first place we feel pain when working at a desk or a typewriter is at the back of the neck and across the shoulders. This is due to holding the head in one position and to holding the shoulders tense or in a hunched position. Lie down, body relaxed. Let the head roll to one side. Now bring it to the midpoint. Notice the tension in the muscles of the neck as the head is moved. Now let it roll to the other side; let it go more and more. (Repeat twice to each side.) Let the head remain quiet and relaxed in any position it assumes. Hunch the shoulders, hold them, now slowly let the muscles relax, more, more, more. (Repeat twice.) Continue to relax neck and shoulders. Remember the keynote of relaxation is doing.

Now let us see what we have covered.

1. You know what is meant by relaxation (the release or reduction of the feeling of tension).
2. You understand the importance of learning to relax regardless of the approach you choose.
3. You have practiced the art of learning to relax.
4. You are now ready to practice and to remember to relax during the day.

Practice the feelings of relaxation and tension during activities throughout the day (sitting in class, watching a movie, waiting for a bus, etc).

Set up cues to test how relaxed you are at different times during the day.

series II: slow controlled movements

This procedure gives the muscles something to do to expel excess tension and, at the same time, to divert your mind from your immediate problems. Lie on your back in a comfortable position. You may turn your arm completely over on a count of 10 or 20 and bring it back to the original position on the same count. Repeat this with the right and left arm, and legs, and by opening and shutting your mouth, fingers, and toes. This is an excellent procedure for getting the most out of a few minutes of rest during the day, or relaxing just before going to sleep or while sitting at work with your eyes closed.

series III: passive approach

This procedure requires mental concentration upon specific parts of the body during each passive phase of breathing. Lie down on your back in a comfortable position with your eyes closed. Turn your attention to your breathing cycle. Slowly extend the exhalation phase of your breathing without forcing it. Now, on each exhalation phase, bring into your consciousness a feeling of looseness, heaviness, formlessness, limpness of the right arm, left arm, both arms, shoulders, throat, right leg, left leg, both legs, chest, abdominal area, face, and jaw. In learning the procedure, consider one part of the body at a time. As you progress, bring into consciousness during your exhalation phase of breathing, the next body part. Your goal is to learn to completely "let go" in all parts of the body at once with each exhalation phase of breathing.

LABORATORY IN RELAXATION

Experiment 1: Test Your Ability to Relax at Will and to Recognize Tension

Directions: Lie down on your back and assume the following position: close your eyes, place your arms at the side of the body, elbows slightly flexed, with fingers lightly touching the floor. The muscles controlling the wrists, elbows, shoulders, knees, legs, and feet are tested by your partner. She will record the results on the chart below. Space for retests is provided.

General Signs of Tension	Subjective Judgment					
	Yes	No	Yes	No	Yes	No
1. Fluttering eyelids						
2. Twitching of fingers						
3. Excessive swallowing						
4. Tightness of lower jaw and lips						
5. Frowning						
6. Short shallow breathing						
Recognition of Tension						
1. Arms						
2. Legs						
3. Face						
4. Head						
5. Chest						

Tension Record

Localized Areas to be Tested	R	L	R	L	R	L
1. Arms Wrist Elbow Shoulder						
2. Legs Knee Hip						
3. Neck Head						
4. Chest Regular breathing No interference with rhythm Extends exhalation slightly on command.						

1. Assistance—You assist your partner in performing the motion.

2. Resistance—You resist the movement that your partner is performing.

3. Posturing or set—You keep the part in a position resisting gravity when your partner takes away her support.

4. Perseverance—You continue the movement begun by your partner after she takes away her support.

1. Your overall evaluation of your ability to relax.   Low   Medium   High
2. Your overall evaluation in recognizing tension.   Low   Medium   High

Experiment 2: Evaluating Relaxation and Leisure Patterns.

Directions: Answer the questions below. Check your answers

Can you change pace? Rest, sleep, positions in daily routines?

Do you:	1st Test Yes	No	2nd Test Yes	No	3rd Test Yes	No
1. Find time to relax, wiggle, and stretch whenever you have a chance during the day?						
2. Take time to relieve held positions required of your work to prevent a feeling of tenseness?						
3. Know how to relax by doing simple movements when you feel yourself become tense because of sustained positions?						
4. Know how to relax when you are put in difficult situations?						
5. Check yourself frequently for habitual tension habits, as scowling, clenched fists, tight jaws, hunched shoulders, or pursed lips?						
6. Relax these evidences of tension at will when you find them?						
7. Automatically relax at will when you recognize you are to face a distressing situation?						
8. Find it easy to relax so that you sleep easily and deeply?						
9. Know how to release tensions so that you can sleep well?						
10. Plan your time so that occasionally you can be away from loud noise and harsh lights?						

Leisure time activities

Do you:						
1. Have interests and hobbies to become completely absorbed in what you are doing?						
2. Plan your day so that you have a time to "do nothing"?						
3. Have the knowledge and understanding to enjoy spectator events, dance, music, art, and sport?						
4. Have social skills to enjoy participating with others?						
5. Play spontaneously, imaginatively, creatively?						
6. Have self-perception of your needs for leisure?						
7. Take responsibility for seeing that you have time for recreation every day?						

1. Explain your primary problem areas in your capacity to change pace—rest, sleep, positions.
2. Describe the main activities that you do in your leisure and off-work time to release tension.

references and sources for additional reading

Jacobson, E., *You Must Relax*. New York: McGraw-Hill Book Company, 1958.

Logan, G.A., and J.G. Dunkleberg, *Adaptations of Muscular Activity*. Belmont, Calif.: Wadsworth Publishing Company, Inc., 1964.

Metheny, E., *Body Dynamics*. New York: McGraw-Hill Book Company, 1952.

Rathbone, J.L., *Corrective Physical Education*. Philadelphia: W.B. Saunders Co., 1944.

Vithaldas, Y., *The Yoga System of Health and Relief from Tension*. New York: Cornerstone Library, Inc., 1961.

exercise and

menstrual function

15 Menstruation is a normal, natural function, and no woman should be inconvenienced by this vital process of her body any more than by digestion, elimination, or breathing. Each person should be able to continue her regular daily activities unless there is an organic reason for internal disequilibrium of the menstrual cycle. This, of course, is a medical problem.

GYNECOLOGICAL CONSIDERATIONS AND PHYSICAL ACTIVITY

Sports and vigorous physical activity for women have long been controversial. It is impossible to present all the facts and ideas concerning this subject in this chapter, but one major concept will be presented. *There is no gynecological evidence to indicate that a healthy girl who is free from menstrual disorder should be barred or restricted in any way from participating in physical activity, swimming, or athletic competition.* A brief examination of the pertinent evidence in support of this follows.

participation and menstrual period

The effects of physical activity on menstruation have been studied by many investigators. In one study on 557 women athletes it was found that 85% noticed no change in their menstrual cycle during intensive sport conditioning programs, 5% noticed favorable change, and 10% noticed unfavorable changes, such as increased flow or pain (1). It should be noted, however, that a similar percentage of unfavorable changes is also found among nonathletes. Another study of 107 top women athletes substantiated the above findings (2). Here, when disturbances were found, they were most marked in swimmers, which was probably due to the extreme temperature changes and prolonged exertion. In 1959 a most authoritative expression of opinion was obtained through a survey of 17 women doctors and gynecologists in this country (3):

12 recommended	no restrictions placed on physical activity, swimming, or competition at any time for girls and women free from menstrual disorders.
1 suggested	limitations during the three day premenstrual phase.
5 suggested	limitations during the first half of the period.
All recommended	no restrictions during the last half of the period.

On the basis of scientific evidence to date, dysmenorrhea (painful menstruation—"cramps") is not a consequence of athletic participation much less of moderate physical activity in which most girls and women participate.

In general, women athletes are able to achieve their usual performance standard at any time during the menstrual cycle. If there are differences in performance standards, they affect about one girl out of four. Such differences occur most often during the premenstrual phase and the first two days of the period (1). Perhaps the question can be settled by women athletes and champions themselves. It is interesting to note that, during the 1956 Melbourne Olympics, six women athletes who were menstruating won gold medals (4). What effect the pill will have on performance in the future will have to be determined through research.

participation and childbearing

Most of the evidence seems to point to the fact that more active women generally have the easiest childbirths. They have these conditions in their favor: general relaxation is particularly good, breathing can be controlled, strong abdominal muscles help them, the ability to relax antagonistic muscles of the pelvic floor (differential relaxation) is favorable (6). It was found that there were fewer complications in pregnancy, shorter and easier labor, and 50% fewer Caesarean sections in women athletes than in their nonathletic counterparts (1). The American Amateur Athletic Union (AAU) study of women athletes (5) disclosed that fertility, gestation, and pelvic measurements were all within normal limits and labor was not unduly long or difficult. In another study (2), it was found that the average duration of labor—from rupture of membranes to delivery—was 102 minutes in athletes and 207 minutes in nonathletes. There are good medical reasons for maintaining regular physical activity during pregnancy (6). But the question of competitive sports participation during this period is another question. It is interesting to note that three women athletes in the 1956 Melbourne Olympics were pregnant at the time, and one double gold medal winner in the Helsinki Olympics was four and one-half months pregnant (4). Draw your own conclusions. It would seem that this is a matter for individual decision, which depends on how each woman athlete perceives herself and the total situation.

EXERCISE AND THE MENSTRUAL PERIOD

What is the role of exercise? Can it help improve menstrual function? Can it help to prevent menstrual discomfort and pain or dysmenorrhea? First, you should know about some of the changes that occur during menstruation and for a few days before. There are biochemical changes taking place and an influx of blood to the pelvic region. You may have some of the following conditions present:

1. increased congestion in the pelvic area
2. a sense of heightened irritability
3. a low threshold for feeling and becoming aware of pain
4. more susceptibility to sudden changes in environmental temperatures
5. a shortening of fascia (connective tissue sheaths) covering muscle structures throughout the body, especially in the low back and pelvic regions, that may cause a decrease in flexibility in these regions.

These conditions should not cause discomfort. They may, however, make you more susceptible to discomfort if your *body lines are unbalanced*; or if you have undue fatigue brought about by improper rest, sleep, or nutrition; if you are experiencing emotional and mental stress; or if you are in situations of extreme environmental conditions. Normal menstrual function depends on:

1. balanced body lines
2. muscle strength
3. flexibility
4. your mental attitude
5. proper daily habits (diet, sleep, activity)
6. medical examination.

exercises for improving your menstrual function

If there is no organic pathology, specific exercises and regular maintenance of physical activity may help to relieve any menstrual discomfort that exists. Exercise and activities may help to prevent discomfort from occurring in the future. Don't be alarmed if you have irregularity in your menstrual cycle during the first two or three months of college life. Any change in immediate surroundings, climate, friends, work, etc. may cause a complete cessation of menstruation or may increase the amount of flow. It is however, advisable that you check with your doctor on any subsequent menstrual irregularity, since it can be a symptom of other organic problems. You may find relief for discomfort during your menstrual period by doing the exercises in Table 15.1.

Table 15.1 Relieving Menstrual Discomfort

Causes	Exercises
Pelvic Congestion: 1. Sluggish circulation due to sitting and insufficient exercise 2. Unbalanced postural lines 3. Constipation.	1. Any exercise that gives total body circulation such as walking or any physical activity. 2. For a period of time change position. Hips higher than chest; knee chest position, lying in bed or kneeling prone. 3. Any twisting, turning exercise that applies pressure on abdominal area and brings about contraction of abdominal muscles.
Tension	1. Relaxation techniques and positioning of the body. 2. Divert your mind with your hobby, listen to music, read, play, watch television. Find something other than problems to absorb your thinking. Be active physically and mentally if possible.
Other	1. Heat (hot water bottle on low back area) may relax tensions, provide depression to nerves, and lessen pain. 2. Clothing—watch constricting clothing especially girdles, tight belts, etc. as this might increase congestion. 3. Check your living habits—warm bath or shower permissible; get proper foods, sleep rest. Watch your apprehension of pain and expectancy of disability. Keep mentally and physically active.

exercises for painful menstruation

Table 15.2 indicates some common causes of painful menstruation and the role of exercises in relieving pain. These exercises have been successfully employed to prevent discomfort and pain from occurring and recurring. These procedures can help stimulate circulation; provide balanced posture; release tight, short muscles and fascia. Perhaps one of the most potent aspects of exercise is in diverting your mind from yourself through enjoyable activity. Your menstrual period should not keep you from your work or play.

At the end of the chapter, you will have an opportunity to evaluate your attitudes toward menstruation. There is also a chart for recording details about your menstrual period. These should help you formulate plans for any needed *postive* action.

Table 15.2 Exercise for Relieving Pain

Causes	Exercises
1. Unbalanced postural lines especially in the alignment of pelvis to trunk and hips	1. Pelvic control exercise (see Chapter 13)
2. Lack of muscle tone and strength in abdominal muscles affecting circulation and elimination	2. Abdominal exercises for strength, tone, and endurance (see Appendix A)
3. Lack of flexibility in hip and low back regions 	3. Billig's Exercise. Stretch fibrous fascial bands so that you have sufficient reserve to prevent nerves from being abnormally irritated during the hormonal changes of menstruation. Stand with left side toward wall and just far enough from wall so that left forearm and hand are on wall at shoulder level, with elbow directly opposite the shoulder joint. Feet together. Place heel of right hand on the rear right hip joint. Reduce tilt of pelvis and hold this position while forcing left hip towards wall with knees straight. Stretching movement must be forced beyond the point of pain. PROGRESSION: Three times a day or three times on each side for a period of three months or more.
4. Lack of movement—no general stimulation of organic systems and release of tensions.	4. Physical recreational activities and other flexibility exercises.
5. Undue muscular tensions	5. Relaxation techniques and exercises.

EXERCISE AND CHILDBEARING

An expectant mother needs preparation for her new task. Having a baby is an athletic feat requiring adherence to the specific rules of the game. Just like any other physical performance in which you hope to achieve optimum performance, you need preparation before the event, preparation during the event, and after the event. What does an expectant mother need for top performance? She needs to keep herself in optimum physical condition with special emphasis on those body regions most involved in the particular task. She needs to keep herself well nourished and at a desirable weight for the specific task. She needs to keep herself well rested and reasonably content in her thinking and everyday life. She needs to know that having a baby should not impair her health, or spoil her figure. All of this is work, new work requiring constant daily adjustments in her food habits, work habits, activity habits, rest and sleep habits, as well as in her thinking habits.

During the past years there has been a shift of emphasis and interest toward the consideration of preventive and post-treatment aspects of particular medical and surgical conditions. Why? Because it was found that use of different therapeutic agents before and after specific treatment hastens the total recovery or shortens the period of convalescence for the patient. One therapeutic agent that has been used increasingly in recent years during the pre- and post-treatment periods has been exercise or activity in all its various forms.

The effects of inactivity have been the objects of considerable medical research. Some varied and rather revolutionary techniques have resulted, especialy with regard to the use of exercise in decreasing the debilitating effects of prolonged inactivity as well as in early restoration of function in the treatment of specific medical and surgical problems. Exercises and body postures have been found helpful in preventing changes associated with prolonged inactivity by maintaining the blood chemistry balance, muscle tone, cardiovascular, respiratory, digestive, and mental-emotional-social adjustment. Some interesting accounts of the use of exercise during childbearing have been reported. With such preparation mothers not only felt better upon getting up, but they regained their normal functions and figure quickly and easily.

In all parts of the world there are varying attitudes toward childbirth as well as specific medical and nursing procedures among peoples of many races. Even in our own culture there are many divergent attitudes and approaches to childbearing. Obviously, there exist many factors that the doctor must consider in outlining a specific program for an expectant mother. Each expectant mother is an individual case and *only her doctor* is in the position to recommend the program that she should follow during her pregnancy. The specific factors and procedures involved in pregnancy are beyond the scope of this book. In other words, a specific exercise program is prescribed by the doctor. However, there are certain principles of exercise which are generally accepted.

exercises for childbearing

The physical or exercise approach to childbearing generally includes the following.

1. exercises for improving and maintaining muscle tone and strength in the abdominal, back, pelvic, and foot muscles
2. exercises for improving and maintaining elastic tone or flexibility in the pelvis, hips, and back
3. exercises for improving body alignment with special emphasis on pelvic control
4. exercises of breathing to promote optimum functioning during pregnancy, labor, and restoration

Table 15.3 Suggested Exercise Approach for the Antenatal Period

Purpose	Name of Exercise	Location of Exercise
To improve *muscle tone* and *strength*		
abdominal wall	Strength and tone Pelvic control	Appendix A Chapter 13
back	Strength and tone	Appendix A
legs	Strength and tone	Appendix A
To improve *elastic tone* or *flexibility*		
pelvis-hips	For hip flexor and hamstring muscles	Appendix A
To achieve *relaxation*		
specific muscle groups	Contract-release and passive (exhalation) techniques	Chapter 14
Effective use of your body	Balanced body lines, up-right position	Chapter 10
Breathing	Special types (costal, sternal, slow and deep) as recommended by your doctor	

Table 15.4 Suggested Exercise Approach for the Postnatal (Puerperium) Period

Purpose	Name of Exercise	Location of Exercise
	Bed exercises	
General stimulation of total body	Fundamental movements arm-leg-trunk	Chapter 7
	Pelvic control	Chapter 13
Relaxation-specific muscle groups	Same as for antenatal period	
	Activities and exercises	
General stimulation of total body and restoration of body functions	Sitting, standing, walking	
Restoration of body lines and pelvic control	Postural alignment	Chapter 13
	Abdominal exercises for antenatal period	
	Pelvic control	Chapter 13
Effective use of your body in daily activities		Chapter 10

5. exercises of relaxation to keep fatigue at a minimum (ability to relax and rest a few minutes each hour as well as to completely relax the skeletal muscles not involved in a particular activity)
6. exercises in how to use your body (form) effectively in everyday tasks, e.g., lifting, carrying, walking, climbing, stooping, lying

Are you surprised to find that this program for childbearing is the same program recommended for all women for optimum living? There is one difference. During childbearing you need to give more attention and time to develop the body regions involved in this specific new task. If you have maintained your physical self (strength, tone, mobility, endurance, posture, weight, effective movements) in your daily activities, your task is an easy one; simply pay attention to the specific parts of your body involved (strength, tone, mobility), and learn how to achieve balanced postures at work and at rest. And, what about the specific procedures outlined for your menstruation? The specific procedures recommended for optimum functioning of your body during menstruation are actually the same as outlined for childbearing. They differ only in degree and in relation to the specific processes involved in carrying the child and restoring the body functions after labor. Just remember that each woman is different and the procedures for each women will depend upon her total well-being—physical, mental, emotional and spiritual.

What type of exercise should you do before the birth of your child? What type of exercise should you do after birth? The period before birth is called the antenatal; the period after birth is called the postnatal, or the puerperium. Tables 15.3 and 15.4 contain general, not specific, recommendations.

SOME CONCLUDING REMARKS

Any specific exercise or position (relaxation, breathing, etc.) recommended during labor by your doctor will depend upon the particular procedure employed at this time. The general procedures recommended above for the antenatal and postnatal period should result in lessening the strain on the back and pelvic viscera, in helping prevent back pain and the general feeling of being "weighted down"; in lessening the early onset of fatigue, thus helping to prevent feelings of tiredness, weakness, and tension; in lessening the feeling of insecurity, thus helping to prevent feelings of loss of poise and looks.

LABORATORY: ASSESSING MENSTRUAL FUNCTION

This section contains three experiments to help you in self-evaluation. First you will find a chart for recording your menstrual periods and evaluating discomfort or pain. The second experiment is a continuum, designed to measure your attitudes towards menstruation. Experiment 3 is a guide to decision making.

Experiment 1: Menstrual Record

Directions: To evaluate pain and discomfort, count the number of days between the start of your period and the start of the one just preceding. Then rate yourself according to the following scale: (a) no pain or discomfort requiring change in routine (3 points); (b) slight pain and discomfort—2 or 3 hours incapacitated, change of routine (2 points); (c) moderate pain and discomfort—½ day incapacitated, change of routine (1 point); (d) severe pain and discomfort,—1 or more days incapacitated, change of routine (0 point). Rate flow as slight, moderate, or heavy, and count the number of days duration.

Month	Days Between	Duration (Days)	Flow (Amount)	Pain (Amount)	What You Do To Relieve Pain/ Discomfort?	What You Do To Prevent Pain/ Discomfort?
September						
October						
November						
December						
January						
February						
March						
April						
May						
June						
July						
August						

Your Rating (Last 3 months) High 3 Medium 2 Low 1

Experiment 2: Attitudes Toward Menstruation

No.	Left	Scale	Right
1.	Normal	1 : 2 : 3 : 4 : 5 : 6 : 7	Abnormal
2.	Shameful	7 : 6 : 5 : 4 : 3 : 2 : 1	Acceptable
3.	Healthy	1 : 2 : 3 : 4 : 5 : 6 : 7	Sick
4.	Painful	7 : 6 : 5 : 4 : 3 : 2 : 1	Painless
5.	Un-noticeable	1 : 2 : 3 : 4 : 5 : 6 : 7	Noticeable
6.	Embarrassing	7 : 6 : 5 : 4 : 3 : 2 : 1	Not embarrassing
7.	Clean	1 : 2 : 3 : 4 : 5 : 6 : 7	Dirty
8.	Good	1 : 2 : 3 : 4 : 5 : 6 : 7	Bad
9.	Stimulating	1 : 2 : 3 : 4 : 5 : 6 : 7	Dull
10.	Nervous	7 : 6 : 5 : 4 : 3 : 2 : 1	Relaxed

Response

Frequency
of
Response
(N = 10)

1	2	3	4	5	6	7

Median
score = _____

(The scoring procedure is described in Chapter 3)

Directions: You already have information on your posture, muscular tone and strength, elastic tone, and flexibility from the laboratory experiments in Chapter 2, and you will find a check on your living habits in Chapter 18 (p. 248). These should help you to assess your status, for evaluation and decision making are entirely up to you. If you feel you have a problem with menstrual function and want to do something about it, answering the questions below should help you to design a personal action plan.

1. Assess and describe your status.

2. What do you think is your primary problem (if you have one)?

3. What do you think causes this problem?

4. Should you be doing something about improving your menstrual function? If so, describe your action plan below.

references and sources for additional reading

1. Erdelyi, G.J., "Gynecological Survey of Female Athletes," *Journal of Sports Medicine and Physical Fitness*, Vol. 2 (September 1942), 174–79.
2. Ingham, O., "Menstruation in Top Class Sportswomen," cited by D. Ryde in *Practitioner*, Vol. 177 (1965), 73.
3. Phillips, M., K. Fox, and O. Young, "Sports Activity for Girls," *Journal of Health, Physical Education, and Recreation*, Vol. 30 (1959), 30.
4. Charles, C. J., "Women in Sport," In *Injury in Sport*, eds., J. R. Armstrong, and W. E. Tucker, Springfield, Ill.: Charles C Thomas, Publisher, 1964.
5. "Effects of Athletic Competition in Girls and Women," *American Athletic Union AAU*, 1953. *Cited in Practitioner*, Vol. 177 (1965), p. 73.
6. Klaus, E. J., and H. Noack, *Frau Und Sport*. Stuttgart, West Germany: Georg Thieme, 1961. Proceedings, National Institutes of Girls Sports (I, II, III, IV, V). Washington, D.C.: American Association of Health, Physical Education, and Recreation.

Rathbone, J., *Corrective Physical Education*, 6th ed. Philadelphia: W.B. Saunders Co., 1959.

Tuttle, W.G. "Women Are Different Than Men," *Science Digest*, Vol. 14 (September 1943), 69.

Ulrich, Celeste, "Women and Sport," In *Science and Medicine of Exercise and Sports*, ed., W.J. Johnson, New York: Harper & Row, Publishers, 1960.

selecting and planning
a personal program in
physical education

16 The purpose of this chapter is twofold: (*1*) to provide you with an objective basis for selecting a personal program in physical education and (*2*) to provide you with the basis for planning and selecting leisure-time physical activities. Very often an individual chooses the physical activities in which she participates quite haphazardly. Her decision may be based on such questions as: Will I have to get dressed or undressed for the activity? Will it fit into my schedule? Will I like it? Will I be too awkward?

You should be aware of and understand the factors that affect your selection. For regardless of the different factors involved, the final decision, as well as its consequences, is yours. The decision you make not only affects you in terms of the present but also the future.

ACTIVITY SELECTION FACTORS

Certain factors should be taken into consideration in selecting and planning a physical education program. A critical analysis of these factors will provide a general framework upon which to design a personal plan for your physical education program as well as for supplemental leisure activities. Some of the more important of these factors will be discussed. These include:

physical performance status

Each activity has physical requirements that must be met if a skill potential is to be realized that will result in a pleasurable and enjoyable experience. Such

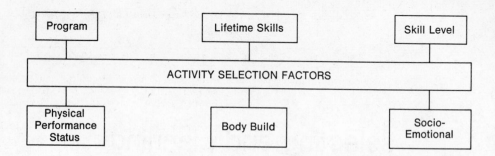

activity requirements were discussed in Chapter 9. It might be well to review them as you review your own health-physical fitness and motor performance status (See experiments 5 and 6 in Chapter 2). Realistic appraisal of one's status and potential should help in decision making. In most instances (as in swimming, tennis, golf, and the like), physical performance and skill increase gradually. Some activities, however, require a certain level of physical performance before even the beginning level of the skill can be realized. Then you may need to supplement skill practice with conditioning activities planned specifically for meeting these requirements. Or you may wish to take a conditioning program to develop a certain level of physical performance before undertaking certain skill courses. Whatever the activity, analyze realistically its physical requirements, estimate your own personal status, and *then* make your decision. This should provide a good basis for estimating your potential success in various activities.

body build

One important factor to consider is body build. Table 16.1 depicts physical activities well suited to each type of body build. Along with other factors, it should be used as a general guide for selecting activities in which you will probably achieve a reasonable degree of skilled performance. Body build is not usually the most crucial factor unless you are involved in very strenuous activities or competitive sports and games. The relative status of weight, fatness and muscle tone should be considered as indicative of the present condition of body build. (Experiment 1 at the end of this chapter should help you gain a more critical analysis of this factor.)

skill level

Present skill level in specific activities is an extremely important factor in planning a personal program. Experiment 2 is designed for you to evaluate the self. A five-point scale is used for rating purposes. If you have average or better skill in a specific activity, you should not take a beginning class in the activity. It may be advisable for you to do intermediate or advanced work

Height and Weight Components	Activities
Endomorphic (soft fat-rotund type)	Activities which demand less agility, speed of movement, or support of body weight such as swimming, golf, archery, bowling, fishing, canoeing, riflery, social dancing, square dancing. With respect to the team sports, may achieve success in different positions such as field hockey goalie, lacrosse goalie, backfield in hockey, and so forth.
Mesomorphic (husky type)	Reasonable success is possible in practically all physical activities.
Ectomorphic (thin-linear type)	Activities in which success is not likely to require support of the body weight, such as running, jumping, apparatus, tennis, basketball, badminton, dancing, tumbling, volleyball. The extreme ectomorph who is low in the other components may be successful in sports, such as bowling, fishing, and dancing. The ectomorph who also has a high mesomorphic component may excel in sports in which the body moves rapidly.

if you desire a higher level of competency. If you have below average skill and are interested in the activity, a beginning class is advisable. The other activity selection factors may help you determine whether you should do this.

Your present and future interests should be considered in selecting a personal program. You may participate for social reasons. You may participate because you have always wanted to, because this activity presents a challenge to your abilities, or because you have a drive for a higher level of competency in this activity.

social-emotional situation

The social characteristics of physical activity relate to your desire and interest in being involved with others. You may enjoy participating with other girls in group physical activities such as hockey and basketball. Or you may find individual sports like tennis, badminton and golf which are mostly co-educational, excellent avenues through which certain social drives may find expression. Emotional tendencies are often closely allied with social drives. Your own temperament will be a determinant. You may be fast at reacting and speedy by nature and find great enjoyment and success in physical activities demanding fast, explosive, overt action and reaction. In that case a slow, steady, evenly controlled activity such as target archery may not be appealing to you. Individuals who are creative and rhythmical will probably find dance activities to their liking. A critical analysis of the social characteristics of physical activities (liking for a group, for small or large group action; being with other young adults) as well as your own personal characteristics (for expression, creativity, release of tensions) should be considered. Experiment 2 provides some objective basis for determining your likes and dislikes of certain activities.

Perhaps with friends or in class you can discuss the social and personal factors that influence these attitudes.

lifetime skills

Those activities in which you can continue to participate throughout your life are considered to have carry-over value. Such activities include golf, bowling, dancing, hunting, fishing, sailing, fencing, and ice skating. Few people continue to play basketball, softball, hockey, lacrosse, and other team sports after leaving the campus. This *does not mean that these skills are not valuable* and should not be learned. Your present physical activity needs may suggest that you participate in some of these activities. Or you may desire to learn these activities because you have never had an opportunity before. Or you may desire to challenge your abilities and improve your present skill level. However, you may be able to satisfy your needs through participation in the intramural program or through your leisure-time activities with others. Before making your decision, look at the material and activities listed in Chapter 20, on recommended physical activities for different ages.

Your future place of residence may have some bearing on the selection of skills. You may not know the exact location. Nevertheless you should have some idea of where you might live. This may provide you with some knowledge of the availability of facilities. You may need to have skills for both the hot-warm months and the cool-cold months. Your physical activity and the joy and satisfaction, as well as relaxation, that can be achieved through your leisure should be a year-round proposition. Modern transportation has made traveling to ski areas or to a warm climate during winter relatively easy!

THE PROGRAM PROFILE

After having considered all the activity factors and having acquired an understanding of your physical self and activity needs, you should be in a position to select activities for your physical education program. Remember, you must carefully evaluate your self-image and plan activities to meet your personal needs if you are to reap the benefits of the "good life." Think carefully; plan wisely. Your selection of activities and your participation in these have significance to you now, and indirectly to the present and future survival and growth of our society. To develop a program profile for the particular situation on your campus, complete Experiment 3.

LABORATORY: WILL YOU BE PHYSICALLY EDUCATED?

When you have completed the physical education courses you have planned for yourself, will you be able to answer these questions positively—*will you be physically educated*? Answer the following questions "yes" or "no."

1. Have you developed your physical potential, making the most of what you have?
2. Do you know and understand your physical capacities?
3. Do you know what needs to be changed and how to change it?
4. Do you understand why your physical potential is important to development of self?
5. Do you understand the importance of your daily living habits in developing and maintaining optimal level of health-physical fitness?
6. Can you dance?
7. Can you swim and save a life?
8. Have you outdoor skills such as canoeing, sailing, walking, gardening, hiking, climbing, camping, hunting, fishing to meet your needs?
9. Have you sport skills such as badminton, tennis, volleyball, golf, archery, table tennis, bowling to meet your needs?
10. Can you make a realistic appraisal of your physical activities—work, off work and leisure—and build optimal levels into your daily routine?

Count 1 point for each yes answer, then circle your rating: *high*, 10; *medium*, 6; *low*, 2.

Experiment 1: Body Build and Physical Performance Level

Directions: Circle the number that best describes your body build (as determined in Chapter 2, p. 24) on the chart below. Then enter your best weight and degree of fatness (p. 24) in the spaces provided.

Weight _____ % of best

Fatness_____ degree of

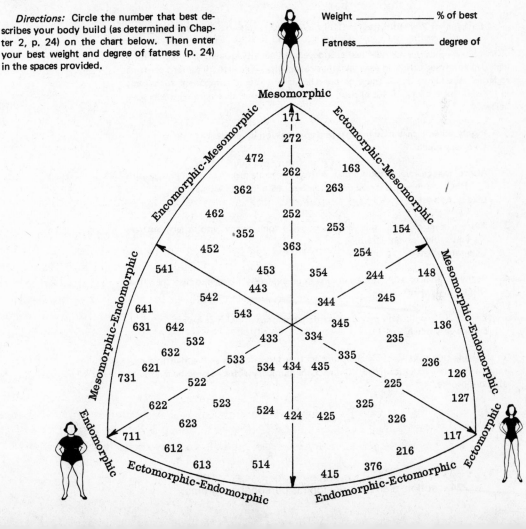

Experiment 1 continued: Record your percentile rank for each motor performance and for health-physical fitness (from pp. 32 and 36) below. Use this data to assess your personal status. Match this with the requirements of the activities you are considering including in your program.

Motor Performance		Health-Physical Performance	
Components	Percentile Rank	Components	Percentile Rank
Power		Strength	
Agility		Muscular endurance	
Speed		Flexibility	
Coordination		C-VR*	
Average**		Average**	

  *Cardiovascular-respiratory endurance
  **Average = total ÷ 4

Experiment 2: Self-Rating of Skill Level and Attitudes Toward Various Sports

Directions: Skill may be defined as a developed activity pattern that allows for a high degree of perfection in a certain physical activity. The activity pattern could be regarded as a habit, but it must be one that is a desirable component for success in the sport or activity. A list of sports follows. Rate yourself according to the scale below.

1   Highly skilled: may play in organized competition if you desire to do so.
    Like very much.

2   Above average level of skill: play with a reasonable degree of competency with
        other young adults if you desire to do so, with joy and satisfaction.
    Like quite a lot.

3   Average level of skill: play with reasonable competency with others, but feel
        you could use more training.
    Like somewhat.

4   Beginning level of skill: just beginning to understand and learn to play the game.
    Dislike somewhat.

5   Zero or little skill: you may have participated once or twice or never.
    Dislike very much.

On the table that follows circle the numbers that indicate your skill and attitude toward each of the activities listed. Connect the numbers with a colored pencil to obtain your profile.

Activities	Skill Ratings					Attitude Ratings				
Individual and Dual										
Archery	1	2	3	4	5	1	2	3	4	5
Badminton	1	2	3	4	5	1	2	3	4	5
Bowling	1	2	3	4	5	1	2	3	4	5
Fencing	1	2	3	4	5	1	2	3	4	5
Golf	1	2	3	4	5	1	2	3	4	5
Ping pong	1	2	3	4	5	1	2	3	4	5
Skiing	1	2	3	4	5	1	2	3	4	5
Ice skating	1	2	3	4	5	1	2	3	4	5
Tennis	1	2	3	4	5	1	2	3	4	5
Track and field	1	2	3	4	5	1	2	3	4	5
Team Sports										
Basketball	1	2	3	4	5	1	2	3	4	5
Field hockey	1	2	3	4	5	1	2	3	4	5
Softball	1	2	3	4	5	1	2	3	4	5
Soccer	1	2	3	4	5	1	2	3	4	5
Speedball	1	2	3	4	5	1	2	3	4	5
Volleyball	1	2	3	4	5	1	2	3	4	5
Aquatics										
Diving	1	2	3	4	5	1	2	3	4	5
Life saving	1	2	3	4	5	1	2	3	4	5
Canoeing	1	2	3	4	5	1	2	3	4	5
Sailing	1	2	3	4	5	1	2	3	4	5
Swimming	1	2	3	4	5	1	2	3	4	5
Synchronized swimming	1	2	3	4	5	1	2	3	4	5
Dance										
Social	1	2	3	4	5	1	2	3	4	5
Folk	1	2	3	4	5	1	2	3	4	5
Square	1	2	3	4	5	1	2	3	4	5
Tap	1	2	3	4	5	1	2	3	4	5
Creative	1	2	3	4	5	1	2	3	4	5

Experiment 3: The Program Profile

Directions: This is a list of courses and activities generally included in physical education, intramural, and extramural offerings on a campus. Each activity has been rated according to the extent to which the activity meets your physical needs, and recreation or carry-over skills (H-high; M-medium; L-low). Make changes in these ratings if you desire, as they apply to you personally.

First, add any activities that are not included if they are offered on your campus. *Second*: Fill in your personal emotional and social ratings (H, M, L) for each activity. *Third*: Write in the term or semester in which these activities are offered in the physical education curriculum. Write an X for each situation where the sport is offered (as an intramural offering, for intercollegiate teams, by a club or special interest group).

| Activities | Factor Rating | | | Life-time Skills | Term-semester offered | Intra-mural offering | Intra-collegiate teams | Clubs/special interest groups on campus |
	Physical	Emotional	Social					
1. Angling, fly, bait, spin.	L	_____	_____	H	_____	_____	_____	_____
2. Archery, field, target.	L-M	_____	_____	H	_____	_____	_____	_____
3. Badminton	M-H	_____	_____	H	_____	_____	_____	_____
4. Basketball	H-M	_____	_____	L	_____	_____	_____	_____
5. Physical conditioning	H	_____	_____	H	_____	_____	_____	_____
6. Bowling	L	_____	_____	H	_____	_____	_____	_____
7. Canoeing	M	_____	_____	H	_____	_____	_____	_____
8. Contemporary dance	H	_____	_____	L	_____	_____	_____	_____
9. Fencing	M-H	_____	_____	L	_____	_____	_____	_____
10. Field hockey	H	_____	_____	L	_____	_____	_____	_____
11. Folk-square dance	M-H	_____	_____	H	_____	_____	_____	_____
12. Golf	L-M	_____	_____	H	_____	_____	_____	_____
13. Gymnastics	H	_____	_____	L	_____	_____	_____	_____
14. Ice skating	M-H	_____	_____	H	_____	_____	_____	_____
15. Lacrose	H	_____	_____	L	_____	_____	_____	_____
16. Life saving	H	_____	_____	H	_____	_____	_____	_____
17. Mountain climbing	H	_____	_____	H	_____	_____	_____	_____

Continued

Activities	Factor Rating			Life-time Skills	Term-semester offered	Intra-mural offering	Inter-collegiate teams	Clubs/special interest groups on campus
	Physical	Emotional	Social					
18. Sailing	L-M	_____	_____	H	_____	_____	_____	_____
19. Shooting, hunting	L-M	_____	_____	H	_____	_____	_____	_____
20. Skiing	H-M	_____	_____	H	_____	_____	_____	_____
21. Skin diving	H-M	_____	_____	H	_____	_____	_____	_____
22. Softball	M	_____	_____	L	_____	_____	_____	_____
23. Social dance	M-L	_____	_____	H	_____	_____	_____	_____
24. Squash	M-H	_____	_____	L	_____	_____	_____	_____
25. Swimming	M-H	_____	_____	H	_____	_____	_____	_____
26. Synchronized swimming	H-M	_____	_____	H	_____	_____	_____	_____
27. Tap dance	M	_____	_____	L	_____	_____	_____	_____
28. Tennis	M-H	_____	_____	H	_____	_____	_____	_____
29. Volleyball	M-H	_____	_____	M	_____	_____	_____	_____
30. Track-field	H	_____	_____	L	_____	_____	_____	_____
31. Water safety instruction	H	_____	_____	H	_____	_____	_____	_____
32. Water skiing	M-H	_____	_____	H	_____	_____	_____	_____
33. Weight training	H-M	_____	_____	H	_____	_____	_____	_____

maintaining
physical potential
throughout
the years

exercise and obesity

17 All of us recognize the desirability of maintaining an optimal body weight in respect to physical appearance. While optimal body weight in and of itself does not insure figure control (good contours and postural lines), it is an essential component. Simply stated, it helps! Most of us recognize that overweight, particularly excessive fat, is detrimental to performing physical activities. This is particularly true where power, agility, and speed are requirements. It is quite obvious that overweight and fatness may lead to more overweight and fatness and to a greater decrease in physical activity. Unless action is taken this vicious cycle will ultimately result in a major health problem—overweight and obesity.

THE PROBLEM: OVERWEIGHT AND OBESITY

Is there a difference?

Weight, according to dictionary definition, is a quality of heaviness or "relative heaviness." Body weight is made up of a number of components that contribute to total weight. Those components that cause the greatest variation in your weight at a given age and height are fat, muscle, and bone. The ratio of bony structure, musculature, and fat distribution is all important in arriving at an assessment of ideal weight. *Overweight*, then, is simply overheaviness relative to some standard and does not carry any direct implication with regard to fatness. *Obesity*, on the other hand, it defined as a bodily condition marked by excessive generalized deposition and storage of fat. Obesity represents one end of the frequency distribution of a continuously distributed variable—fatness. No exact data are available to determine what degree of fat or overweight is the dividing point between obesity and nonobesity. Some state that a deviation between 10 and 20% above the average or so-called best, ideal, or desirable weight constitutes an obese condition. Others consider a 20% deviation the outside limit of normal weight. An even higher percentage has been used as the cutoff point.

In general, overweight and obesity are not differentiated in insurance statistics and other studies on morbidity and mortality associated with excess weight. In most instances, the data reported are in terms of weight and not in terms of fatness. At present it is not known which is the greater hazard to health or, if both are involved, what their relative contributions are to health problems. But there is little doubt that the markedly overweight individual is obese. There seems to be little question that the part of excess weight that should be reduced is the fatty component, i.e., excess body fatness.

prevalence

Although no statistics for the incidence of overweight and obesity in the total population exist, various reports have discussed their increasing prevalence (1, 2, 3). Some estimate that one person out of five is overweight. Data reported by the National Center for Health Statistics showed that obesity was at the top of the list of 25 chronic diseases, with a rate of 129 per 1,000 population (4). There is little question, however, that many factors combine to reduce the accuracy of general estimates of its prevalence: Among these are population samples (mostly from insured individuals) and varying criteria used to define overweight and obesity. But no matter how crude and meager the statistical data are, overweight and obesity afflict an increasing number of persons in this country among all age groups and at all levels of income. These data show a considerable increase in overweight in women as they get older. Excessive weight gains most often occur after age 20, during pregnancy, and after the menopause.

In general, in young adults, the prevalence of overweight is about equal for both sexes, with more women becoming overweight after age 30. But there are some striking differences: In one study of white and Negro subjects, Negro women in all age groups tended to be heavier than white women of corresponding height (4). No marked differences were found among the men. Recent data indicate an inverse relationship between the socio-economic status of a group and the prevalence of obesity in that group (1). That is, as overweight increases, socio-economic status decreases except for the lowest group—the laborers. Some of the racial differences may be accounted for by these factors. By way of conclusion, the data available do indicate that a high proportion of our population weighs more than is considered desirable for optimum health. Individuals who are excessively overweight are probably also obese, having excessive body fatness. Statistics compiled by the Bureau of Health Education of the American Medical Association indicate the following.

1. The problem of overweight begins early in life and is as much a matter of overeating as of underactivity.
2. Physically active persons have less body fat than a comparable group of inactive persons of similar age and weight.
3. Some 25% of the population is overweight, many dangerously so, with a correspondingly greater incidence of chronic and degenerative diseases.

implications for general
health and longevity

The generally accepted position is that overweight and obesity are health hazards, and at least contributory causes of life-threatening conditions for otherwise healthy individuals. Insurance data and comparable population statistics supply strong evidence of the health risks associated with obesity and overweight for people who are otherwise healthy (1, 5, 6), namely:

1. Susceptibility to gall bladder disease, gout, diabetes mellitus, hypertension, and possibly atherosclerosis.
2. Increased risks in surgery and pregnancy, impairment of ambulation in such diseases as arthritis and in recovery from fractures and cerebral strokes.
3. Respiratory or pulmonary difficulties; the work of breathing is twice that of persons of normal weight, posing a greater problem in oxygenating the blood supplying the extra fat tissue, thereby reducing tolerance to exercise and increasing resistance for respiratory infections.
4. Increased functional disability in the aged by decreasing physical activity and producing a decline of vitality.

Insurance statistics suggest also that the association between overweight and mortality is real, but the causal relationship is obscure. Table 17.1 presents some causes of death and shows the excess mortality among overweight men and women (5).

Figure 17.1 shows the association between degree of overweight among men and women and reduced length of life (5). Life insurance data have limitations that make it impossible to interpret them as unequivocal evidence that obesity predisposes an individual to early mortality. Such data do not distinguish between total body weight and obesity; therefore, it is impossible to determine if excess mortality is due to fatness or to other factors such as the effects of body type or the presence of hypertension or hypercholesteremia, which increase the risk of developing coronary heart disease (7). Yet, recognizing these limitations, one must rely on existing studies. Present materials appear to indicate that overweight is at least an indirect cause of diminished general health and longevity.

Table 17.1   Excess Mortality Among Overweight Men and Women

Some Major Causes of Death	Excess Mortality (%)	
	Men	Women
Cardiovascular-renal diseases		
Heart and circulatory diseases	43	51
Vascular lesions of central nervous system	53	29
Nephritis	73	–
Cancer	16	13
Diabetes mellitus	133	83
Influenza and pneumonia	32	27

Age: 15-69 years; men 20% overweight, women 15% overweight. Comparisons made between people considered standard risks.

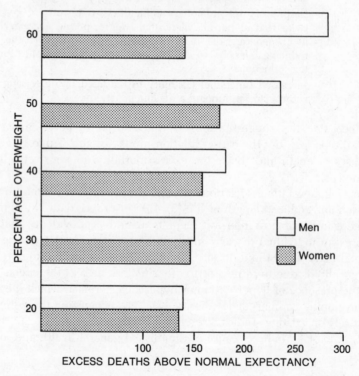

Figure 17.1   Excess Deaths above Normal Expectancy among Overweight Men and Women

Weight reduction, therefore, is desirable for all overweight individuals. Weight control is essential for developing and maintaining optimal levels of health-fitness.

implications for personal well-being

Perhaps of equal or even greater importance to you are the effects of overweight on personal or psychological well-being. There is some evidence that overweight may seriously affect the development of emotional maturity; body mastery in sports, games, and activities; the attainment of optimal levels of health-physical fitness at maturity; and scholastic achievement (8, 9, 10). A number of recent studies (10, 11) show that obese children—obese girls in particular—have many characteristics of minority groups: obsessive concern with their condition, passivity, withdrawal, and expectation of rejection. Also, a decreased tendency toward motion is common among obese adults and children, and to a large degree the inactivity antedates the obesity in the individual (6, 12). Immediate justification for weight reduction and weight control appears warranted when one considers the benefits of improved physical appearance, better social acceptance, greater vitality, and feelings of personal well-being, rather than more delayed expectations of lessened morbidity and improved longevity (6).

THE INFLUENCE OF CALORIC BALANCE

Weight is a matter of balance—balance of energy intake (food) and energy expenditure (physical activity). Both food and physical activity are measured in calories. When energy intake and energy outgo are equal, the individual is in caloric balance or equilibrium. If the energy intake exceeds the energy outgo, the individual is in positive energy balance. Energy is neither lost nor gained but only changed to a different form (Law of Conservation of Energy); for this reason, the energy is deposited in the form of body fat. If energy outgo is greater than intake, the individual is in negative energy balance, and energy deposited as body fat will be consumed (burned) to supply the fuel needed; weight will be lost.

Getting only a few more calories each day than are needed can produce weight gains. Conversely, expending a few more calories per day than are consumed can produce weight loss. The case in point is that small gains or losses tend to be cumulative and produce telling effects in a few years' time. In general, one pound of body fat is equal to about 3,500 calories. Examine Table 17.2 and you will understand the importance of caloric balance.

Many factors adversely modify the caloric balance, and this leads to excessive fatness (6). Recent research and some of the more common contributing factors will be discussed briefly. It is almost impossible to isolate or separate cultural, genetic, and physiological effects; but for ease of presentation, these

Table 17.2 Overweight is a Matter of Balance—Faulty Caloric Balance

Energy Intake Food	Energy Outgo (Activity)		Total Energy Balance per day		Weight Status
2,400 cal.	2,400 cal.	=	Balance	=	No change
2,550 cal. (extra snack)	2,400 cal.	=	Positive balance or 150 cal. surplus	=	Gain: 1 lb. per mo. or 12 lbs. per year
2,400 cal.	2,550 cal. (vigorous physical activity ½ hour a day)	=	Negative balance or 150 cal. deficit a day	=	Loss: 1 lb. per mo. or 12 lbs. per year
2,400 cal.	2,250 cal. (changed to electric typewriter)	=	Positive balance or 150 cal. surplus a day	=	Gain: 1 lb. per mo. or 12 lbs. per year

factors have been categorized arbitrarily under family and environmental influences.

family influences

The genetic effect is doubtless important. In one study, it was found that 8 to 9% of the children of normal weight parents were obese. Where one parent was fat, 40% of the children were overweight; and where both parents were fat, the proportion rose to 80% (13). Studies of adopted children showed their weights bore little relationship to those of the adoptive parents (14). This seems to indicate that overweight is not just a matter of family eating habits. (*Racial* and *socio-economic* factors have been previously discussed.)

There is evidence that *metabolic mechanisms* are operating, which may or may not be of genetic origin. A glandular condition (underactive thyroid) is an uncommon cause of simply obesity. Some research (15) is examining critically the metabolic mechanisms, glucose and fat metabolism, and the workings of a satiety center in the brain ("switches" that turn hunger on and off, letting an individual know when she has eaten enough). Other research is directed toward the *function of adipose tissue or fat cells*: Fat acquired in childhood appears to establish the number and size of a person's fat cells. These shape the adult figure and may create reducing problems, making food turn into fat faster than in slender persons (16).

Recent evidence has shown that obese individuals, particularly obese young children, have *endomorphic characteristics* and are also more mesomorphic than their nonobese counterparts (17). *Such evidence would imply that children should be watched carefully and desirable food and exercise habits should be particularly emphasized.*

environmental influences

An overabundance of food, low level of physical activity, and stress are all factors that may lead to positive calorie balance and fatness (6). Diet in this country tends to be a concentrated source of calories with a high fatness content. Food plays a role in everyone's life that is beyond its physiological function (11). *Stress* may predispose an individual to fatness. For some individuals food may be a deterrent to anxiety and tension or may be used to alleviate boredom and frustrations. Conversely, other individuals may refrain from eating when experiencing the same feelings. Thus, the way an individual responds to stress may predispose her to overeating and fatness. In this light, obesity is not an accidental accompaniment to overeating, but it is a process of living, involving body and psyche, by which the individual adapts to "stressors." It is clearly apparent that such obesity cannot be easily altered without establishing new ways for the individual to maintain internal equilibrium.

In our highly automated society, labor-saving devices have *decreased physical activity* in occupational activities as well as in leisure pursuits. If food intake is not correspondingly decreased, the result is a positive energy balance and a subsequent weight gain. The mechanism for regulating food intake apparently is not adapted to functioning at extremely low levels of physical activity. When there is a decrease in physical activity, voluntary food intake generally decreases—but not proportionally. In some instances, food intake may stabilize; but, at very low levels of activity, food intake increases, and fatness is the automatic consequence. In addition, if a decrease in physical activity occurs along with an increased food intake, the excess calories resulting seem to have a greater effect on weight status than for individuals who remain active. Seemingly, the active person has two factors operating in her favor: the increase in resting energy expenditure and the cost of moving body weight. Both of these are proportional to a great extent to total body weight. The inactive person, on the other hand, has only resting expenditure, which is the minor factor. She will show a greater weight increase than her active counterpart.

An increase in physical activity, though it increases caloric intake, does not result in increased body weight. Jean Mayer, of the School of Public Health at Harvard University, found (15) that fat girls actually ate less and were less well nourished than their slimmer friends. The slimmer girls were more active physically and ate more. More of them participated regularly in dancing and sports than did the fat girls. *Such evidence would seem to imply that a reorganization of one's life to include regular physical activity and a nutritious diet is essential for maintaining optimal weight.* The role of physical activity in weight control programs has been succinctly stated by Jean Mayer, "Inactivity is the most important factor explaining the frequency of 'creeping overweight' in modern Western Society" (15).

SOME CONCLUDING REMARKS

From the foregoing, there can be little doubt that obesity must be regarded as a complex condition. Perhaps the concept of *obesities* is a better way to look at this problem. The variation in the causes indicate that not all obesity is the same. Further research will eventually throw light on the actual mechanism of the development and treatment of obesity. In the meantime, preventive measures should be taken. These are commonly based on direct action to modify food intake and energy expenditure. Permanent weight control depends upon reorganizing one's eating and physical activity habits. Strenuous activity on an irregular basis for obese individuals with low levels of health-fitness is not encouraged.

Should you go on a weight reduction program? Before making that decision, you need to determine your best or most desirable weight, based on your actual weight, your appearance, and some idea of your subcutaneous fat pads as indicated by skinfold measurements. To help you make such appraisal, laboratory experiments have been devised. The principles underlying prevention or weight control are similar to those underlying weight reduction. Strong motivation and sufficient knowledge are the keys to effective programs for getting and keeping your best weight. A plan that can be a base for weight control is one that incorporates principles of diet and physical activity. Such a program, together with the underlying principles, is presented in Chapter 12. Special dietary plans for weight reduction or gain are considered modifications of the normal diet. This means adjustment in caloric level and not in essential food nutrients, i.e., proteins, fats, carbohydrates, minerals, vitamins, and water.

references and sources for additional reading

1. Hathaway, M.L., and E.D. Foward, *Heights and Weights of Adults in the United States*, Home Economics Research Report No. 10., Agricultural Research Service., U.S. Department of Agriculture. Washington, D.C., 1960.

2. Society of Actuaries, *Build and Blood Pressure Study*, vols. 1 and 2. Chicago: Society of Actuaries, 1959.

3. National Center for Health Statistics, *Weight, Height and Selected Body Dimensions of Adults*, Public Health Service Series 11, No. 8. U.S. Department of Health, Education and Welfare. Washington, D.C., 1965.

4. National Center for Health Statistics, *Weight by Height and Age of Adults, United States, 1960–62*. Vital and Health Statistics. Public Health Service, Pub. No. 1000-Series 11, No. 14. Washington, D.C.: Government Printing Office, May 1966.

5. Metropolitan Life Insurance Company, "Overweight: Its Prevention and Significance," a series of articles reprinted from *Statistical Bulletin*, 1960.

6. U.S. Department of Health, Education and Welfare, *Obesity and Health: A Source Book of Current Information for Professional Health Personnel*, National Center for Chronic Disease Control. Arlington, Va.

7. Kagan, A., *et al.*, "The Coronary Profile," *Annals of the New York Academy of Science*, Vol. 97 (March 1963), 883.

8. Hopwood, H. H., and S. S. Van Iden, "Scholastic Underachievement as Related to Sub-par Physical Growth," *Journal of School Health*, Vol. 35 (October 1965), 337.

9. Stunkard, A., and M. Mendelson, "Disturbance in Body Image of Some Obese Persons," *Journal of American Dietetic Association*, Vol. 38 (April 1961), 328.

10. Bullen, B.A., R. B. Reed, and J. Mayer, "Physical Activity of Obese and Non-

obese Adolescent Girls Appraised by Motion Picture Sampling," *American Journal of Clinical Nutrition* Vol. 14, (March 1964), 211.

11. Burch, H., "Psychological Aspects of Obesity," *Borden Review of Nutritional Research*, Vol. 19, (April 1958).

12. Wessel, J., *et al.*, "Influences of Physical Activity on Functional Responses to Submaximal Work and Body Composition in Women, 20–69 Years." In Proceedings 7th International Congress of Gerontology, Vienna, Austria, June 26-July 2, 1966.

13. Johnson, M.L., B.S. Burke, and J. Mayer, "Relative Importance of Inactivity and Overeating in the Energy Balance of Obese High School Girls," *American Journal of Clinical Nutrition* Vol. 4 (October 1956), 37.

14. Withers, R.F.J., "Problems in Genetics of Human Obesity," *Eugenics Review*, Vol. 52 (1964), 81.

15. Mayer, J., "Genetic, Traumatic, and Environmental Factors in the Etiology of Obesity," *Physiological Review*, Vol. 33 (December 1953), 472.

16. ———, "Obesity: Physiological Considerations," *American Journal of Clinical Nutrition*, Vol. 9 (1961), 530.

17. Seltzer, C.C., and J. Mayer, "Body Build and Obesity: Who Are the Obese?" *Journal of the American Medical Association,* Vol. 189 (May 1964), 677.

Mayer, J. *Overweight.* Prentice-Hall, Inc. 1969.

"Weight Control." A Collection of Papers presented at the Weight Control Colloquium, Iowa State College, Ames, Iowa, 1955.

Weight Control Source Book, Chicago: National Dairy Council.

exercise to
your heart's content

18   Until recent years, physical activity has been a way of life. Human muscular effort accomplished the many tasks that were part of existence. With the tremendous increase in technology and resulting mechanical devices for the home, office, and industry, physical activity has been reduced. Even leisure activities for children and adults require less physical activity. The concern in this chapter is with physical activity as a way of life specifically related to keeping healthy hearts healthy and with the possible role of physical activity in preventing the onset of cardiovascular disease.

Does physical activity keep healthy hearts healthy?

Does physical activity as a way of life help to prevent the onset of coronary heart disease?

THE PROBLEM: CARDIOVASCULAR DISEASES

It is assumed by many that because the United States has one of the highest standards of living in the world, that it is also the healthiest country and that its people live longer. Many countries, however, have a lower incidence of infant mortality, and the United States is far down the list in terms of average life expectancy. Table 18.1 shows that our men rank eighteenth in life expectancy, while our women rank tenth.

Some authorities attribute early death in men to the pressures involved in their work, particularly in business and the professions. As more and more women assume positions in management and professions, they will also become prone to what are often spoken of as the stress diseases—cardiovascular disease, ulcers, intestinal inflammation.

It is a fact that the white male has a far greater chance of dying prematurely from cardiovascular disease than his wife or nonwhite neighbor of either sex. Various reasons have been advanced for the protection that women enjoy. In part it may be that women are far more weight and figure conscious than men; yet they carry proportionally more body weight than men for their height. Women may have natural protection through the operation of the estrogen hormone group. These hormones may stave off the advance of *atherosclerosis*. Men have been found to develop atherosclerotic conditions by the ages of 18–29; few women in this age group do. Women with atherosclerotic deposits in their arteries have been found to have a lower than average level of circulating estrogen. When women have their ovaries removed (these are responsible for the production of most estrogens), they begin to develop atherosclerosis. However, the pill may change this picture. With the onset of menopause, women generally begin to lose their resistance to heart disease. As the buildup of fatty deposits takes a considerable time to reach the danger level, protection gained during the early years of life continues to give women an advantage.

Figure 18.1 shows the relationship between sex, race, and the risk of premature death from heart disease in the United States for people between the ages of 45 and 54; the figures represent deaths per 100,000 people. It is believed that the high rate among white men is due to their greater addiction to smoking, their greater incidence of obesity, their greater representation in occupations of highest mental stress and tension, and their higher blood

TABLE 18.1 Life Expectancy of Men and Women in Selected Countries*

Male Ranking	Life Expectancy in Years	Female Ranking	Life Expectancy in Years
1. Netherlands	71.4	Sweden	75.4
2. Sweden	71.3	Iceland	75.0
3. Norway	71.1	Netherlands	74.8
4. Israel	70.9	Switzerland	74.8
5. Iceland	70.7	Norway	74.7
6. Denmark	70.4	Canada	74.2
7. Switzerland	69.5	France	74.1
8. Canada	68.4	England and Wales	73.9
9. New Zealand	68.2	Denmark	73.8
10. England and Wales	68.0	UNITED STATES	73.4
11. Spain	67.3	U.S.S.R.	73.0
12. Puerto Rico	67.3	Israel	73.0
13. Czechoslovakia	67.2	New Zealand	73.0
14. France	67.2	Czechoslovakia	72.8
15. Japan	67.2	Australia	72.8
16. Australia	67.1	West Germany	72.4
17. West Germany	66.9	Japan	72.3
18. UNITED STATES	66.6	Puerto Rico	72.1

*Adapted from R. L. Williams, ed., *The Healthy Life*, Special Report (New York: Time-Life Books Div. of Time Inc., 1966), p. 9.

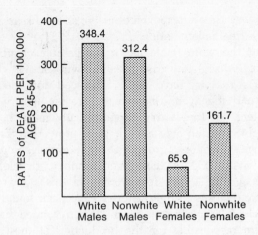

Figure 18.1 Relationship Between Sex, Race, and Death from Cardiovascular Disease
Adapted from R.L. Williams, ed., *op. cit.*, p. 21.

chloresterol levels than nonwhite males. The reason for the striking difference between the rates for white women and nonwhite women cannot be adequately explained at the present time.

Since 1900 the pattern of causes of death in the United States has greatly changed. Then the major causes were tuberculosis and pneumonia (acute diseases); now they are coronary heart disease, cancer, and stroke (chronic diseases). In part, these changes reflect medical advances in the control of acute disorders. Vaccines, immunization, antitoxins, antibiotics, and advances in diagnostic medicine have all helped to reduce the incidence of acute diseases in the United States.

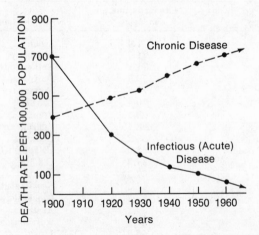

Figure 18.2 Prinicpal Cause of Death in the United States Between 1900 and 1960. Because of advances in medical science and technology, the rate of death from infectious disease has declined and that from chronic disease increased.

TABLE 18.2   Major Causes of Death in the United States*

Cause of Death	Number of Deaths in 1963	% of Total Deaths
Coronary heart disease	707,830	39.0
Cancer	291,870	15.7
Stroke	201,166	11.1
Accidents (automobile and other)	100,669	5.6
Influenza and pneumonia	70,761	3.9
Other circulatory causes	74,508	4.1
All other causes	366,745	20.6

*Adapted from R. L. Williams, ed., *op. cit.*, p. 20.

As can be seen from Table 18.2, coronary heart disease is the most common cause of death in the United States. Some of the conditions that seem to influence a person's potential for coronary heart disease will be briefly presented. Some available evidence related to conditions most commonly associated with coronary heart disease is discussed. If you wish additional information, it is readily available. The data presented may help you reach decisions about your own way of life and about your future role as homemaker (especially your part in *keeping your husband alive and well!*).

THE INFLUENCES

The information is organized under two major headings: Family Influences and Environmental Influences. These categories are used for ease of presentation. It is difficult, almost impossible, to separate cultural background from genetic effects and physiological influences. It is not our intent to demonstrate exact cause and effect relationships but to indicate significant conditions that seem to predispose a person to coronary heart disease. No one single condition can be isolated, but together the implications may become clearly apparent.

family influences

Family History. There is evidence that genetic effects may predispose one to greater susceptibility to coronary heart disease (1). *Body type.* Data relating to the endomesmorphic body type are accumulating which appear to indicate a predisposition for coronary heart disease among such individuals (2). *Sex and race.* In the United States, white males are most susceptible and their susceptibility begins quite early. Women are less susceptible than males (white and nonwhite), and white women less so than nonwhite women. *Obesity.* As the degree of obesity increases, the risk increases for both men and women (1). (It is more often thought that the term "obesities" should be used because of the many different origins of fatness.) Obesity may be genetic in origin, may be due to simple overeating and underexercising, or to certain metabolic mechanisms. Whatever its origin, persons more than 10–20% above acceptable body weight for their height and age run a definite risk. If a person is 30% or more overweight, that person has 2.5 times greater likelihood of contracting heart disease. *Diets.* Many food habit patterns are deeply entrenched in family, religious, ethnic, and social life. Diets with a high amount of fat and highly saturated fats may predispose one to heart disease. *Blood cholesterol levels.* The actual role of cholesterol in coronary heart disease is still subject to research. High levels of cholesterol (above 275 mg.) provide a diagnostic index or predictor (1). This factor may be genetic in origin. The level of cholesterol is evaluated along with other factors in a medical examination. An individual who has a combination of high blood pressure, a high level of cholesterol, and heavy smoking runs 12 times the risk of suffering coronary heart disease than his normal counterpart (1). *Hypertension.* A person with high blood pressure is 4 times as likely to develop coronary heart disease as his normal counterpart. High blood pressure provides a diagnostic index or good predictor of one's potential for coronary heart disease (1). This, too, can be genetic.

environmental influences

Under present-day conditions in the United States, children as well as adults have low levels of energy expenditure and high levels of stress and tension in adapting to changing patterns of sociocultural life. *Stress and tension.* There is some evidence that undue emotional stress and tension may predispose or be a condition that can even predict one's potential for coronary heart disease (1). *Physical activity.* There is some evidence to support the belief that a lack of physical activity may significantly hasten the onset of coronary heart disease (3). Most of this evidence has come from population studies and animal experimentation. In the next section, some studies will be presented.

THE ROLE OF EXERCISE

The old superstition that athletes generally die young because of enlarged hearts is incorrect. Athletic performance has been shown to have no detrimental effect upon the lives of athletes. Indeed, studies have indicated no difference in longevity, morbidity, or cause of death between athletes and nonathletes (4). Other studies show that athletes tend to be less active after they give up competition, so it is possible that protection given to them by their vigorous exercise early in life may be dissipated in middle age.

In studying the incidence of coronary heart disease among various public servants in Britain, Morris found that those people who were more active in their jobs (conductors of double deck buses rather than bus drivers, postmen rather than clerical assistants in the post office) generally gained protection from the onset of coronary heart disease. He found that the more active workers suffered 50% fewer fatal attacks than the sedentary group. Active workers who had heart attacks had them later in life. Such attacks were less likely to be fatal, and more likely to be of the comparatively milder version of angina pectoris (5). There was a greater incidence of heart disease among individuals in occupations involving little physical activity. In another study (6) autopsies revealed twice as many scars on the heart muscle (representing previous heart disease) of people engaged in light occupations as among people working in jobs requiring strenuous physical labor. The same generalization may be made for women. Activity on the job and in homemaking may provide a protection from coronary heart disease. If this activity is further supplemented by a program of regular endurance-type exercise, more protection may be gained.

atherosclerosis

Closely related to the problem of coronary heart disease is atherosclerosis. This condition is caused by the deposit along the inner walls of the arterial blood vessels of a fatty substance (such as cholesterol) which builds up to an extent that may eventually block blood flow completely. The problems involved with research into this complaint with human subjects are obvious, and most of the longitudinal research has been done with animals. Wong et al. (7, 8) and Kobernick et al. (9) found that the incidence of atherosclerotic deposits in the abdominal aorta of animals was reduced by forcing them to exercise on a daily basis. Orma (10) fed cockerels a stock diet and found that restriction in activity had no effect. When he fed them a high cholesterol diet and exercise was again restricted, there was a marked increase in the deposition of atherosclerotic plaque material on the inner walls of the major arteries. Exercise is not the only factor in the reduction of the incidence of coronary heart disease and atherosclerosis, but it is of sufficient importance to warrant a strong supporting statement in its favor as a mediating factor.

cholesterol

As previously stated, the relationship between cholesterol levels and the onset of coronary heart disease is part of a complex of other co-existing relationships. It has been shown that cholesterol level is a good indicator of potential heart trouble, that inactive people have higher blood cholesterol levels than active people, and that this level can be greatly reduced by exercise (11). Mann of Harvard University demonstrated that blood cholesterol levels, in people who were overfed, increased, and that these levels diminished when the diet was normalized. When the same subjects were overfed but placed on a program of vigorous exercise, their cholesterol levels did not increase if the body was able to burn up the additional food intake (12, 13). The evidence is clear that cholesterol levels are reduced by exercise; this definitely provides a form of protection from coronary heart disease, although the manner in which this occurs is still to be determined.

vascularization (collateral circulation)

In the event of a blockage of the arterial supply of blood to the muscles of the heart, it would be of advantage to the individual to have developed a network of alternative pathways. With these, the blood could circumvent the blocked area. This network is called a "collateral circulation," and is similar to the development of extra capillaries in working muscles that makes oxygen supply and metabolite egress from the cells more efficient. At the moment evidence for the development of a collateral circulation as a residual effect of exercise is not completely established for normal people, but there is strong support for its acceptance. Eckstein used dogs as experimental subjects, and various degrees of constriction were applied to the coronary arteries. He found that exercise promoted collateral growth above that which occurred in the control subjects with moderate to severe constrictions to the coronary arteries. He concluded that "judicious use of early and continued exercise may reduce the clinical manifestation of coronary heart disease" (14, 15). He also stated that it was important for middle-aged people to exercise before the onset of any cardiovascular disease symptoms so as to gain a degree of protection. But as a study during the Korean War (16) showed significant deposits of cholesterol in the arteries of young men (averaging 22.1 years of age), is it essential that exercise programs be started during adolescence. This is as important for women as men, as an increasing proportion of women are suffering from heart disease early in life.

obesity and overweight

As has been discussed, excessive fatness is associated with coronary heart disease. The food intake center in the brain does not appear to be adapted to function well at very low levels of activity. As physical activity decreases to very low levels of energy expenditure, food intake stabilizes at higher levels and may even increase. Fatness is the consequence. Inactivity can contribute significantly to the development of obesity (17). The role of physical activity and weight control has been discussed in detail in Chapter 13.

stress and tension

The association between stress and tension and coronary heart disease has been indicated. Some research data have been accumulated on the role of physical activity in alleviating stress and tension and possible heart deterioration. The heart responds to mental-emotional stress as well as to physical stimuli or exercise stress. The response to mental-emotional stress is often spoken of in medicine as the anticipatory rate or tension rate. It is this response that makes the heart a unique muscle.

Kraus and Raab brought attention to the fact that endurance training not only improves the heart's vagal tone (lower resting heart level), but also decreases its sympathetic tone (17). The heart is regularly controlled by two opposing autonomic nerve influences—the vagal tone that slows it down and the sympathetic tone that speeds it up. The sympathetic nervous system combined with the output of adrenalin tends to speed up the heart. When a high level of adrenalin in the blood reaches the heart, it causes it to increase in rate and strength of contraction. Adrenalin is a very important factor in stepping up heart function to meet the energy demands in exercise. However, there appears to be good evidence that constant stimulation with adrenalin in resting stages puts the heart at a disadvantage and may be damaging to heart muscle. Raab was able to show that persons with endurance training increased the vagal tone and at the same time reduced the amount of sympathetic activity, thus, decreasing the adrenalin threat to the heart. He found that persons who are easily stirred up have greater sympathetic tone. Persons who exercised regularly in an endurance-type activity were not so easily emotionalized, i.e., their hearts didn't beat at an excessively fast rate in response to emotional stress. Thus, it would appear that a healthy, efficient heart is less affected by adrenalin. As yet, why this occurs is not known, but possibly it is due to more efficient utilization or decreased production of adrenalin. A healthy, efficient heart responds better and seemingly has a built-in degree of protection regardless of the type of stimuli (exercise or emotional stress).

CONCLUDING REMARKS

Is the evidence worthy of your concern for self, and for your future family? Are the facts and explanations sufficient to draw health implications for the role of physical activity? Is the evidence clear enough to indicate a relationship between physical activity habit patterns and protection from the onset of cardiovascular disease? What conditions that predispose a person to coronary heart disease are controllable? If you believe that diet, physical activity, and abstinence from cigarette smoking can help provide you with a built-in protective mechanism, what do you plan to to about it—if anything? Are your present health-fitness habits of diet and physical activity sufficient to provide you with a healthy, efficient heart and optimal body weight and shape?

What about the future? Male members of our society have been major targets of early coronary heart disease in the past. Women have been given some protection by their circulating estrogen hormones until menopause. The pill may provide additional protection through an extended period of time. However, the trend for women to hold positions in the upper echelons of business and in the professions is clearly apparent and is likely to accelerate during your lifetime and your children's. Associated with this is a gradual increase in incidence of heart and circulatory disease in women. If physical activity and the regulation of diet can give a measure of protection to men who occupy stressful work roles, then the same protection can be given women.

From the information presented on organic tone (cardiovascular-respiratory endurance) relative to developing and maintaining a healthy, efficient heart, how would you answer the questions at the beginning of this chapter? Two questionnaires follow that may help you take stock of your health-fitness attitude as well as provide you with insight into your daily living habits.

LABORATORY: ASSESS YOUR WELL-BEING

Questionnaire 1: Physical Potential and Total Well-Being

Directions: Check your answers below as you perceive your real self-image. This is not a test, but a self-rating technique. Add your points: Yes (3); Somewhat (2); No (1). Rate yourself on the scale: High (45-36); Medium (35-27); Low (26-1).

Do You Think You Have the Capacity to:	Yes	Somewhat	No
1. Think, reason, and find solutions to your problems and carry the solutions out?			
2. Persevere until your work is done?			
3. Have insight into your physical condition?			
4. Have insight and knowledge of your present level of energy expenditure?			
5. Have knowledge and understanding of how to improve the health efficiency of your heart?			
6. Have adequate cardiovascular-respiratory endurance?			
7. Have self-sufficiency to build physical activity into your way of life?			
8. Feel secure?			
9. Make a home and maintain a healthy family?			
10. Know how to keep your husband alive?			
11. Play with enthusiasm, joy, and skill a minimum of three times per week?			
12. Face reality and make decisions about the role of physical activity in your life?			
13. Feel confident of your present health-fitness status?			
14. Enjoy people, to work with them, and to play with them?			
15. Have a keen enjoyment of life?			

Total points: _____

Subtotals

Your rating: _____

Directions: Check your answers below as you perceive your real self now. This is not a test. It is a self-rating technique to help you become aware of what you actually do. Add your points: Always (3); Sometimes (2); Rarely (1). Rate yourself on the scale: High (45-36); Medium (35-27); Low (26-1).

Do You:	Always	Sometimes	Rarely
A. Physical factors			
1. Check with your doctor once a year?			
2. Check with your dentist once a year?			
3. Have regular eliminations?			
4. Practice cleanliness with respect to body, teeth, hair, clothing, and your total appearance?			
5. Select appropriate equipment at the proper height to prevent undue joint-muscular strain?			
B. Mental and emotional health factors			
6. Actually do tasks rather than getting tired by thinking of what you have to do?			
7. Have an awareness of your potential?			
8. Feel secure and self-sufficient?			
C. Nutritional factors			
9. Eat well-balanced meals each day (the recommended allowance of the four basic food groups)?			
10. Match your caloric output with your intake?			
D. Rest-sleep factors			
11. Get your proper amount of sleep, eight to ten hours out of every twenty-four?			
12. Take time to relax or rest a little each day?			
13. Recognize undue tensions and take time to relax?			
14. Have an absorbing outlet to divert your mind from fundamental problems and to refresh yourself?			
15. Find time to be physically active each day by walking, swimming, or participating in similar pursuits in excess of daily demands?			

Total points: _____
Your rating: _____   Sub-totals

references and sources for additional reading

1. Williams, R.L., *The Healthy Life*, Special Report. New York: Time-Life Books, Div. of Time, Inc., 1966.
2. Parnell, R.W., *Behaviour and Physique*. London: Edward Arnold (Publishers) Ltd., 1958.
3. Montoye, H.J., "Summary of Research on the Relationship of Exercise to Heart Disease." Paper presented at the 7th Annual Meeting, American College of Sports Medicine, Miami Beach, Florida, April 23, 1960.
4. ———, "Sports and Length of Life," in *Science and Medicine of Exercise and Sports*, ed. W.R. Johnson. New York: Harper & Row, Publishers, 1960.
5. Morris, J. N., P.A.B. Raffle, C.G. Roberts, and J.W. Parks, "Coronary Heart Disease and Physical Activity of Work," *Lancet*, Vol. 365 (1953) 1053-7.

6. Morris, J.N., and M.C. Crawford, "Coronary Heart Disease and Physical Activity of Work," *British Medical Journal*, Vol. 2 (1958) 1485–96.

7. Wong, H.Y.C., R.L. Simmons, and E. W. Hawthorne, "Effects of Controlled Exercise on Experimental Atherosclerosis in Androgen-treated Chicks," *Federation Proceedings*, Vol. 15 (1956) 203.

8. Wong, H.Y.C., M.B. Anderson, J.K. Kim, D.J. Liu, and E.W. Hawthorne, "Hypocholesterolizing Effect of Exercise on Cholesterol-Fed Cockerels," *Federation Proceedings*, Vol. 16 (1957) 138.

9. Kobernick, S.D., C. Niwayana, and A.C. Zuchlewski, "Effect of Physical Activity on Cholesterol Atherosclerosis in Rabbits," *Proceedings of the Society for Experimental Biology and Medicine*, Vol. 96 (1957) 623–8.

10. Orma, E.J., "Effect of Physical Activity on Atherogenesis. An Experimental Study in Cockerels," *Acta Physiologica Scandinavica*, Suppl. 142, Vol. 41 (1957) 1–75.

11. Spain, D.M., D.J. Nathan, and M. Gillis. "Weight, Body Type and Prevalance of Coronary Atherosclerotic Heart Disease in Males." *American Journal of Medical Science*. Vol. 245 (April 1963) 63–69.

12. Mann, G.V., "Importance of Caloric Disposition in Cholesterol and Lipo Protein Metabolism of Human Subjects," *Federation Proceedings*, Vol. 14 (1955) 442.

13. Mann, G.V., K. Teel, O. Hayes, A. McNally, and D. Bruns, "Exercise in the Disposition of Dietary Calories," *New England Journal of Medicine*, Vol. 253 (1955) 349–55.

14. Eckstein, R.W., "Effect of Exercise and Coronary Artery Narrowing on Coronary Collateral Circulation," *Circulation Research*, Vol. 5 (1957) 230–5.

15. ———, "Effect of Exercise and Coronary Arterial Narrowing on Growth of Interarterial Coronary Anastomoses," *Federation Proceedings*, Vol. 15 (1956) 54

16. Enos, W.F., R. H. Holmes, and J. C. Beyer, "Coronary Disease Among United States Soldiers Killed in Action in Korea," *Journal of the American Medical Association*, Vol. 152 (1953) 1090–3.

17. Kraus, H., and W. Raab, *Hypokinetic Disease*. Springfield, Ill.: Charles C Thomas, Publisher, 1961.

exercise and stress

19 Mental stress has always been present in life. In spite of the fact that life has changed markedly from primitive to modern times, stress is probably no more severe now that it was then. Since the Industrial Revolution, life has undergone drastic change; and new and different stressors (stress-producing situations or agents) have replaced the old. No one doubts that even more drastic alterations in patterns of life will produce different stressors, demanding further adaptation for the survival and growth of each person and of society itself. Today, as in the past and in the future, adaptation to stress is a critical problem. In the United States, more than 300 million dollars are spent yearly on tranquilizers to quiet the jitters and relieve anxiety and tension. The situation has been satirically characterized in poetic form by an eminent physiologist, Dr. Steinhaus (1).

> We are advised to
> Wake up with Caffeine,
> Keep going on Nicotine,
> Move bowels on Serutan,
> Kill pain with aspirin,
> Stay alive on Geritol,
> Drown worries in alcohol,
> Grow slender with effortless Ella,
> Adjust the stomach on Tums,
> Lift your arches with steel.
> Hold your belly with a three-way stretch,
> Write examinations on Benezedrine,
> Quiet tensions with tranquilizers,
> Dispel nagging backaches with kidney pills,

Go to sleep on barbiturates,
Start the new day with bubbling alkalizers to get rid of yester-
day's brown taste
To make room for to-day's.[1]

SOME CONCEPTS ABOUT EXERCISE AND STRESS

No one denies that there are many diverse forces and pressures in life today that are stress-producing and manifest themselves in anxiety and tension states. It is important to recognize that you must change to meet change, adjusting your environment or yourself to meet each challenge according to your own potential. Some of the more dominant forces or conditions producing change and creating new demands for adaptation today are depicted in Table 19.1.

stress and adaptation

Stress is essential to life: stress is the process of living, and the process of living is reacting or adapting to stress. Stress-producing stimuli induce anxiety and

[1]Arthur H. Steinhaus, *Toward an Understanding of Health and Physical Education* (Dubuque, Iowa: Wm. C. Brown Company Publishers, 1900), p. 287. Reproduced by permission of the publisher.

TABLE 19.1 Change and Adaptation

Dominant Forces of Change	Demands on Adaptability Potential
1. Explosion of scientific and technological knowledge and communication advances.	1. Find means of handling explosion of knowledge; of keeping up with the times; of decision making—what knowledge is of most worth; of utilizing advances and dealing with the impact of mass media.
2. Demand for specialization as industry and technology expand, create new positions, and require new skills.	2. Make priority decisions for development of talents and skills; promote continual learning throughout life.
3. Bigness, complexity, and automation in all aspects of life, including the future of the school.	3. Counteract the personal identity crisis, alienation and dehumanization; promote personally satisfying, pleasurable recreative activities.
4. Changing roles of men and women; changes in family patterns and role of family unit.	4. Reinforce personal security and inner balance; counteract feelings of personal insecurity; find means of maintaining emotional tone.
5. Population explosion and ever-increasing advances in transportation and mobility.	5. Emphasize sharing, other directedness, empathy and sensitiveness to others, evaluate the role of "the pill."
6. Shift in value orientation in the American way of life and value crises—racial strife, population mobility, urban and suburban crises, nuclear weapons.	6. Evaluate value systems, decision-making values to live by, use of knowledge and technology for bettering mankind.

tension. Dealing with these is a matter of balancing incoming stimuli with outgoing energy—energy expended in some pleasant activity. For total well-being, there must also be a balancing of effort with rest and sleep. Each person is continually involved in adaptive effort to maintain internal equilibrium or homeostasis. *Homeostasis* is the physiological maintenance of internal equilibrium in which the autonomic nervous system and endocrine system are intimately involved. From your own personal experience, the contribution of rest and sleep for stabilization and maintenance of an internal equilibrium must be clearly apparent. Recent investigations are directed toward determining the role of physical activity in helping to maintain the homeostasis balance of the body—the adaptation potential of the body.

Hans Selye, a Canadian endocrinologist, has dedicated his life to research on the physiology of stress in an investigation of a unified theory of disease (2). Selye has attempted to identify specific body responses to general non-specific stimuli. *Stress*, as he uses the concept, is the body's reaction or response to a stressor, through a specific stress syndrome of physiologically induced change. A *stressor* is any trying circumstance, condition, or agent that elicits physiological changes that make the body mobilize its resources and increase its energy expenditure. Whatever the stressors, the pattern of body response is consistent; such a response may be local or general. The General Adaptation Syndrome (GAS), or general response of the body to resist or combat these stressors, consists of three stages: the alarm reaction, the resistance stage, and the exhaustion stage. During the alarm reaction, the response to the stressor is both local and general (via the nervous system to the endocrine system). After the alarm reaction has been activated, the major symptoms of stress begin to be noticeable; but, if the stress-producing stimuli are prolonged, the body enters the resistance stage, and the symptoms disappear. It is in the resistance stage that the balancing of "pro-inflammatory" hormones and "anti-inflammatory" hormones, secreted by the adrenal cortex, occurs. The balancing of these facilitating and inhibiting vital forces results in adaptation—the ability to resist the stressor and maintain homeostasis. Lack of the ability to adapt or adjust to the stressor brings about the exhaustion stage, which eventually is fatal.

The implications of Selye's stress theory are that some kinds of stressors may be prophylactics for the deleterious effects of other kinds of stress. Exercise, for example, may be a stressor that enhances one's potential for adaptation. It is a stress-producing stimulus that elicits body responses and through progressive conditioning, produces beneficial changes in body function. These adaptations may facilitate the body's adjustment to other stress-producing stimuli; that is, regular exercise may provide built-in protective or adaptative mechanisms. Such a concept has been proposed by Kraus and Raab (3). These investigators use the term "hypokinetic disease" (*hypo*—under; *kinetic*—motion, exercise) to express the relationship between lack of exercise and the stress syndrome. They postulate that some diseases are induced by lack of exercise. Such diseases not only affect the musculoskeletal system (resulting in pain in tension target areas) but also directly affect the cardiovascular system, hormonal balance, and psychological well-being. Kraus and Raab are convinced that lack of habitual physical activity coupled with muscular deficiency (low level of health-physical fitness) and suppression of the *fight* and *flight* physiological responses to anxiety and tension become manifest in generalized stress reactions and diseases. The hypokinetic disease concept is illustrated in Figure 19.1.

The stress concept may not entirely present or resolve the crucial health problems facing each of us today. However, it does provide guidelines for living in a healthy way. Whatever the stress-provoking situation, one thing is certain, the degree of manifestation of the stress syndrome (your reactions) is

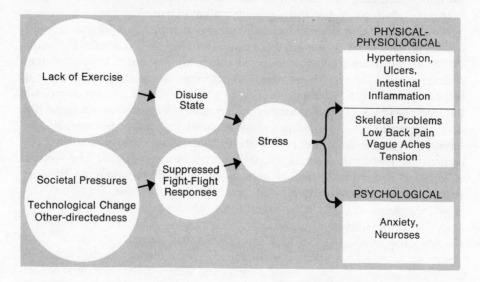

Figure 19.1   Schema of the Hypokinetic Disease Concept of Kaus and Raab (3)

an individual matter. How your body responds will depend upon your perception of the situation, your level of health-physical fitness, and your memory of past situations. Some individuals enjoy, even thrive on the challenge of competition such as examinations and sports. For others the stress effects of these events are very potent and deplete their energy resources. Stress is here to stay, and it is up to you to appraise the stress-provoking conditions in your life. Evaluate your energy resources. Determine how long you can keep on adapting to stress without excessive tiredness and tensions or depletion of your energy stores. Some of the warning signs and symptoms of undue tensions that foreshadow a chronically tired and physically tense condition are:

1. sleeplessness
2. getting up feeling tired after a night's rest
3. being restless, cross, impatient, or irritable
4. taking more time to do the tasks you once did easily
5. feelings of tiredness brought on by just thinking of all you have to do

6. being unenthusiastic, bored and feeling stale
7. dreading getting up in the morning and facing the day
8. disliking meeting new people and facing new situations
9. having vague aches and pains in tension areas
10. being addicted to work and unable to change pace.

muscular tension and emotional states

Emotional stressors, of whatever origin, produce increased tension or tonus in skeletal muscles; that is, there is a neuromuscular manifestation of various psychologically induced anxieties and tensions. Much of the evidence supporting this concept has been provided by Edmund Jacobson (4). He made electronic measurements of tension by attaching electrodes to the skin to pick up small electrical changes in different muscles which were recorded. By electromyography, it is possible to gain insight into a person's emotional states and nervousness. Relationships were found between certain electromyographical measurements of selected skeletal muscular activity and such clinical states as headache, backache, and emotional states. Muscle tension itself is not the critical problem. What is important is excessive or prolonged muscle tension (residual neuromuscular hypertension), which may imply a more serious problem—nonadjustment.

THE EXERCISE APPROACH TO RELAXATION

Your aptitude and achievement in the art and science of relaxation is of the utmost importance to your personal well-being. *Relaxation* is the release of tensions. Exercise techniques for relaxation have a twofold purpose: (*1*) to reduce unnecessary neuromuscular tension and (*2*) to re-energize or refresh one's self—emotionally and physically. Life is based upon the cycle of building energy stores, utilizing these stores, and recovering from use. Regular habitual exercise may be one way to counteract the potentially dangerous stress effects of excessive tensions and anxieties that have no vicarious outlets. Adjustment takes thought. You must develop a capacity to meet change with change. This requires the ability to balance all the things that make up the process of living; such as work with play, physical effort with rest, calmness with turmoil, being a spectator with being an active participant, and energy intake with energy outgo.

The fundamental approach to reducing emotional states of excessive tension and anxiety is recognizing the underlying problems and stress-provoking conditions. Removing the causes or changing the environment to permit adaptation is primarily the task of professionally trained personnel; however, the exercise approach to relaxing and reducing tension lies within your realm. Two techniques are involved in this: recreation and progressive muscular relaxation.

recreation: the leisure approach to relaxation

This approach is carried out through personal involvement in pleasurable leisure activities that are balanced with work, rest, and sleep. Two primary results of recreation are the desirable outcomes of refreshment and relaxation.

Leisure is a fundamental human need. And without a capacity to *recreate*, you lose an essential attribute of the so-called "good life." As you find more and more time available from your working day, your leisure and the use you make of it will assume an increasingly important role in your *life*. It is through leisure that you have the opportunity for continued growth, individual enrichment, and a better society.

Why is leisure important? Here are some answers you should evaluate. It may provide the joy and satisfaction of being with others. It may reduce tensions by diverting the mind from its immediate problems. It may provide opportunities for creativity, ingenuity, and a firing of the imagination. It may be a tonic, a refresher, an avenue or outlet for muscular energies and emotional release. It may provide moments of aesthetic enjoyment of the beauty of nature, of the beauty of human movement in dance and excellence in sports. It may be a way of attaining physical skills within the cultural milieu. These are some of the reasons that make leisure important to everyone.

Physical activities help to divert the mind from everyday problems by providing new directions and different problems to solve. They help utilize excess neuromuscular tension in the accomplishment of specific pleasurable goals. The physical activity selected should be vigorous enough to bring about a feeling of refreshment and a pleasant feeling of physical tiredness that can come only from muscular activity. Such activities should be planned and balanced with life's other activities. If spaced and balanced properly, they help prevent undue tensions and the resulting feelings of chronic tiredness, hypertension, and irritability.

Perhaps the case for recreation is best made by W.C. Menninger, of the famous Kansas clinic, who perceives recreation as a way of insuring mental health (5):

> Recreation has not only played an important part in the treatment program of many mental illnesses, but it has been a considerable factor in enabling former patients to remain well. Therefore, psychiatrists believe that recreative activity can also be a valuable preventative for mental illness. There are, however, ways one can reduce the risks of being waylaid by it . . . (1) competitive games provide an unusually satisfactory outlet for the instinctive aggression drive, (2) the psychological values in certain kinds of recreation lie in the opportunity to create (rugs, music, poetry, baking), (3) relaxation through entertainment, through catering to the passive desires of many of us as well as to provide an opportunity for vicarious participation (listening to music, seeing a ball game, reading a mystery book, or studying art masterpieces) . . . .
>
> Mentally healthy people participate in some form of volitional activity to supplement their required daily work. . . . Their satisfaction

from these activities meet deep-seated psychological demands, quite beyond the superficial rationalization of enjoyment. . . . By comparison with two generations ago, there is today a greater need for recreative play. People now have little opportunity to express their aggressive needs, to pioneer, or to explore. . . . The psychiatrist can make certain recommendations: good mental health is directly related to the capacity and willingness to play. Regardless of his objections, resistances, and past practices, any individual will make a wise investment for himself if he does plan time for his play and takes it seriously. . . . If we could encourage and guide more people to creative activity, we could and would make a major contribution to our national and international peace of mind.

progressive relaxation

Relaxation is required not only for rest and sleep (zero muscular activity), and for maintaining internal equilibrium, but also for smooth, efficient performance of an athlete or dancer. Utilizing only as much energy and muscular tension in the parts directly involved as required to perform a task is called "differential relaxation." It applies to every task we do—even sitting or lying, resting or walking. It has been demonstrated that individuals can improve their ability to achieve voluntary relaxation.

Complete relaxation in all parts of the body or differential relaxation lies with the integration of brain, nerve, and muscles. Muscular tensions are only possible when nerve impulses are received by muscle fibers. Therefore, the basis for controlling muscle tension resides in the central nervous system. It is possible to increase or decrease muscular tension through thought and mental concentration. There are special techniques by which you can learn to relax at will and facilitate effective rest and sleep, or to relieve tension-creating situations. Here again there are individual differences in the capacity to relax at will. Some of us automatically relax; we let go of the excess tensions in our muscles when we feel ourselves becoming tense or when we assume a position of rest or sleep. Some of us have the ability to relax but, because we do not know the difference between the feeling of tension and the feeling of relaxation in our muscles, this knowledge is of little benefit to us. Others have a great deal of neuromuscular tension and have difficulty in recognizing the tension and in releasing it at will.

Jacobson used the term *residual tension* to describe excessive tenseness residing in the muscles. The method of relaxation he proposed has been widely applied by many others. The term used to describe his method is "progressive relaxation" (4). It depends upon teaching the individual to recognize progressively decreasing levels of voluntary muscular tension by applying the principles of kinesthetic perception. Once the individual's perceptive powers are great enough to identify tension in different parts of the body, she can learn to completely relax one muscle group or body region after another until her whole body is completely relaxed.

The need for sleep and rest is illustrated very clearly by our physiological processes. The human body is not a perpetual motion machine; it needs time to fuel up and replenish its energy supplies at regular intervals. When sleep overtakes us, our conscious mind relinquishes control, and one by one our senses begin to depart. Vision is first, taste follows, then smell, hearing, and touch. It is at this point that our energy consumption (basal metabolism) reaches its lowest ebb. Our recuperative processes accelerate, reaching the depleted cells of the body and mind. Sleep should mean rest. It is not the quantity of sleep that counts, but the quality of the sleep. It is possible to sleep without getting any rest, and to rest without getting any sleep. The physical benefits of the period of recuperation depend upon how restful our sleep is. Sleep needs vary just as do other physiological functions. It is common experience to find that usually eight hours of sleep are needed for normal recuperation—studies show that while it may take four hours to restore physical energies, it may take twice as long to replenish energy expended by mental effort.

Restful sleep is impossible if mind and body are keyed up with nervous and emotional tensions. Such a state keeps the recuperative processes from functioning properly and may be the reason for one to wake in the morning actually more tired than when he went to bed. This is the kind of sleep that interferes with replenishment of our energies. Tests show that a series of rest periods during the day can actually do more to recuperate mind and muscles than troubled hours of shallow slumber. Scientists agree that how well we sleep is a vital factor, not only for how we feel but for how productive our life span is.

Variations in sleep needs are clearly seen in infancy, childhood, and adulthood. With aging, the need for sleep and rest appears to increase. It is quite common for persons past sixty to need an additional hour or two of rest during the day. Sleep and rest are both preventive and restorative. Learning how to rest between activities during the day will conserve energy and make for greater efficiency in the total work output. Sleep and rest in proper proportions to your work are essential for your lifetime energy resources.

Relaxation, the release of neuromuscular tension, is the key to restful sleep, and progressive muscular relaxation is one of the most effective techniques for producing rest and sleep. Sleep is a state of almost complete relaxation: the heart rate, breathing rate, blood pressure are lowered; the body stores food or energy supplies and filters waste products from the blood by the kidneys.

SOME CONCLUDING REMARKS

The thesis of the chapter is this: In order to have the capacities and the potential for undergoing and adapting to change, you need to move—to become activated. But more than merely moving, you need to channel your talents and energy. What you do in your leisure can be a great energizing force for your personal well-being and for the society in which you live. Take time in your daily routine to change your pace. Take time for a vacation. Assume personal responsibility for recreating yourself daily throughout your life. Leisure may be the best tonic or refresher, the best protector or developer of self that you can find.

references and sources for additional reading

1. Steinhaus, A.H., *Toward an Understanding of Health and Physical Education.* Dubuque, Iowa: William C. Brown Company, Publishers, 1963, p. 287.
2. Selye, H., *The Physiology and Pathology of Exposure to Stress.* Montreal: Acta, Inc., 1950.
3. Kraus, H., and W. Raab, *Hypokinetic Disease.* Springfield, Ill.: Charles C Thomas, Publisher, 1961.
4. Jacobson, E., *Progressive Relaxation.* Chicago: University of Chicago Press, 1934.
5. Menninger, W.C., "Recreation and Mental Health," *Recreation*, Vol. 42 (November 1948), 340–46.

movement patterns

through the years

20 Throughout this book the self-image concept has been presented to enable you to make a realistic estimate of your physical potential, the physical activity or movement patterns in your daily life, and their value in modern living. Through measurement and self-evaluation procedures, your present status was assessed and personal activity needs identified. Techniques of physical conditioning and the underlying principles for designing action plans to accomplish specific purposes were presented. The general framework upon which to build a personal program in physical education during your college years was presented. This chapter deals primarily with you, as an adult, designing a personal program to maintain your physical potential throughout your life. In addition, brief discussions of the value of physical activity for young children and the new image of physical education for children and youth are presented.

FOR THE ADULT

physical activity and aging

To be a fully functioning human being throughout one's life rather obviously requires physical as well as intellectual and emotional capacities. Evidence from research constantly bolsters the belief that physical activity significantly delays the aging process and helps to preserve physical and mental capacities longer than would otherwise be the case (1). Although strength, flexibility, endurance, speed, reaction time, and other physical capacities reach their maximum somewhere during the late teens and twenties and then show a gradual decline with advancing age, a general level of physical activity may

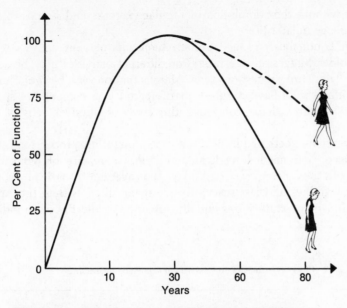

Figure 20.1 Biological Curve of Functional Capacities.
Question: Can activity delay the aging process as suggested by the broken line?

help to prevent or delay age changes per se. Results of studies undertaken in our laboratory on age, physical activity, and functional characteristics of girls and women from 20 to 69 years clearly indicate that declining efficiency in adjustment to physical effort with age is attributable both to aging processes and to the decrease in the level of habitual physical activity (2, 3). Figure 20.1 presents these concepts schematically.

Of equal importance is understanding postural changes with aging. Obviously it takes time to develop the optimal body lines of an adult. This fact is illustrated in Figure 20.2. Can one speculate on the kind of body form one

Figure 20.2 Stages of Development

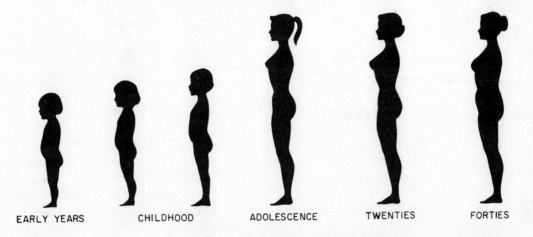

EARLY YEARS   CHILDHOOD   ADOLESCENCE   TWENTIES   FORTIES

might have without the stimulation of regular exercise, and its possible effect on the self-image in later life?

You should judiciously reduce the strenuousness of your activity levels as you grow older. Suggested age range for different activities may be found in Table 20.1. These are suggestions only. Many situations can be found in which older individuals who have regularly participated in a competitive sport and are in good condition have continued this form of physical activity despite advancing years.

The preventive effects of physical activity, along with proper food, enough rest and sleep, and needed medical and dental care, are of particular importance with advancing years. Today the average American woman is statistically healthier and less susceptible to many diseases than the American man. But after menopause she is equally susceptible, and there are indications

TABLE 20.1 Physical Activities and Suggested Age Recommendation

Sport Activities	Age range recommended	Recreational Games	Age range recommended	Dance Activities	Age range recommended	Outdoor Recreation	Age range recommended
Badminton	Under 50	Archery	All ages	Folk	All ages	Fishing Bait	All ages
Basketball	40	Croquet		Square		Fly Deep sea	
Fencing	50	Darts		Social		Gardening	
Hockey	40	Bicycling		Modern		Hunting	
Gymnastics	40	Bowling		Tap		Shooting	
Handball	50	Deck tennis				Pistol Rifle Skeet	
Lacrosse	40	Horseshoes				Trap	
Skiing	60	Golf				Hiking	
Soccer	40	Table tennis				Canoeing	
Softball	40	Lawn bowling				Sailing	
Tennis	50	Shuffleboard				Motoring	
Water polo	30	Swimming				Camping and outing	
Squash	50	Riding					
Volleyball	50	Skating					

that she is becoming increasingly susceptible even before menopause. Of particular importance for health-fitness are control of body weight, release of tension and emotional stress, and maintenance of good bodily function. Excessive body fatness, lack of muscle tone or atrophy, lack of elastic tone or joint stiffness, decreased cardiovascular-respiratory capacity, postural imbalance, vague aches and pains, and impairment of various metabolic functions are all now considered possible effects of prolonged inactivity (4). Further, there is not much doubt that physical activity, i.e., muscular effort, is among the best means for releasing tensions and emotional stresses and alleviating chronic tiredness and fatigue.

Despite gaps in our knowledge about the role of physical activity in modern life, we firmly believe that each individual must not only design a personal program to meet her needs but must also incorporate it into her way of life if she is to maintain her physical potential and a wholesome self-image throughout life. Such a program should enable her to

1. maintain her energy, vitality, and interest in life
2. preserve her physical and mental capacities and maintain a good appearance
3. have an inner balance—an emotional tone on which her relationships with others and with her environment depends
4. have a capacity and willingness to play—to enjoy physical activities commensurate with her age and physical condition
5. survive without unusual dependency on others
6. gain protection from chronic degenerative conditions.

Health-physical fitness values and skills in physical activities are not ends in themselves, but rather the means to carry on one's life work competently with personal satisfaction and joy. Physical activity should be engaged in for the pleasure it gives and for aid in remaining an effectively functioning human being throughout life. It must not simply be a strenuous competitive effort to keep fit or to prevent specific disease. It must, as the theme of this book states, be a case of *making the most of one's self through physical activity as a way of life*. Examples of exercise plans for keeping fit and liking it may be found in the reference material (5–8) at the end of the chapter.

simple ways to evaluate self

The self-image concept and movement characteristics have been presented in detail to make possible a realistic estimate of your physical self and your movement patterns in daily use. The chart that follows is intended as a guide for self-evaluation in the years ahead. We have divided physical activity into four broad groups and suggested simple tests in each area. Checking yourself with this chart in future years will enable you to evaluate how well your movement habits provide you with the exercise, interest, and avenues of self-expression you need to keep your appearance, health, and spirits in top shape.

Simple Ways to Evaluate Yourself
Four Activity Groups and Their Contribution to Movement Characteristics

1. Muscular Tone

Desirable body proportions?

Test: push-feel firm?   same as at age 25?

2. Elastic Tone

Bend easily?

touch ankles
or toes?   touch knees
to forehead?   bend foot,
curl toes?

Free and easy body lines?

Tests: free and easy?   stiff?   collapsed?   pass wall test?

Extend easily?

pass floor test?

Free and easy motion?

Tests: free and easy?   stiff?   collapsed?   touch fingers
on upper back?

Turn-twist easily?

twist 90°?

3. Organic Tone

Desirable weight and fat deposit?

Tests: same as age 25–30?   pinch only 1 inch of fat?   change position, stretch?   relax under tension?   change pace?

Optimim energy outgo?

Tests: swim ½ mile without stopping?   run-walk a mile in 10 minutes?   self-expression?   self-development?   achievement of skills?

Optimum recuperation powers?

Tests: recover quickly after physical activity?*   awaken refreshed?   tense or relaxed?   meaning of movement?

*Breathlessness and pounding of heart noticible after 10 minutes; marked fatigue persisting after 2 hours; sleep disturbed or undue weakness the following day—these are all signs that the exercise was too severe.

4. Psycho-Social Tone

Release of tension?

Self-interest?

Insight into self and others?

the preschool child

As the child grows and develops, particular movements of the body, at first random and reflexive, combine into more general and complex movement patterns for postural control, locomotion, and arm-hand coordination. There is an orderly sequence of motor development as the child proceeds at his own pace (9, 10). Figure 20.3 outlines the sequential development of fundamental motor patterns in young children.

Details of information slowly being provided through research fit into the general concept that early motor activity experiences (from birth to about 6 or 7 years) are an important factor in learning and development (11, 12). Active play is seen as the way the child explores and experiments with the many objects and events that make up his world. In this light, he learns by experimenting with his emerging motor abilities; by developing an awareness of self, his own body image, and body parts and of what he can do; and by perceiving his relationship to others and to objects in space and time. Thus, through his active play in motor activities, the young child is not only maturing but also "learning to move as he moves to learn." In the past few years there have also been new approaches to remedial and motor therapy programs for children with learning problems or disabilities. Some material is included at the end of this chapter for those who wish to learn more about this area.

Perhaps, as Dr. Arthur Steinhaus has stated (16), the mother is the first physical educator. As such, there are certain things she (and you as a future parent) should know. One concerns enabling the child to feel free to seek activity and to explore, to experiment in activities of his choice. Each child has differences, which are apparent at an early age in his preference of one form of active play over another, as well as differences in his degree or level of activity. Much more needs to be learned about variations in motor activity as related to influences within individuals and to external factors in their environment. As someone has said, "understanding nuclear physics is child's play compared with understanding child's play." It is probable, however, that the enthusiasm and play-fun values given by his parents to particular activities and to physical activity as a way of life influence the young child's value of activity.

Another thing a parent should know concerns providing plenty of space to permit the child freedom to explore, to experiment, and to practice managing his body in a variety of situations. All kinds of equipment to encourage general bodily movement and locomotion and manipulating objects for hand-eye-leg coordination should be provided. Active play or motor activity experiences will serve to improve bodily functioning and muscular development. That "Play's the Thing"—the title of an article by Eli Bower (17)—should be emphasized. Its immediate satisfaction is fun, joy, imagination, and the creativity of the activity itself; the long-range goal is individual and social competency (18). "Play cannot be prescribed, assigned or done to order. It

LEVELS OF
MATURITY

5 years	56.4 months	Backward heel-to-toe walking (4.7 years)
	54 months	Balances on one foot for 10 seconds (4.5 years)
4 years	46.8 months	Catches bounced ball (3.9 years)
	43.2 months	Heel-to-toe walk (3.6 years)
	40.8 months	Hops on one foot (3.4 years)
	38.4 months	Balances on one foot for 5 seconds (3.2 years)
3 years	33.6 months	Broad jump (2.8 years)
	30 months	Balances on one foot for 1 second (2.5 years)
2 years	23.9 months	Pedals tricycle
	22.3 months	Jumps in place
	20 months	Kicks ball forward
	19.8 months	Throws ball overhand
	17 months	Walks up stairs
	14.3 months	Walks backwards
1 year	12.1 months	Walks well
	11.6 months	Stoops and recovers
	11.5 months	Stands well alone
	9.8 months	Stands momentarily
9 months	9.2 months	Walks, holding on to furniture
	8.3 months	Thumb-finger grasp
	7.6 months	Gets to sitting
	7.6 months	Pulls self to stand
6 months	5.8 months	Stands holding on
	5.5 months	Sits without support
	4.2 months	Pulls to sit, no head lag
	4.2 months	Bears some weight on legs
	3.6 months	Reaches for object
	3.3 months	Grasps rattle
3 months	2.9 months	Prone — chest up, arm support
	2.8 months	Rolls over
	2.2 months	Prone — head up 90°
	2.2 months	Hands together
	1.9 months	Prone — head up 45°
	0.7 month	Prone — lifts head
	Birth	

Figure 20.3   Development of Fundamental Motor Patterns in Children*

*Adapted from W. K. Frankenburg and J. B. Dodds, "The Denver Developmental Screening Test," *Journal of Pediatrics*, Vol. 71, No. 2 (1967), 181–91; and A. Gesell and C. S. Amatruda, *Developmental Diagnosis* (New York: Harper & Row, Publishers, 1941.)

is voluntary. It is fun. It is important, indeed mandatory for animal and human existence" (17).

the school-age child and youth

Several related discoveries in different fields of study have led to new insights into the learning process at all levels of education. These discoveries, along with the explosion of knowledge and a rapidly changing, complex society, have given impetus to the search for the answer to what knowledge is of most worth and how can it best be transmitted so as to transform the child into a fully functioning integrated person (19, 20). Educational theory and practice are being revolutionized. The development of new curricula in mathematics, science, and social studies, and new approaches to aiding children with learning problems are the results. In fact, every subject is undergoing a similar transformation. As bases for decision making, parents and community leaders should be aware of all new curricula, the problems and needs, and possible solutions to be utilized in implementating changes and evaluating results.

What then is the new approach in physical education for school-age children and youth? Through the years, physical education curricula have progressed through three major stages. The major emphasis of these stages has been health-physical fitness; skills in games, sports, and dance and recreational participation; and socialization—working, playing and interacting with others according to rules and a sense of fair play. The emergent concepts and ideas of a rapidly developing fourth stage integrate these earlier stages with an emphasis on an understanding of self, movement, and the environment and the ways in which individuals may organize their own physical activity to insure optimal development of their physical potential to accomplish the significant purposes of their lives. The ultimate goal, then, of present-day physical education is the transformation of the whole child into a fully functioning integrated person—a physically educated person.

The new curriculum, the new image of physical education, from kinder-

TABLE 20.2 Educational Goals

Focuses	For Desired Outcomes
1. Self-image	A more realistic body image for building a wholesome self-concept throughout life: How I look, What I can do, How I do it, and Why I do it.
2. Controlling and adjusting to the environment	Efficiency of movement in fundamental movement patterns and specified skills in games, sports, dance, and exercise deemed of worth in the culture for work and play.
3. Survival	Improved functioning of the heart, lungs, muscles, and other organic systems to respond effectively to increased demands and stresses.
4. Play	Joy, enthusiasm, creativity, imagination, emotional tone, and stability; working, playing, and interacting with others according to the sense of fair play; socially approved patterns of behavior.

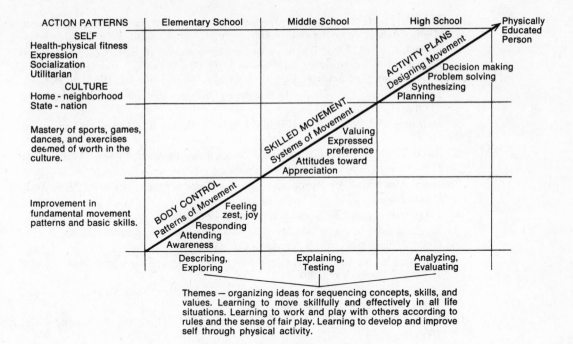

Figure 20.4 Schema of Physical Education

garten through twelfth grade is an integrated program organized around underlying themes and carefully ordered concepts, skills, and values, growing in complexity as the child advances into adolescence. For all children this provides a firm foundation on which they may be guided to a better understanding of self, movement, and the environment. Each teaching-learning situation enables the child to explore and describe his universe—self, movement, others, objects, and events in his environment; to seek orderly explanations of the objects, others, and events explored; and to test his explanations through a variety of situations and activities. The learning experiences focus on developing understandings, skills, and values of purposeful physical activity or movement patterns throughout life.

Two new curricula approaches utilizing this conceptual structure are indicated in the reference material. Figure 20.4 illustrates such an approach to physical education schematically.

As an adult, a potential mother, and a potential community leader—if you are truly physically educated—you should be aware of such new approaches in physical education programs in your school and community.

references and sources for additional reading

1. "Exercise and Fitness," *Journal of the American Medical Association*, Vol. 188 (May 4, 1964), 433–36.

2. Wessel, J., *et al.*, "Age and Physiological Responses to Exercise in Women 20–69 Years of Age," *Journal of Gerontology*, Vol. 23 (July 1968), 269.

3. Wessel, J., *et al.*, "Age Trends of Various Components of Body Composition and Functional Characteristics in Women Aged 20–69 Years," *Annals of the New York Academy of Science*, Part II, Vol. 110 (September 26, 1963), 608.

4. Kraus, H., and W. Raab, *Hypokinetic Disease*. Springfield, Ill.: Charles C Thomas, Publisher, 1961.

5. Steinhaus, A., *How to Keep Fit and Like It*. Chicago: The Dartnell Corporation, 1963.

6. *Adult Physical Fitness*. President's Council on Physical Fitness. Washington, D.C., Government Printing Office, 1966.

7. *Royal Canadian Air Force Exercise Plans for Physical Fitness*. New York: Pocket Books, 1961.

8. Cooper, K.H., and K. Brown, *Aerobics*. New York: M. Evans & Co., Inc., 1968.

9. Breckenridge, M., and M. Murphy, *Growth and Development of the Young Child*. Philadelphia: W. B. Saunders Co., 1964.

10. Espenscade, A., and H. Eckert, *Motor Development*. Columbus, Ohio: Charles E. Merrill Books, Inc., 1967.

11. Piaget, Jean, *The Origins of Intelligence in Children*. New York: International Universities Press, 1966, pp. 21–341.

12. Hebb, D.O., *A Textbook of Psychology*. Philadelphia: W. B. Saunders Co., 1958.

13. Delacato, C.H., *The Diagnosis and Treatment of Speech and Reading Problems*. Springfield, Ill.: Charles C Thomas, Publisher, 1963.

14. Kephart, N.C., *The Slow Learner in the Classroom*. Columbus, Ohio: Charles E. Merrill Books, Inc., 1962.

15. Smith, Hope, "Motor Activity and Perceptual Development," *Journal of Health, Physical Education, and Recreation* (February 1968) 28.

16. Steinhaus, A., *Toward Understanding Health and Physical Education*. Dubuque, Iowa: William C. Brown Company, Publishers, 1963.

17. Bower, Eli, "Play's the Thing," *Today's Education* (September 1968), 10–16.

18. ———, *Fostering Maximum Growth in Children*. Department of Elementary Kindergarten-Nursery Education, National Education Association, Washington, D.C., 1969.

19. *This Is Physical Education*, American Association for Health, Physical Education, and Recreation, Washington, D.C.

20. Wessel, J., *Fitness for the Modern Teen-Ager*. New York: The Ronald Press Company, 1963.

21. *Health Education. A Conceptual Approach to Curriculum Design*, School Health Education Study. St. Paul, Minnesota, 1967.

22. *The Battle Creek Physical Education Project—Title III*, Physical Education Department, Battle Creek, Michigan, 1969.

appendix A

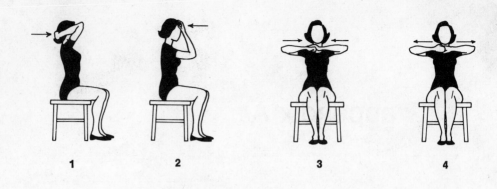

Skeletal Muscles and Body Regions

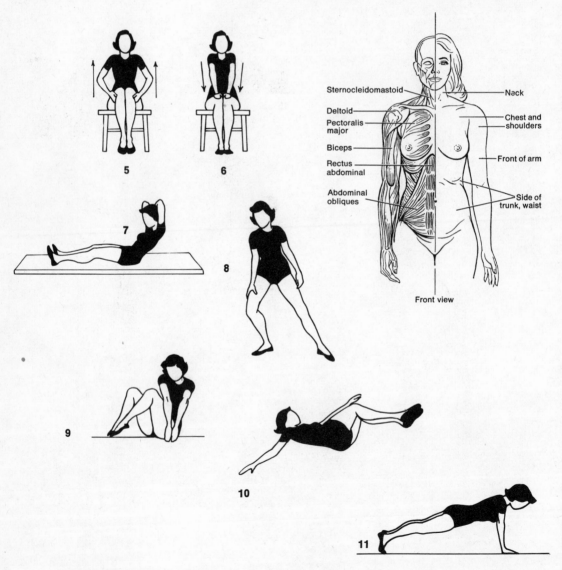

Sternocleidomastoid

Deltoid

Pectoralis major

Biceps

Rectus abdominal

Abdominal obliques

Neck

Chest and shoulders

Front of arm

Side of trunk, waist

Front view

chart 1: trunk, arms, shoulders

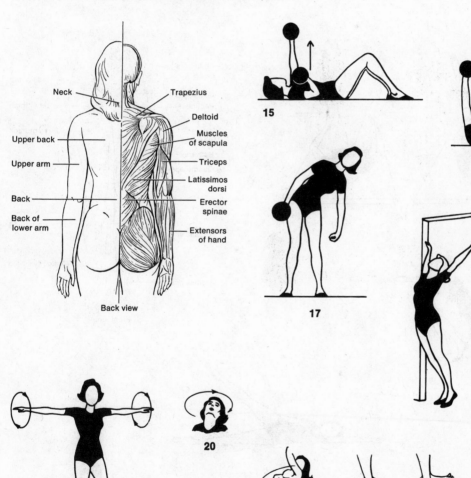

Neck
Trapezius
Deltoid
Upper back
Muscles of scapula
Upper arm
Triceps
Latissimos dorsi
Back
Erector spine
Back of lower arm
Extensors of hand

Back view

1

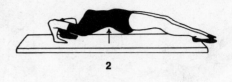

2

Skeletal Muscles and Body Regions

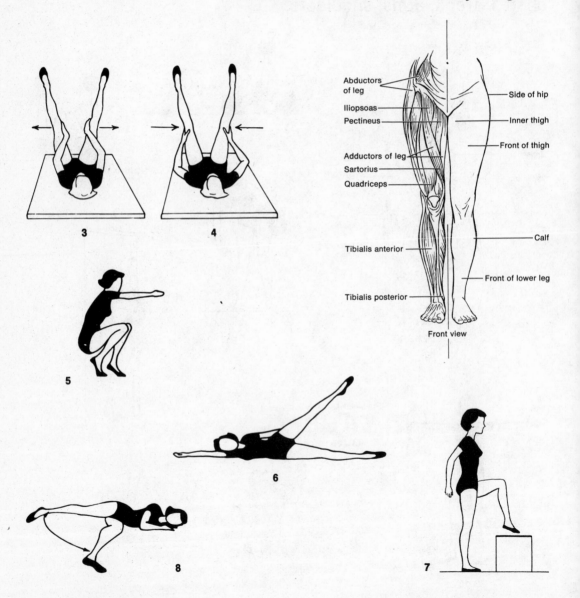

3

4

Abductors of leg

Iliopsoas

Pectineus

Adductors of leg

Sartorius

Quadriceps

Side of hip

Inner thigh

Front of thigh

Tibialis anterior

Tibialis posterior

Calf

Front of lower leg

Front view

5

6

7

8

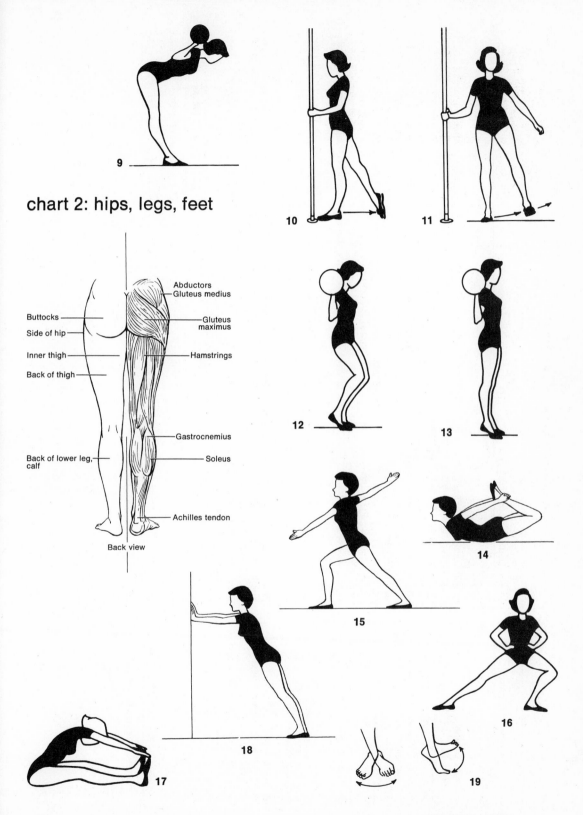

chart 2: hips, legs, feet

Back view

- Abductors
- Gluteus medius
- Buttocks
- Gluteus maximus
- Side of hip
- Inner thigh
- Hamstrings
- Back of thigh
- Gastrocnemius
- Back of lower leg, calf
- Soleus
- Achilles tendon

9

10

11

12

13

14

15

16

17

18

19

Exercises Accompanying Muscle Chart 1*

Exercise Movement	Primary Muscles Exercised and Body Regions Developed	Exercise Movement	Primary Muscles Exercised and Body Regions Developed
Isometrics		**Weight Lifting**	
1. Neck flexion	Sternomastoid—front of neck	13. Shoulder extension	Posterior deltoid, infraspintus, teres major—upper back, back of shoulder or scapular muscles
2. Neck extension	Erector spinae, trapezius—upper back	14. Shoulder extension, elbow flexion, and scapular adduction	Latissimus dorsi, teres major, trapezius, rhomboids, biceps and brachialis—upper back, back of shoulder, front of upper arm
3. Shoulder horizontal flexion	Pectoralis major, serratus anterior—front of chest	15. Shoulder flexion, elbow extension, and scapular abduction	Deltoid, pectoralis major, serratus anterior, triceps—chest, front of shoulder, back of upper arm
4. Shoulder horizontal extension-abduction	Trapezius, rhomboids—upper back	16. Shoulder horizontal flexion abduction	Pectoralis major, serratus anterior—front of chest
5. Elbow flexion	Biceps, brachialis—front, upper arm	17. Trunk lateral flexion	Obliques—Side of trunk (waist)
6. Elbow extension	Triceps—back of upper arm	**Flexibility**	
7. Trunk flexion	Obliques, rectus abdominis—front of trunk (abdominals)	18. Shoulder stretcher	Pectoralis major, serratus anterior, latissimus dorsi, teres major—front of chest, back
8. Trunk lateral flexion	Obliques—Side of trunk (waist)	19. Arm circle	Pectoralis major, serratus anterior—front of chest
Calisthenics		20. Head circle	Sternomastoid, trapezius, erector spinae—front of the neck and upper back
9. Trunk flexion (curl)	Obliques, rectus abdominis—front of trunk (abdominals)	21. Trunk twister	Obliques, erector spinae—trunk (side, front, back)
10. Pelvic rotation	Obliques—Side of the trunk (waist)	22. Trunk bender	Erector spinae—upper and lower back
11. Shoulder horizontal flexion-adduction	Pectoralis major, serratus anterior, triceps—chest, back of upper arm		
12. Trunk extension with scapular adduction	Erector spinae, trapezius, rhomboids—Trunk and upper back		

*The numbers are keyed with those in the illustration on pages 272-73

Exercises Accompanying Muscle Chart 2*

Exercise Movement	Primary Muscles Affected and Body Regions Developed
Isometrics	
1. Knee flexion	Quadriceps—*Front of thigh*
2. Trunk extension	Erector spinae, hamstrings, gluteus maximus—*back, buttocks, neck regions*
3. Hip adduction	Adductor longus, adductor magnus, pectineus—*Inner thigh*
4. Hip abduction	Gluteus medius, gluteus minimus tensor fasciae latae—*Side of hip*
Calisthenics	
5. Leg flexion	Quadriceps, gastrocnemius, sartorius gluteus maximus—*front of thigh, calves*
6. Hip abduction	Adductor longus, adductor magnus—*inner thigh*
7. Leg extension	Quadriceps, gastrocnemius, soleus, gluteus maximus—*Front of thigh, calves*
8. Leg flexion and extension	Iliopsoas, gluteus maximus, gluteus gluidus, quadriceps—*Side of hip, buttocks*
Weight Lifting	
9. Trunk flexion	Erector spinae, gluteus maximus—*back, buttocks*
10. Leg extension	Gluteus maximus, hamstrings—*buttocks, back of thigh*
11. Leg abduction	Gluteus medius, tensor fasciae latae—*Side of hip*
12. Leg flexion	Quadriceps, gastrocnemius, soleus, gluteus maximus—*front of thigh, calves*
13. Ankle extension	Gastrocnemius, soleus—*calves*
Flexibility	
14. Knee flexion and hip extension	Quadriceps, iliopsoas—*Front of thigh and hip*
15. Hip extension	Iliopsoas, pectineus—*Front of hip*
16. Hip abduction	Adductor longus, adductor magnus—*inner thigh*
17. Trunk flexion	Hamstrings, erector spinae—*Back of lower leg, back*
18. Ankle flexion	Gastrocnemius, soleus—*calves*
19. Foot circling with toe flexion	Anterior tibial, posterior tibial, peroneals, long toe flexions and extensions—*Front and side of ankle foot*

*The numbers are keyed with those in the illustrations on pages 274-75

appendix A 277

Activity	General Pace	M.S.	M.E.	CV-R E.	Flx.	P-S.	Energy Expenditure Rating
Volleyball	Slow to moderate		3		2	1	Low to medium
Walking on level	2.7 m.p.h.		2	1			Low
Playing ping pong	Moderate		3		2	1	Low to medium
Swimming-backstroke	Pleasure-25 yd. per min.		1	2	3	4	Medium
Sailing						1	Low to medium
Swimming-breaststroke	Pleasure-20 yd. per min.		1	2	3	4	Medium
Calisthenics	Moderate to hard	2	3	4	1		Medium
Bicycling	Level roads-moderate		1	2		3	Medium
Golfing	Slow to moderate		3	4	2	1	Low to medium
Gardening	Slow		3		2	1	Low to medium
Walking	Level-4.5 m.p.h.		2	1		3	Medium
Tennis	Moderate		3	4	2	1	Medium
Basketball	Moderate		1	3	2	4	Medium to high
Swimming-crawl	Pleasure-45 yd. per min.		1	2	3	4	Medium to high
Swimming-breaststroke	Pleasure-40 yd. per min.		1	2	3	4	Medium to high
Modern dancing	Pleasure		3	4	2	1	Medium to high
Mountain climbing	Moderate	3	1	2		4	Medium to high
Skating	Moderate		1		2	3	Medium to high
Squash/Handball	Moderate to hard		1	2	3	4	Medium to high
Skiing	Moderate	3	1	4	2	1	Medium to high
Weight training	Moderate to hard	1	2	4	3		Medium to high
Circuit training	Moderate to hard	1	2	3	2		Medium to high
Distance running	Moderate		2	1	3		High
Sprinting	Repeated	3	1	2	4		High

M.S. = Muscular Strength
M.E. = Muscular Endurance
CV-R E. = Cardiovascular-respiratory Endurance
Flx. = Flexibility
P-S = Psycho-Social Benefits

appendix B

The values shown in the table that follows are in terms of common units of measure: one cup, one ounce, or a piece of specified size. The quantities of foods thus shown can be converted readily to particular serving portions. The one-cup amount, for example, can be reduced or multiplied in estimating servings of various sizes. A dash (—) indicates a lack of reliable evidence; tr. (trace) means a value too small to be measured. The figures for food energy (calories) have been rounded off to the nearest 5 calories.

The source of the data on pp. 280-309 is the *Agricultural Handbook* No. 8: Composition of Foods—Raw, Processed, Prepared, compiled by the Agricultural Research Service, U.S. Department of Agriculture (revised December 1963).

Nutritive Values of Foods

Food	Weight gm.	Approximate Measure	Calories	Protein gm.	Fat gm.	Total Carbohydrate gm.	Water gm.	Minerals Calcium mg.	Iron mg.	Vitamins Vitamin A I.U.	Thiamine mg.	Riboflavin mg.	Niacin mg.	Ascorbic Acid mg.
Almonds, shelled	15	12-15 nuts	90	3.0	8.0	3	1	35	0.7	0	0.04	0.14	0.5	tr.
Apples														
Fresh, E.P.	150	1 med, large, 3 in. diam.	90	0.3	0.9	22	127	11	0.5	140	0.05	0.03	0.2	6
Baked, unpared	115	1 large, 2 tbsp. sugar	195	0.5	0.2	49		12	0.6	180	0.04	0.05	0.3	2
Apple juice, fresh or canned	100	1/2 cup, scant	50	0.1	tr.	12	88	6	0.6	—	0.01	0.02	0.1	1
Applesauce														
Sweetened	125	1/2 cup	115	0.3	0.1	30	95	5	0.6	50	0.03	0.01	tr.	1
Unsweetened	125	1/2 cup	50	0.3	0.3	13	111	5	0.6	50	0.03	0.01	tr.	1
Apricots														
Fresh	100	2-3 medium	50	1.0	0.2	13	85	17	0.5	2700	0.03	0.04	0.6	10
Canned, heavy syrup pack	120	4 halves, 2 tbsp. juice	105	0.7	0.1	26	92	13	0.4	1990	0.02	0.02	0.5	5
water pack	100	4 halves, 2 tbsp. juice	40	0.7	0.1	10	89	12	0.3	1830	0.02	0.02	0.4	4
Dried, sulfured, raw	30	4-6 medium halves	80	1.5	0.2	20	8	20	1.7	3270	tr.	0.05	1.0	4
unsweetened (cooked)	140	1/2 cup fruit and liquid	120	2.0	0.3	30	106	31	2.5	4200	tr.	0.07	1.4	4
Apricot nectar, canned	125	1/2 cup	70	0.4	0.1	18	106	11	0.3	1180	0.01	0.01	0.3	4
Artichokes, French, A.P.	200	1 large, cooked	50	5.5	0.4	20	173	102	2.2	300	0.14	0.08	1.4	16

Food	Weight gm.	Approximate Measure	Calories	Protein gm.	Fat gm.	Total Carbohydrate gm.	Water gm.	Minerals Calcium mg.	Iron mg.	Vitamin A I.U.	Vitamins Thiamine mg.	Riboflavin mg.	Niacin mg.	Ascorbic Acid mg.
Asparagus														
Fresh, green, cooked	100	1/2 cup cut, 6-7 spears	20	2.0	0.2	4	94	21	0.6	900	0.16	0.18	1.4	26
Canned, green	100	1/2 cup cut, 6-7 spears	20	2.0	0.4	3	93	19	1.9	800	0.06	0.10	0.8	15
Avocados														
Fuerte, California	100	1/2 pear, about 4 in. long	170	2.0	17.0	6	74	10	0.6	290	0.11	0.20	1.6	14
Florida	125	1/2 pear, about 4 in. long	160	2.0	14.0	11	98	13	0.8	360	0.14	0.25	2.0	18
Bacon, broiled, drained	25	3 strips, crisp	155	8.0	13.0	0.8	2	4	0.8	0	0.13	0.09	1.3	—
Beans														
Canned, with pork and tomato sauce	130	1/2 cup	160	8.0	3.0	25	92	70	2.3	170	0.10	0.04	0.8	3
Canned, with pork and sweet sauce	130	1/2 cup	195	8.0	6.0	27	86	82	3.0	—	0.08	0.05	0.7	—
Lima, fresh, boiled	80	1/2 cup, drained	90	6.0	0.4	16	57	38	2.0	220	0.14	0.08	1.0	14
Red, canned, solids and liquids	125	1/2 cup	115	7.0	0.5	21	95	36	2.3	tr.	0.06	0.05	0.8	—
Snap, green, fresh or frozen, cooked	100	3/4 cup, drained	25	1.5	0.2	5	92	50	0.6	540	0.07	0.09	0.5	12
Snap, green, canned	100	3/4 cup, drained	25	1.0	0.2	5	92	45	1.5	470	0.03	0.05	0.3	4
Soy, dry weight	30	1/2 cup, scant, after cooking	120	10.0	5.0	10		68	2.5	20	0.33	0.09	0.7	—

Beef

Food	(g)	Approximate measure												
Corned, canned	85	3 slices, 3 x 2 x 1/4 in.	185	21.5	10.0	0	50	17	3.7	—	0.02	0.20	2.9	0
hash, canned	115	1/2 cup	230	10.0	17.0	9		30	1.4	tr.	0.03	0.16	3.3	0
Dried, creamed	120	1/2 cup	210	16.0	13.0	6		106	2.1	440	0.07	0.30	1.6	0
Hamburger, broiled market ground	85	4 from pound	245	20.5	17.0	0	46	9	1.7	30	0.08	0.18	4.6	—
lean ground	85	4 from pound	185	23.0	10.0	0	51	10	3.0	20	0.08	0.20	5.1	—
Roast, chuck, braised or pot roasted	100	2 slices, 4 x 1-1/2 x 1/2 in.	375	24.0	30.0	0	45	10	3.1	60	0.04	0.19	3.8	—
oven, relatively lean	100	1 slice, 4-1/2 x 3 x 1/2 in.	345	23.5	27.0	0	48	10	3.1	50	0.06	0.18	4.3	—
rib, choice grade	100	1 slice, 4-1/2 x 3 x 1/2 in.	440	20.0	39.0	0	40	9	2.6	80	0.05	0.15	3.6	—
Steak, round, broiled	100	1 piece, 4-1/2 x 3-1/2 x 1/2 in.	260	28.5	15.0	0	55	12	3.5	30	0.08	0.22	5.6	—
sirloin, broiled	100	1 piece, 4-1/2 x 2-1/2 x 1 in.	410	22.0	35.0	0	42	10	2.9	60	0.06	0.18	4.6	—
Beets, cooked or canned	85	1/2 cup, drained solids	30	1.0	tr.	6	77	12	0.4	20	0.03	0.03	0.3	5
Biscuits, baking powder, from mix	100	3 biscuits, 2 in. diam.	325	7.0	9.0	52	29	68	2.3	tr.	0.27	0.25	2.0	tr.
Blackberries, dewberries, boysenberries, and youngberries, fresh	100	2/3 cup	60	1.0	0.9	13	85	32	0.9	200	0.03	0.04	0.4	21
Blueberries, fresh	100	2/3 cup	60	0.7	0.5	15	83	15	1.0	100	0.03	0.06	0.5	14

Bread

Food	(g)	Approximate measure												
Boston brown	100	3 slices, 1/2 in. thick	210	5.5	1.0	46	45	90	1.9	70	0.11	0.06	1.2	0

Food	Weight gm.	Approximate Measure	Calories	Protein gm.	Fat gm.	Total Carbohydrate gm.	Water gm.	Minerals Calcium mg.	Iron mg.	Vitamin A I.U.	Vitamins Thiamine mg.	Riboflavin mg.	Niacin mg.	Ascorbic Acid mg.
Corn, from mix	40	1 piece, 2 in. square	95	2.5	3.0	13	20	34	0.5	110	0.06	0.08	0.5	tr.
French or Vienna, enriched	23	1 slice	70	2.0	0.7	13	7	10	0.5	tr.	0.06	0.05	0.6	tr.
Raisin	23	1 slice	60	1.5	0.6	12	8	16	0.3	tr.	0.01	0.02	0.2	tr.
Rye, American	23	1 slice	55	2.0	0.3	12	8	17	0.5	0	0.04	0.02	0.3	0
White, unenriched	23	1 slice	60	2.0	0.7	12	8	19	0.2	tr.	0.02	0.02	0.3	tr.
enriched	23	1 slice	60	2.0	0.7	12	8	19	0.6	tr.	0.06	0.05	0.6	tr.
Whole wheat	23	1 slice	55	2.5	0.7	11	8	23	0.5	tr.	0.06	0.03	0.7	tr.
Broccoli	100	2/3 cup, boiled, drained	25	3.0	0.3	5	91	88	0.8	2500	0.09	0.20	0.8	90
Brussel sprouts	70	5-6 sprouts, boiled drained	25	3.0	0.3	4	62	22	0.8	360	0.06	0.10	0.6	61
Butter	10	1 pat, 45 per pound	70	tr.	8.0	tr.	2	2	0	330	—	—	—	0
	14	1 tbsp.	100	tr.	11.0	tr.	2	3	0	460	—	—	—	0
Cabbage, headed														
Raw	100	1 cup, shredded	25	1.5	0.2	5	92	49	0.4	130	0.05	0.05	0.3	47
Cooked	100	1-1/3 cup	20	1.0	0.2	4	94	42	0.3	120	0.02	0.02	0.1	24
Cakes														
Angel, from mix	40	2 in. sector of 8-in. cake	105	2.5	0.1	24	14	38	0.1	0	tr.	0.04	tr.	0
Chocolate, fudge icing	100	2 in. sector of 8-in. cake	370	4.5	16.0	56	22	70	1.0	160	0.02	0.10	0.2	tr.

Food		Measure												
Gingerbread, from mix	55	2 x 2 inches	150	1.5	4.0	28	20	50	0.9	tr.	0.02	0.05	0.4	tr.
Plain cake or cupcake, iced	100	2 in. sector of 8-in. cake or 2 medium cupcakes	370	3.5	12.0	63	21	50	0.3	200	0.02	0.07	0.1	tr.
Pound cake, plain	30	1 slice, 2-3/4 x 3 x 5/8 in.	125	2.0	6.0	16	6	12	0.2	90	0.01	0.03	0.1	tr.
Yellow cake, iced, from mix	100	2 in. sector of 8-in. cake	335	4.0	11.0	58	26	91	0.6	140	0.02	0.08	0.2	tr.
Candy														
Caramel, plain or chocolate	30	1 oz.	120	1.0	3.0	23	2	44	0.4	3	0.01	0.05	0.1	tr.
Chocolate, milk, plain	30	1 oz.	155	2.5	10.0	17	0.3	68	0.3	80	0.02	0.10	0.1	tr.
with almonds	30	1 oz.	160	3.0	11.0	15	0.5	69	0.5	70	0.02	0.12	0.2	tr.
Fudge, with nuts	30	1 oz.	130	1.0	5.0	21	23	24	0.4	tr.	0.01	0.03	0.1	tr.
Hard	30	1 oz.	115	0.0	0.3	29	0.4	6	0.6	0	0	0	0	0
Marshmallow	30	1 oz.	100	0.6	tr.	24	5	5	0.5	0	0	tr.	tr.	0
Peanut brittle	30	1 oz.	125	2.0	3.0	24	0.6	11	0.7	0	0.05	0.01	1.0	0
Cantaloupe, See Melons														
Carrots														
Raw	50	1 carrot, 5-1/2 x 1 in. or 1/2 cup grated	20	0.6	0.1	5	44	19	0.4	5500	0.03	0.03	0.3	4
Boiled, drained	100	2/3 cup, diced	30	0.9	0.2	7	91	33	0.6	10500	0.05	0.05	0.5	6
Cauliflower														
Raw	100	1 cup flower buds	25	2.5	0.2	5	91	25	1.1	60	0.11	0.10	0.7	78
Boiled, drained	100	3/4 cup	20	2.5	0.2	4	93	21	0.7	60	0.09	0.08	0.6	55

Food	Weight gm.	Approximate Measure	Calories	Protein gm.	Fat gm.	Total Carbohydrate gm.	Water gm.	Calcium mg.	Iron mg.	Vitamin A I.U.	Thiamine mg.	Riboflavin mg.	Niacin mg.	Ascorbic Acid mg.
Celery														
Raw	100	2 lg. stalks or 1 cup diced	15	0.9	0.1	4	94	39	0.3	270	0.03	0.03	0.3	9
Boiled, drained	100	3/4 cup, diced	15	0.8	0.1	3	95	31	0.2	240	0.02	0.03	0.3	6
Cereals														
Ready to eat														
Bran Flakes, 40%, added nutrients	30	3/4 cup	90	3.0	0.5	24	0.9	21	1.3	0	0.12	0.05	1.9	0
Corn Flakes, added nutrients	25	1 cup	95	2.0	0.1	21	1	4	0.4	0	0.11	0.02	0.5	0
Rice, puffed, added nutrients	14	1 cup	55	0.8	0.1	13	0.5	3	0.3	0	0.06	0.01	0.6	0
Wheat Flakes, added nutrients	25	1 cup	90	3.0	0.4	20	0.9	10	1.1	0	0.16	0.04	1.2	0
Wheat, puffed, added nutrients	12	1 cup	45	2.0	0.2	9	0.4	3	0.5	0	0.07	0.03	0.9	0
Wheat, shredded	40	1 large biscuit	140	4.0	0.8	32	3	17	1.4	0	0.09	0.04	1.8	0
Cooked (figured from 1 oz. dry weight)														
Cornmeal, white or yellow unenriched	120	1/2 cup	60	1.0	0.2	13	105	1	0.2	70	0.02	0.01	0.1	0
enriched	120	1/2 cup	60	1.0	0.2	13	105	1	0.5	70	0.07	0.05	0.6	0

Food													
Corn grits, white, degerm., unenriched	120	1/2 cup	1.0	0.1	13	105	1	0.1	tr.	0.02	0.01	0.2	0
enriched	120	1/2 cup	1.0	0.1	13	105	1	0.4	tr.	0.05	0.04	0.5	0
Oatmeal	65	2/3-3/4 cup	2.0	1.0	12	104	11	0.7	0	0.10	0.02	0.1	0
Wheat, Cream of, reg. (Farina)													
unenriched	50	2/3-3/4 cup	2.0	0.1	10	107	5	0.2	0	0.01	0.01	0.1	0
enriched	50	2/3-3/4 cup	2.0	0.1	10	107	5	0.4	0	0.05	0.04	0.5	0
Wheat, whole meal (e.g., Ralston)	55	1/2 cup	2.0	0.4	11	105	8	0.6	0	0.07	0.02	0.7	0
Cheeses													
Natural													
Cheddar, American	30	1 oz. or 4 tbsp., grated	7.5	10.0	0.6	11	225	0.3	390	0.01	0.14	tr.	0
Cottage, large or small curd, creamed	55	1/4 cup or 2 rounded tbsp.	7.5	2.0	2.0	43	52	0.2	90	0.02	0.14	tr.	0
uncreamed	55	1/4 cup or 2 rounded tbsp.	9.5	0.2	2.0	44	50	0.2	5	0.02	0.15	tr.	0
Cream	110	1 oz. or 2 tbsp.	2.5	11.0	0.6	15	19	0.1	460	0.01	0.07	tr.	0
Swiss, domestic	110	1 oz.	8.5	8.0	0.5	12	278	0.3	340	tr.	0.12	tr.	0
Pasteurized processed													
American	110	1 oz.	7.0	9.0	0.6	12	209	0.3	370	0.01	0.12	tr.	0
Cheese food (e.g., Velveeta)	95	1 oz.	6.0	7.0	2.0	13	171	0.2	290	0.01	0.17	tr.	0

Food	Weight gm.	Approximate Measure	Calories	Protein gm.	Fat gm.	Total Carbohydrate gm.	Water gm.	Minerals Calcium mg.	Iron mg.	Vitamins Vitamin A I.U.	Thiamine mg.	Riboflavin mg.	Niacin mg.	Ascorbic Acid mg.
Cheese spread, American	30	1 oz.	85	5.0	6.0	3.0	15	170	0.2	260	tr.	0.16	tr.	0
Cherries														
Raw, sweet	100	15 large, 20-25 small	70	1.5	0.3	17	80	22	0.4	110	0.05	0.06	0.4	10
Red, canned, heavy syrup	120	1/2 cup, pitted, with syrup	95	1.0	0.2	25	94	18	0.4	70	0.02	0.02	0.2	4
Red, canned, water pack	100	1/2 cup, pitted with juice	50	1.0	0.2	12	87	15	0.3	60	0.02	0.02	0.2	3
Chicken														
broiled	100	3 1/2 oz., flesh only	135	24.0	4.0	0	71	9	1.7	90	0.05	0.19	8.8	—
canned, flesh only	100	3 1/2 oz.	200	21.5	12.0	0	65	21	1.5	230	0.04	0.12	4.4	4
Creamed	177	3/4 cup	310	26.5				124	1.6	490	0.06	0.27	5.7	tr.
Fryer, breast	100	Approx. 1/2 breast, fried	205	32.5	6.0	2	58	12	1.7	90	0.05	0.22	14.7	—
thigh and drumstick	100	1 of each, med. size, fried	235	29.0	11.0	3	56	13	2.3	200	0.06	0.48	6.8	—
Roasted	100	3-1/2 oz., flesh and skin	250	27.0	15.0	0	57	11	1.8	420	0.08	0.14	8.2	—
Chickpeas or *garbanzos*, dry weight	30	1/2 cup, after cooking	110	6.0	1.0	18	—	45	2.1	15	0.10	0.03	0.6	—
Chickory or *endive*, curly	25	10 small leaves	5	0.5	0.1	1	23	22	0.2	1000	0.02	0.03	0.1	6
Chili con carne, canned														
With beans	250	1 cup	335	19.0	15.0	31	181	80	4.3	150	0.08	0.18	3.3	—

Food		Measure												
Without beans	250	1 cup	500	26.0	37.0	15	167	95	3.5	380	0.05	0.30	5.5	—
Chocolate (beverage) all milk	220	1 cup, small, 6 oz. milk	210	7.0	8.0	32	—	222	0.5	295	0.08	0.32	0.1	1
Chocolate, bitter or baking	30	1 oz. or 1 square	150	3.0	16.0	9	1	23	2.0	20	0.02	0.07	0.5	0
Clams, canned, solids and liquid	100	1/2 cup	50	8.0	0.7	3	86	55	4.1	—	0.01	0.11	1.0	—
Cocoa (beverage), all milk	200	1 cup, small, 6 oz. milk	174	7.0	9.0	20	—	224	0.9	295	0.08	0.34	0.3	2
Cola type beverages, See *Soft Drinks*														
Coconut, dried, sweetened	15	2 tbsp., shredded	80	0.5	6.0	8	1	2	0.3	0	0.01	tr.	0.1	—
Collards, boiled, drained	100	1/2 cup	30	2.5	0.6	5	91	152	0.6	5400	0.14	0.20	1.2	46
Cookies, assorted, commercial	25	3 small or 1 large, 3 in. diameter	120	1.5	5.0	18	1	9	0.2	20	0.01	0.01	0.1	tr.
Corn, sweet														
Fresh	100	1 small ear, cooked	90	3.5	1.0	21	74	3	0.6	400	0.12	0.10	1.4	9
Canned, drained	100	1/2 cup, scant	85	2.5	0.8	20	76	5	0.5	350	0.03	0.05	0.9	4
Cream style, canned	100	1/2 cup, scant	80	2.0	0.6	20	76	3	0.6	330	0.03	0.05	1.0	5
Cornmeal See under *Cereals*														
Corn syrup, light or dark	20	1 tbsp.	60	0	0	15	5	9	0.8	0	0	0	0	0
Cowpeas or blackeye peas,														
Immature, fresh	160	1 cup, cooked	170	13.0	1.0	29	115	38	3.4	560	0.48	0.18	2.2	27
Mature, dried	125	1/2 cup, cooked	95	6.5	0.4	17	100	21	1.6	12	0.20	0.05	0.5	—
Crabmeat, canned or cooked	100	5/8 cup	100	17.5	3.0	1	77	45	0.8	—	0.08	0.08	1.9	—

Food	Weight gm.	Approximate Measure	Calories	Protein gm.	Fat gm.	Total Carbo-hydrate gm.	Water gm.	Calcium mg.	Iron mg.	Vitamin A I.U.	Thia-mine mg.	Ribo-flavin mg.	Niacin mg.	Ascorbic Acid mg.
Crackers														
Graham, plain	7	1 cracker, 2-1/2 in. sq.	25	0.6	0.7	5	0.4	3	0.1	0	tr.	0.01	0.1	0
Ry-Krisp	13	2 wafers, 1-7/8 x 3-1/2 in.	45	1.5	0.2	10	0.8	7	0.5	0	0.04	0.03	0.2	0
Saltines	4	1 cracker, 2 in. square	17	0.4	0.5	3	0.2	1	0.1	0	tr.	tr.	tr.	0
Soda, plain or oyster	10	2 crackers, 2-1/2 in. sq. or 10 oyster	45	0.9	1.0	7	0.4	2	0.2	0	tr.	0.01	0.1	0
Cranberry, jelly, sweetened	20	1 level tbsp.	30	tr.	tr.	8	12	1	tr.	4	tr.	tr.	tr.	tr.
Sauce, unstrained	15	1 level tbsp.	25	tr.	tr.	7	8	1	tr.	3	tr.	tr.	tr.	tr.
Cream														
Half-and-half	60	1/4 cup or 4 tbsp.	80	2.0	7.0	3	48	65	tr.	290	0.02	0.10	0.1	1
Heavy or whipping	60	1/4 cup or 4 tbsp.	210	1.5	23.0	2	34	45	tr.	920	0.01	0.07	tr.	1
Light, coffee or table	60	1/4 cup or 4 tbsp.	130	2.0	12.0	3	43	61	tr.	500	0.02	0.09	0.06	1
Cucumber, raw, pared	50	1/2 medium	7	0.3	0.1	2	48	9	0.2	tr.	0.02	0.02	0.1	6
Custard See under *Puddings*														
Dates, dried or fresh	100	1/2 cup pitted or 12 average	275	2.0	0.5	73	23	59	3.0	50	0.09	0.10	2.2	0
Doughnuts														
Cake type	30	1 average	120	1.5	6.0	15	7	12	0.4	24	0.05	0.05	0.4	tr.
Yeast	30	1 average	125	2.0	8.0	11	9	11	0.5	20	0.05	0.05	0.4	0

Eggs

Food	Weight (g)	Measure											
Raw, whole, E.P.	50	1 large, 24 oz per doz.	80	6.5	6.0	0.5	37	27	1.2	590	0.06	0.15	0.1	0
white	32	1 white	16	3.5	tr.	0.3	29	3	tr.	0	tr.	0.09	tr.	0
yolk	18	1 yolk	64	3.0	5.5	3.1	9	24	0.9	580	0.04	0.07	tr.	0
Omelet or scrambled	100	2 small eggs with milk	175	11.0	13.0	2.0	72	80	1.7	1080	0.08	0.28	0.1	0
Eggplant, raw	100	2 slices or 1/2 cup pieces	25	1.0	0.2	6	92	12	0.7	10	0.05	0.05	0.6	5
Fats														
Cooking, vegetable	100	1/2 cup	885	0	100.0	0	0	0	0	—	0	0	0	0
solid or oil	12.5	1 tbsp.	110	0	13.0	0	0	0	0	—	0	0	0	0
Figs														
Fresh	100	2 large or 3 small	80	1.0	0.3	20	78	35	0.6	80	0.06	0.05	0.4	2
Canned, heavy syrup	100	3 figs and 2 tbsp. syrup	85	0.5	0.2	22	77	13	0.4	30	0.03	0.03	0.2	1
Dried	20	1 large	55	0.9	0.3	14	5	25	0.6	20	0.02	0.02	0.1	0
Fish														
Cod, steak, baked	100	4 oz, before cooking	170	28.5	5.0	0	65	31	1.0	180	0.08	0.11	3.0	—
Fish sticks	110	5 sticks, or 4 oz., cooked	195	18.0	10.0	7	72	12	0.4	0	0.04	0.08	1.8	—
Flounder or sole	100	4 oz, before cooking	200	30.0	8.0	0	58	23	1.4	—	0.07	0.08	2.5	—
Haddock, cooked, fried	100	4 oz, before cooking	165	19.5	6.0	6	66	40	1.2	—	0.04	0.07	3.2	2
Halibut, broiled	100	3-1/2 oz, cooked	171	25.0	7.0	0	67	16	0.8	680	0.05	0.07	8.3	—
Mackerel, Atlantic	100	3-1/2 oz, cooked with butter	235	22.0	16.0	0	62	6	1.2	530	0.15	0.27	7.6	—
Salmon, fresh, broiled	100	3-1/2 oz, cooked	180	27.0	7.0	0	63	—	1.2	160	0.16	0.06	9.8	0

Food	Weight gm.	Approximate Measure	Calories	Protein gm.	Fat gm.	Total Carbohydrate gm.	Water gm.	Minerals		Vitamins				
								Calcium mg.	Iron mg.	Vitamin A I.U.	Thiamine mg.	Riboflavin mg.	Niacin mg.	Ascorbic Acid mg.
Canned, pink	110	1/2 cup	155	23.0	7.0	0	78	216	0.9	80	0.03	0.20	8.8	—
Canned, sockeye or red	110	1/2 cup	190	22.0	10.0	0	74	285	1.3	250	0.04	0.18	8.0	—
Sardines, Atlantic, packed in oil	85	3 oz. drained solids	175	20.5	9.0	—	52	371	2.5	190	0.03	0.17	4.6	—
Swordfish, broiled	100	3-1/2 oz., cooked with butter	175	28.0	6.0	0	65	27	1.3	2050	0.04	0.05	10.9	—
Tuna, canned, in oil	100	5/8 cup, drained	195	29.0	8.0	0	61	8	1.9	80	0.05	0.12	11.9	—
water pack	100	5/8 cup, solids and liquids	125	28.0	0.8	0	70	16	1.6	—	—	0.10	13.3	—
Flours														
Rye, light	80	1 cup, sifted	285	8.0	0.8	62	9	18	0.9	0	0.12	0.06	0.5	0
Wheat, patent, all purpose, unenriched	110	1 cup, sifted	400	11.5	1.0	84	13	18	0.9	0	0.07	0.06	1.0	0
enriched	110	1 cup, sifted	400	11.5	1.0	84	13	18	3.2	0	0.48	0.29	3.9	0
whole grain	120	1 cup, stirred	400	16.0	2.0	85	14	49	4.0	0	0.66	0.14	5.2	0
Fruit cocktail														
(heavy syrup)	100	1/2 cup, scant	75	0.4	0.1	20	80	9	0.4	140	0.02	0.01	0.4	2
Gelatin, dry, plain	10	1 tbsp.	35	8.5	tr.	0	1	—	—	—	—	—	—	—
Gelatin dessert														
Plain	120	1/2 cup	70	2.0	0.0	17	101	—	—	—	—	—	—	—

Food	Weight (g)	Measure												
With fruit	120	1/2 cup	80	1.5	0.1	20	98	—	—	—	—	—	—	4
Grapefruit														
Raw, pulp only	100	1/2 med., 4-1/4 in. diam.	40	0.5	0.1	11	88	16	0.4	80	0.04	0.02	0.2	38
Canned, in syrup	100	1/2 cup, scant, solids and liquid	70	0.6	0.1	18	81	13	0.3	10	0.03	0.02	0.2	30
Grapefruit juice, canned														
Unsweetened	180	6 oz., 3/4 cup	75	0.9	0.2	18	161	14	0.7	20	0.05	0.04	0.4	61
Sweetened	180	6 oz., 3/4 cup	95	0.9	0.2	23	155	14	0.7	20	0.05	0.04	0.4	56
Grapes														
American type (slip-skin)	100	22-24 avg. size	70	1.5	1.0	16	82	16	0.4	100	0.05	0.03	0.3	4
European type (adherent skin)	100	22-24 avg. size	65	0.6	0.3	17	81	12	0.4	100	0.05	0.03	0.3	4
Grape juice	195	6 oz., 3/4 cup	130	0.4	tr.	32	162	21	0.6	—	0.08	0.04	0.4	tr.
Griddle cakes, from mix, with milk	25	1 med., 4 in. diam.	50	1.5	1.0	8	14	55	0.2	30	0.04	0.06	0.2	tr.
Ham, smoked														
Cooked	100	3-1/2 oz., 2-3 small slices	290	21.0	22.0	0	54	9	2.6	0	0.47	0.18	3.6	—
Canned	100	3-1/2 oz.	195	18.5	12.0	0.9	65	11	2.7	0	0.53	0.19	3.8	—
Heart, beef, braised	85	3 oz.	160	27.0	5.0	0.6	52	5	5.0	30	0.21	1.04	6.5	1
Honey, strained	20	1 tbsp.	60	0.1	0	16	3	1	0.1	0	tr.	0.01	0.1	tr.
Ice cream, plain, factory pack	100	3/4 cup (12% fat)	205	4.0	13.0	21	62	123	0.1	520	0.04	0.19	0.1	1
Ice milk (dessert)	100	2/3 cup	150	5.0	5.0	22	67	156	0.1	210	0.05	0.22	0.1	1
Ices, water, lime	100	1/2 cup	80	0.4	tr.	33	67	tr.	tr.	0	tr.	tr.	tr.	1

Food	Weight gm.	Approximate Measure	Calories	Protein gm.	Fat gm.	Total Carbohydrate gm.	Water gm.	Calcium mg.	Iron mg.	Vitamin A I.U.	Thiamine mg.	Riboflavin mg.	Niacin mg.	Ascorbic Acid mg.
Jams, jellies, preserves, marmalade	20	1 tbsp.	55	0.1	tr.	14	6	4	0.2	tr.	tr.	0.01	tr.	tr.
Kale, boiled, drained	55	1/2 cup, leaves only	20	2.5	0.4	3	48	103	0.9	4570	0.06	0.10	0.9	51
Kidney														
Beef, raw	100	3-1/2 oz.	130	15.0	7.0	0.9	76	11	7.4	690	0.36	2.55	6.4	15
Lamb, raw	100	3-1/2 oz.	105	17.0	3.0	0.9	78	13	7.6	690	0.51	2.42	7.4	15
Kohlrabi, boiled, drained	75	1/2 cup diced	20	1.5	0.1	4	69	25	0.2	15	0.05	0.02	0.2	32
Lamb, (choice grade)														
Chop, loin, broiled lean and fat	100	1 avg, 3-1/2 oz., 3/4 in. thick	360	22.0	29.0	0	47	9	1.3	—	0.12	0.23	5.0	—
lean only	66	2.4 oz.	125	19.0	5.0	0	41	8	1.3	—	0.10	0.18	4.0	—
Leg, roasted lean and fat	100	3-1/2 oz., 2 sl. 4 x 3 x 1/4 in.	280	25.5	19.0	0	54	11	1.7	0	0.15	0.27	5.5	—
lean only	85	3 oz.	160	24.0	6.0	0	53	11	1.9	—	0.14	0.26	5.3	—
Shoulder, roasted lean and fat	100	3-1/2 oz.	340	22.0	27.0	0	50	10	1.2	—	0.13	0.23	4.7	—
lean only	75	2.7 oz.	155	20.0	8.0	0	46	9	1.4	—	0.11	0.21	4.3	—
Lard	110	1/2 cup	990	0	110.0	0	0	0	0	0	0	0	0	0
	14	1 tbsp.	125	0	14.0	0	0	0	0	0	0	0	0	0
Lemon juice	100	1/2 cup, scant	25	0.5	0.2	8	91	7	0.2	20	0.03	0.01	0.1	46

Food	g	Measure	Cal.	Protein	Fat	Carboh.								
Lemonade concentrate frozen	15	1 tbsp.	5	0.1	tr.	1	14	1	tr.	tr.	0.01	0.01	tr.	7
Lemonade	250	1 cup, diluted as directed	110	0.3	tr.	29	221	3	tr.	tr.	tr.	0.02	0.2	18
Lentils, dried, cooked	100	1/2 cup	105	8.0	tr.	19	72	25	2.1	20	0.07	0.06	0.6	0
Lettuce, raw														
Compact head	50	2 lg. or 4 small leaves	7	0.5	0.1	1	48	17	1.0	485	0.03	0.03	0.2	4
Iceberg type	90	1/5 head, 4-3/4 in. diam.	12	0.8	0.1	3	86	18	0.5	300	0.05	0.05	0.3	5
Loose leaf	50	2 lg. or 4 small leaves	9	0.7	0.2	2	47	34	0.7	950	0.03	0.04	0.2	9
Liver														
Beef, fried	75	2 slices 3 x 2-1/4 x 3/8 in.	170	20.0	8.0	4	42	8	6.6	40050	0.20	3.14	12.4	20
Lamb, broiled	75	2 slices 3 x 2-1/4 x 3/8 in.	195	24.0	9.0	2	38	12	13.4	55880	0.37	3.83	18.7	27
Pork, fried	75	2 slices 3 x 2-1/4 x 3/8 in.	180	22.0	9.0	2	41	11	21.8	11180	0.26	3.27	16.7	17
Lobster, canned or cooked	100	2/3 cup meat	95	18.5	2.0	0.3	77	65	0.8	—	0.10	0.07	—	—
Macaroni or Spaghetti														
Unenriched, tender	140	1 cup, cooked 14-20 min.	155	5.0	0.6	32	101	11	0.6	0	0.01	0.01	0.4	0
Enriched, tender	140	1 cup, cooked 14-20 min.	155	5.0	0.6	32	101	11	1.3	0	0.20	0.11	1.5	0
Baked with cheese	220	1 cup	475	19.0	24.0	44	128	398	2.0	950	0.22	0.44	2.0	tr.
Margarine, fortified	10	1 pat, 1/45 lb.	70	0.1	8.0	tr.	2	2	0	330	—	—	—	0
Margarine, fortified	14	1 tbsp.	100	0.1	11.0	0.1	2	3	0	460	—	—	—	0
Melons, E.P.														
Cantaloupe or muskmelons	100	1/2 of 4-1/2 in. melon	30	0.7	0.1	8	91	14	0.4	3400	0.04	0.03	0.6	33
Casaba	100	3-1/2 oz., 1 avg. serving	35	0.8	0.3	8	91	14	0.4	40	0.04	0.03	0.6	23

Food	Weight gm.	Approximate Measure	Calories	Protein gm.	Fat gm.	Total Carbohydrate gm.	Water gm.	Minerals Calcium mg.	Iron mg.	Vitamin A I.U.	Vitamins Thiamine mg.	Riboflavin mg.	Niacin mg.	Ascorbic Acid mg.
Watermelon	100	1/2 cup, balls or cubes	25	0.5	0.2	6	93	7	0.5	590	0.03	0.03	0.2	7
	900	1/6 of a 10 x 16 in. melon	235	4.5	2.0	58	833	63	4.5	5310	0.27	0.27	1.8	63
Milk														
Whole, fresh	244	8 oz, 1 cup or full glass	165	8.5	9.0	12	213.0	285	0.1	370	0.07	0.41	0.2	2
Skim or buttermilk	246	1 cup	85	9.0	0.2	13	223.0	298	0.1	tr.	0.10	0.44	0.2	2
Half and Half	242	1 cup	325	8.0	28.0	11	193.0	261	tr.	1160	0.07	0.39	0.2	2
Evaporated	126	1/2 cup or 1 cup reconstituted	170	9.0	10.0	12	93.0	318	0.1	400	0.05	0.43	0.3	1
Condensed (sweetened)	20	1 tbsp.	65	1.5	2.0	11	5.0	52	tr.	70	0.02	0.08	tr.	tr.
Dried, whole	8	1 tbsp.	40	2.0	2.0	3	0.2	73	tr.	90	0.02	0.12	0.1	1
skim (nonfat solids)	7.5	1 tbsp.	25	2.5	0.1	4	0.2	98	tr.	tr.	0.03	0.14	0.1	1
Malted, plain, dry	8	1 tbsp.	35	1.0	0.7	6	0.2	23	0.2	80	0.03	0.04	tr.	0
Chocolate drink commercial	250	1 cup (skim milk used)	190	8.0	6.0	27	207.0	270	0.5	200	0.10	0.40	0.3	3
Yogurt, low-fat	246	1 cup	125	8.5	4.0	13	219.0	295	tr.	170	0.10	0.44	0.2	2
Muffins														
Bran	35	1 medium	90	2.5	3.0	15	12	50	1.3	80	0.05	0.08	1.4	tr.
Cornmeal (yellow, enriched)	45	1 medium	140	3.0	5.0	21	15	47	0.8	140	0.09	0.10	0.7	tr.

White flour, enriched	40	1 medium	120	3.0	3.0	4	15	42	0.6	40	0.07	0.09	0.6	tr.
Mushrooms, raw	100	3-1/2 oz.	30	2.5	0.3	4	90	6	0.8	tr.	0.10	0.46	4.2	3
Mustard greens, boiled, drained	100	2/3 cup	25	2.0	0.4	4	93	138	1.8	5800	0.08	0.14	0.6	48
Mustard, prepared, brown or yellow	15	1 tbsp.	11	1.0	1.0	1	12	13	0.3	—	—	—	—	—
Noodles, egg														
Unenriched	100	2/3 cup, cooked	125	4.0	2.0	23	70	10	0.6	70	0.03	0.02	0.4	0
Enriched	100	2/3 cup, cooked	125	4.0	2.0	23	70	10	0.9	70	0.14	0.08	1.2	0
Nuts, mixed, shelled	15	8-12 average nuts	95	2.5	9.0	3	—	14	0.5	tr.	0.09	0.02	0.6	tr.
Oils, salad or cooking	110	1/2 cup	970	0	110.0	0	0	0	0	—	0	0	0	0
	14	1 tbsp.	125	0	14.0	0	0	0	0	—	0	0	0	0
Okra, boiled, drained	100	9 pods, 3 in. long	30	2.0	0.3	6	91	92	0.5	490	0.13	0.18	0.9	20
Olives, E.P.														
Green	5	1 large or 2 small	5	tr.	0.6	0.1	4	3	0.08	15	—	—	—	—
Ripe (Mission)	5	1 large or 2 small	10	0.1	1.0	0.2	4	5	0.09	5	tr.	tr.	—	—
Onions, green (scallions), raw	8.5	1 medium, without tops	5	0.1	tr.	0.9	7	3	0.05	tr.	tr.	tr.	0.03	2
Onions, mature, dry — Raw	100	1 onion, 2-1/2 in. diam.	40	1.5	0.1	9	89	27	0.5	40	0.03	0.04	0.2	10
	10	1 tbsp., chopped	4	0.2	tr.	0.9	9	3	0.05	5	tr.	tr.	0.02	1
Boiled, drained	100	1/2 cup, 3-4 small	30	1.0	0.1	7	92	24	0.4	40	0.03	0.03	0.2	7
Oranges, raw, E.P.	150	1 medium, 3 in. diam.	75	1.5	0.3	18	129	62	0.6	300	0.15	0.06	0.6	75
Orange juice														
Fresh or canned	185	6 oz., 3/4 cup, 1 sm. glass	80	1.0	0.4	19	163	20	0.4	370	0.17	0.06	0.7	93

Food	Weight gm.	Approximate Measure	Calories	Protein gm.	Fat gm.	Total Carbo-hydrate gm.	Water gm.	Calcium mg.	Iron mg.	Vitamin A I.U.	Thia-mine mg.	Ribo-flavin mg.	Niacin mg.	Ascorbic Acid mg.
Frozen (concentrate or diluted)	185	6 oz., 3/4 cup, 1 sm. glass	80	1.0	0.2	20	163	17	0.2	370	0.17	0.02	0.6	83
Oysters, raw														
Eastern	120	5-8 medium	80	10.0	2.0	4	102	113	6.6	370	0.17	0.22	3.0	—
Pacific and Olympia	120	5-8 medium or 3-1/2 oz. Olympia	110	13.0	3.0	8	95	102	8.6	—	0.14	—	1.6	36
Oyster stew (1 part oysters, 3 parts milk)	230	1 cup, 3-4 oysters	200	11.0	12.0	11	193	269	3.2	640	0.14	0.41	1.6	—
Pancakes. See *Griddle cakes*														
Papayas, raw	100	1/2 cup, cubed	40	0.6	0.1	10	89	20	0.3	1750	0.04	0.04	0.3	56
Parsley, raw	3.5	1 tbsp., chopped	2	0.1	tr.	0.3	3	7	0.2	300	tr.	0.01	tr.	6
Peaches														
Raw, yellow, E.P.	115	1 med. peach, 2 in. diam.	45	0.7	0.1	11	103	10	0.6	1530	0.02	0.06	1.2	8
Canned, heavy syrup	120	2 halves, 2 tbsp. juice	95	0.5	0.1	24	95	5	0.4	520	0.01	0.02	0.7	4
water pack	120	1/2 cup, sliced, with liquid	40	0.5	0.1	10	109	5	0.4	540	0.01	0.04	0.7	4
Dried, sulfured, cooked, unsweetened	135	1/2 cup, 5-6 halves, 3 tbsp. liquid	110	1.5	0.3	29	103	20	2.6	1650	tr.	0.08	2.0	3
Peanuts, shelled, roasted	15	15-17 nuts (without skins)	90	4.0	8.0	3	tr.	11	0.3	—	0.05	0.02	2.6	0
Peanut butter	16	1 tbsp.	90	4.0	8.0	3	tr.	10	0.3	—	0.02	0.02	2.4	0
Pears														
Raw, including skin	180	1 pear, 3 x 2-1/2 in. diam.	110	1.5	0.7	28	148	14	0.5	40	0.04	0.07	0.2	7

Food	Measure														
Canned, heavy syrup	2 halves and 2 tbsp. syrup	120	90	0.2	0.2	24	96	6	0.2	tr.	tr.	0.01	0.02	0.1	1
water pack	2 halves and 2 tbsp. juice	120	40	0.2	0.2	10	109	6	0.2	tr.	tr.	0.01	0.02	0.1	1
Peas															
Green, fresh or frozen	1/2 cup, boiled, drained	80	55	4.5	0.3	10	65	18	1.4	430	0.22	0.09	1.8	16
Canned, drained	1/2 cup	80	65	4.0	0.3	12	63	20	1.4	550	0.09	0.05	0.8	6
Split, dry, cooked	1/2 cup (from 1 oz. dry wt.)	125	145	10.0	0.4	26	88	14	2.1	50	0.19	0.11	1.1	—
Peas and carrots, frozen, cooked	1/2 cup	75	40	2.5	0.2	8	64	19	0.8	6980	0.14	0.05	1.0	6
Pecans	12 halves or 2 tbsp. chopped	15	105	1.0	11.0	2	1	11	0.4	20	0.13	0.02	0.1	tr.
Peppers															
Green, raw, E.P.	1 medium shell	65	15	0.8	0.1	3	61	6	0.5	270	0.05	0.05	0.3	83
	1 tbsp., chopped	10	5	0.1	tr.	0.5	9	1	0.1	40	0.01	0.01	tr.	13
Red, canned (pimentos)	1 medium	40	10	0.4	0.2	2	37	3	0.6	920	0.01	0.02	0.2	38
Pickles, cucumber															
Dill	1 large, 4 x 1-3/4 in.	135	15	0.9	0.3	3	126	35	1.4	140	tr.	0.03	tr.	8
Sweet	1 pickle, 2-3/4 x 3/4 in.	20	30	0.1	0.1	7	12	2	0.2	20	tr.	tr.	tr.	1
Relish, sweet or mixed	1 tbsp.	13	20	0.1	0.1	4	8	3	0.1	0	0	0	0	0
Pies															
Apple	1/6 of 9 inch pie	160	410	3.5	18.0	61	76	13	0.5	50	0.03	0.03	0.6	2

Food	Weight gm.	Approximate Measure	Calories	Protein gm.	Fat gm.	Total Carbohydrate gm.	Water gm.	Minerals		Vitamins				
								Calcium mg.	Iron mg.	Vitamin A I.U.	Thiamine mg.	Riboflavin mg.	Niacin mg.	Ascorbic Acid mg.
Blackberry	160	1/6 of 9 inch pie	390	4.0	18.0	55	82	30	0.8	140	0.03	0.03	0.5	6
Cherry	160	1/6 of 9 inch pie	420	4.0	18.0	61	75	22	0.5	700	0.03	0.03	0.8	tr.
Chocolate meringue	160	1/6 of 9 inch pie	405	7.5	19.0	54	77	110	1.1	300	0.05	0.19	0.3	tr.
Custard	160	1/6 of 9 inch pie	350	10.0	18.0	37	93	154	1.0	370	0.08	0.26	0.5	0
Lemon meringue	140	1/6 of 9 inch pie	360	5.0	14.0	53	66	20	0.7	240	0.04	0.11	0.3	4
Mince	160	1/6 of 9 inch pie	435	4.0	18.0	66	69	45	1.6	tr.	0.11	0.06	0.6	2
Pumpkin	150	1/6 of 9 inch pie	320	6.0	17.0	37	89	77	0.8	3710	0.50	0.15	0.8	tr.
Pineapple														
Raw	100	2/3 cup, no sugar	50	0.4	0.2	14	85	17	0.5	70	0.09	0.03	0.2	17
Canned, crushed, heavy syrup	130	1/2 cup, solids and liquid	95	0.4	0.1	25	104	14	0.4	70	0.10	0.03	0.3	9
sliced	120	2 small or 1 large slice, 2 tbsp. juice	90	0.4	0.1	23	96	13	0.4	60	0.10	0.02	0.2	8
water pack	100	2 small or 1 large slice, 2 tbsp. liquid	40	0.3	0.1	10	89	12	0.3	50	0.08	0.02	0.2	7
Pineapple juice, canned, unsweetened	185	6 oz, 3/4 cup, 1 sm. glass	100	0.7	0.2	25	158	28	0.6	90	0.09	0.04	0.4	17
Pineapple and grapefruit juice	185	6 oz, 3/4 cup	100	0.4	tr.	25	159	9	0.4	20	0.04	0.02	0.2	30

	Wt. (g)	Measure												
Plums														
Raw, hybrid type	100	2 medium	50	0.5	0.2	12	87	12	0.5	250	0.03	0.03	0.5	6
Canned, purple (Italian) heavy syrup	120	3 med., 2 tbsp. syrup	100	0.5	0.1	26	93	11	1.1	1450	0.02	0.02	0.5	2
Popcorn, with oil and salt	15	1 cup	70	2.0	3.0	9	1	1	0.3	—	—	0.01	0.3	0
Pork														
Chops, broiled, E.P.														
lean and fat	66	1 medium thick chop	245	15.0	20.0	0	30	7	1.9	0	0.33	0.15	3.2	—
lean only	48	(from above serving)	110	13.5	6.0	0	28	6	1.8	0	0.29	0.13	2.6	—
Loin, roasted														
lean and fat	90	2 slices, 3-1/2 x 3-1/4 in.	335	20.0	28.0	0	41	9	2.6	0	0.45	0.21	4.4	—
lean only	70	(from above serving)	165	20.0	9.0	0	40	8	2.5	0	0.43	0.20	3.9	—
Potatoes														
Baked	100	1 medium	95	2.5	0.1	21	75	9	0.7	tr.	0.10	0.04	1.7	20
Boiled, pared before cooking	100	1 medium	65	2.0	0.1	15	83	6	0.5	tr.	0.09	0.03	1.2	16
French-fried	100	20 pieces, 2 x 1/2 x 1/2 in.	275	4.5	13.0	36	45	15	1.3	tr.	0.13	0.08	3.1	21
frozen (reheated)	100	20 pieces, 2 x 1/2 x 1/2 in.	220	3.5	8.0	34	53	9	1.8	tr.	0.14	0.02	2.6	21
Mashed, milk and table fat added	100	1/2 cup	95	2.0	4.0	12	80	24	0.4	170	0.08	0.05	1.0	9

Food	Weight gm.	Approximate Measure	Calories	Protein gm.	Fat gm.	Total Carbohydrate gm.	Water gm.	Calcium mg.	Iron mg.	Vitamin A I.U.	Thiamine mg.	Riboflavin mg.	Niacin mg.	Ascorbic Acid mg.
Potato chips	20	10 chips, 2 in. diam.	115	1.0	8.0	10	tr.	8	0.4	tr.	0.04	0.01	1.0	3
Prunes, dried														
Softened	32	4 prunes, medium	80	0.7	0.2	22	9	16	1.2	510	0.03	0.05	0.5	1
Cooked, unsweetened	135	8-9 med., 2 tbsp. juice	160	1.5	0.4	42	90	32	2.4	1010	0.04	0.09	0.9	1
Prune juice, canned	180	6 oz., 3/4 cup	140	0.7	0.2	34	144	25	7.4	—	0.02	0.02	0.7	4
Puddings														
Apple Brown Betty	100	1/2 cup	150	1.5	4.0	30	65	18	0.6	100	0.06	0.04	0.4	1
Chocolate, cooked or instant (from mix)	130	1/2 cup	160	4.5	4.0	30	91	133	0.4	170	0.03	0.20	0.1	tr.
Custard	100	1/2 cup	115	5.5	6.0	11	77	112	0.4	350	0.04	0.19	0.1	tr.
Junket (mix) with milk	130	1/2 cup	125	4.0	5.0	17	104	152	tr.	200	0.04	0.21	0.1	1
Prune whip	65	1/2 cup	100	3.0	0.1	24	37	14	0.8	300	0.01	0.09	0.3	1
Rice, with raisins	145	2/3 cup	210	5.0	5.0	39	95	142	0.6	160	0.04	0.20	0.3	tr.
Tapioca, cream	100	1/2 cup	135	5.0	5.0	17	72	105	0.4	290	0.04	0.18	0.1	1
Vanilla, home recipe, with starch	130	1/2 cup	145	5.0	5.0	21	99	152	tr.	210	0.04	0.21	0.1	1
Pumpkin, canned	120	1 cup	40	1.0	0.4	10	108	30	0.5	7680	0.04	0.06	0.7	6
Radishes, raw, common	40	4 small	7	0.4	tr.	1	38	12	0.4	5	tr.	tr.	0.1	10
Raisins, natural														

	Grams	Measure												
unbleached	40	1/4 cup	115	1.0	0.1	31	7	25	1.4	4	0.02	0.01	0.1	tr.
	10	1 tbsp.	30	0.1	tr.	8	2	6	0.3	1	tr.	tr.	tr.	tr.
Raspberries														
Black, fresh	100	2/3 cup	75	2.0	1.0	16	81	30	0.9	tr.	0.03	0.09	0.9	18
Red, fresh	100	2/3 cup	55	1.0	0.5	14	84	22	0.9	130	0.03	0.09	0.9	25
Red, canned, water pack	100	1/2 cup, solids and liquid	35	0.7	0.1	9	90	15	0.6	90	0.01	0.04	0.5	9
Rhubarb, cooked, with sugar	135	1/2 cup, fruit and syrup	190	0.7	0.1	49	85	105	0.8	110	0.03	0.07	0.4	8
Rice														
Brown, cooked	100	2/3 cup	120	2.5	0.6	26	70	12	0.5	0	0.09	0.02	1.4	0
White, enriched, cooked	100	2/3 cup	110	2.0	0.1	24	73	10	0.9	0	0.11		1.0	0
Precooked, instant	100	2/3 cup	110	2.0	tr.	24	73	3	0.8	0	0.13		1.0	0
Rolls and buns (enriched)														
Plain (pan rolls)	28	1 small	85	2.5	2.0	15	9	21	0.5	tr.	0.08	0.05	0.6	tr.
Hamburger bun	38	1 large	115	3.0	2.0	20	12	28	0.7	tr.	0.11	0.07	0.8	tr.
Hard	52	1 large	160	5.0	2.0	31	13	24	1.2	tr.	0.14	0.12	1.4	tr.
Rye wafers, See Crackers														
Salad dressings (commercial)														
Blue Cheese	16	1 tbsp.	80	0.8	8.0	1.0	5	13	tr.	30	tr.	0.02	tr.	tr.

Food	Weight gm.	Approximate Measure	Calories	Protein gm.	Fat gm.	Total Carbohydrate gm.	Water gm.	Minerals Calcium mg.	Iron mg.	Vitamins Vitamin A I.U.	Thiamine mg.	Riboflavin mg.	Niacin mg.	Ascorbic Acid mg.
French	15	1 tbsp.	60	0.1	6.0	3.0	6	2	0.1	—	—	—	—	—
low-calorie	15	1 tbsp.	15	0.1	0.6	2.0	12	2	0.1	—	—	—	—	—
Mayonnaise	14	1 tbsp.	100	0.2	11.0	0.3	2	3	0.1	40	tr.	0.01	tr.	—
Salad dressing (mayonnaise type)	15	1 tbsp.	65	0.2	6.0	2.0	6	2	tr.	30	tr.	tr.	tr.	—
low-calorie	15	1 tbsp.	20	0.2	2.0	0.7	12	3	tr.	30	tr.	tr.	tr.	—
Thousand Island	15	1 tbsp.	75	0.1	8.0	2.0	5	2	0.1	50	tr.	tr.	tr.	tr.
Boiled, home recipe	17	1 tbsp.	30	0.7	2.0	3	12	15	0.1	80	0.01	0.03	tr.	tr.
Sauces														
Butterscotch sauce	44	2 tbsp.	205	0.5	7.0	41		41	1.4	300	tr.	tr.	tr.	tr.
Cheese sauce	38	2 tbsp.	65	3.0	5.0	2		88	0.1	210	0.01	0.08	0.1	tr.
Chocolate syrup, thin	40	2 tbsp.	100	0.9	0.8	25	13	7	0.6	tr.	0.01	0.03	0.2	0
Fudge type	50	2 tbsp.	165	3.0	7.0	27	13	64	0.7	80	0.02	0.11	0.2	tr.
Custard sauce, avg.	36	2 tbsp.	40	2.0	2.0	5		39	0.2	120	0.01	0.12	0.1	tr.
Hard sauce	21	2 tbsp.	95	0.1	6.0	12		2	tr.	230	tr.	tr.	tr.	0
Hollandaise, true	50	1/4 cup, scant	180	2.5	19.0	0.4		23	0.9	1030	0.03	0.04	tr.	tr.
Tartar sauce	20	1 tbsp.	105	0.3	12.0	0.8	7	4	0.2	40	tr.	tr.	tr.	tr.

Food	Measure	Weight (g)	Food energy (calories)	Protein (g)	Fat (g)	Carbohydrate (g)	Calcium (mg)	Phosphorus (mg)	Iron (mg)	Vitamin A (I.U.)	Thiamine (mg)	Riboflavin (mg)	Niacin (mg)	Ascorbic acid (mg)
Tomato catsup or chili sauce	1 tbsp.	17	20	0.3	0.1	4	4	12	0.1	240	0.02	0.01	0.3	3
White sauce, medium	1/2 cup	133	215	5.0	17.0	12	153	98	0.3	610	0.05	0.23	0.3	tr.
Sauerkraut, canned	2/3 cup, solids and liquid	125	20	1.0	0.3	5	45	116	0.6	60	0.04	0.05	0.3	18
Sausages														
Bologna, all meat	1 oz., 1 slice 4-1/4 x 1/8 in.	30	85	4.0	7.0	1	—	17	—	—	—	—	—	—
Frankfurter	1 average, cooked	50	150	6.0	14.0	0.8	3	29	0.8	—	0.08	0.10	1.3	—
Liverwurst, fresh	1 oz.	30	90	5.0	8.0	0.5	3	16	1.6	1910	0.06	0.39	1.7	—
Luncheon meat, pork, cured, canned or pkg.	1 oz.	30	90	5.0	8.0	0.4	3	17	0.7	0	0.09	0.06	0.9	—
Pork sausage, link, cooked	3 links	60	285	11.0	27.0	tr.	4	21	1.4	0	0.47	0.20	2.2	—
Salami, dry	1 oz.	30	135	7.0	11.0	0.4	4	9	1.1	—	0.11	0.08	1.6	—
Vienna sausage, canned	2 oz., 1/2 can	60	145	8.5	12.0	0.2	5	38	1.3	—	0.05	0.08	1.6	—
Scallops														
Raw	3-1/2 oz.	100	80	15.5	0.2	3	26	80	1.8	—	—	0.06	1.3	—
Frozen, breaded, fried	3-1/2 oz., reheated	100	195	18.0	8.0	11	—	60	—	—	—	—	—	—
Sherbet, orange	1/2 cup	100	135	0.9	1.0	31	16	67	tr.	60	0.01	0.03	tr.	2
Shrimp, canned	3 oz., meat only	85	100	20.5	0.9	0.6	98	60	2.6	50	0.01	0.03	1.5	—
Sirup, table, cane and maple	1 tbsp.	20	50	0	0	13	3	7	tr.	0	0	0	0	0

Food	Weight gm.	Approximate Measure	Calories	Protein gm.	Fat gm.	Total Carbohydrate gm.	Water gm.	Minerals Calcium mg.	Iron mg.	Vitamin A I.U.	Vitamins Thiamine mg.	Riboflavin mg.	Niacin mg.	Ascorbic Acid mg.
Soft Drinks														
Cola type	170	1 bottle, 6 oz.	65	0	0	17	153	—	—	0	0	0	0	0
Dietary drink (less than 1 Cal./oz.)	170	1 bottle, 6 oz.	—	0	0	—	170	—	—	0	0	0	0	0
Ginger Ale	170	1 bottle, 6 oz.	50	0	0	14	156	—	—	0	0	0	0	0
Root Beer	170	1 bottle, 6 oz.	70	0	0	18	152	—	—	0	0	0	0	0
Soups, canned, diluted, ready to serve														
Asparagus or celery, cream of, made with water	190	3/4 cup	70	1.0	4.0	7	175	38	0.4	150	0.02	0.04	tr.	tr.
made with milk	190	3/4 cup	130	5.0	7.0	12	163	154	0.6	300	0.04	0.21	0.6	2
Bean, with pork	185	3/4 cup	125	6.0	4.0	16	156	46	1.7	480	0.09	0.06	0.7	2
Bouillon, broth or consomme	180	3/4 cup	20	4.0	0	2	172	tr.	0.4	tr.	tr.	0.02	0.9	—
Chicken, cream of,	190	3/4 cup	75	2.5	5.0	6	175	19	0.4	320	0.02	0.04	0.4	tr.
with rice	185	3/4 cup	40	2.5	0.9	4	175	6	0.2	110	tr.	0.02	0.6	—
Clam chowder (Manhattan)	190	3/4 cup	60	2.0	2.0	10	175	27	0.8	680	0.02	0.02	0.8	—
Mushroom, cream of	190	3/4 cup	105	2.0	8.0	8	170	32	0.4	60	0.02	0.10	0.6	tr.

Food	g	Measure												
Pea, split	185	3/4 cup	110	7.0	2.0	16	158	22	1.1	330	0.19	0.11	1.1	tr.
Tomato	185	3/4 cup	65	1.5	2.0	12	167	11	0.6	760	0.04	0.04	0.9	9
Vegetable beef	185	3/4 cup	60	4.0	2.0	7	170	9	0.6	2040	0.04	0.04	0.7	—
Soups, dehydrated, add water as directed														
Chicken noodle	185	3/4 cup	40	1.5	1.0	6	175	6	0.2	40	0.06	0.04	0.4	tr.
Onion	185	3/4 cup	30	1.0	0.9	4	177	7	0.2	tr.	tr.	tr.	tr.	2
Spaghetti, canned, tomato sauce with														
Cheese	100	2/3 cup	75	2.0	0.6	15	80	16	1.1	370	0.14	0.11	1.8	4
Meat balls	100	2/3 cup	100	5.0	4.0	11	78	21	1.3	400	0.06	0.07	0.9	2
Spinach, fresh or frozen, boiled	90	1/2 cup, drained	20	3.0	0.3	3	83	84	2.0	7290	0.06	0.13	0.5	25
Squash														
Summer, boiled, drained	100	1/2 cup	15	0.9	0.1	3	96	25	0.4	390	0.05	0.08	0.8	10
Winter, baked	100	3-1/2 oz. (yellow)	65	2.0	0.4	15	81	28	0.8	4200	0.05	0.13	0.7	13
boiled, drained	100	1/2 cup	40	1.0	0.3	9	89	20	0.5	3500	0.04	0.10	0.4	8
Starch, pure (arrowroot, corn, etc.)	8	1 tbsp.	30	tr.	tr.	7	1	0	0	0	0	0	0	0
Strawberries														
Fresh	100	2/3 cup	35	0.7	0.5	8	90	21	1.0	60	0.03	0.07	0.6	59
Frozen, sweetened, whole	100	3-1/2 oz.	90	0.4	0.2	24	76	13	0.6	30	0.02	0.06	0.5	55

Food	Water gm.	Approximate Measure	Calories	Protein gm.	Fat gm.	Total Carbohydrate gm.	Water gm.	Calcium mg.	Iron mg.	Vitamin A I.U.	Thiamine mg.	Riboflavin mg.	Niacin mg.	Ascorbic Acid mg.
Sugar														
Brown	110	1/2 cup, firmly packed	410	0	0	106	2	94	3.7	0	0.01	0.03	0.2	0
White, granulated	100	1/2 cup	385	0	0	100	1	0	0.1	0	0	0	0	0
	12	1 tbsp. or 3 level tsp.	45	0	0	12	tr.	0	tr.	0	0	0	0	0
powdered	128	1 cup stirred before meas.	495	0	0	127	1	0	0.1	0	0	0	0	0
	8	1 tbsp.	30	0	0	8	tr.	0	tr.	0	0	0	0	0
loaf	7	1 cube or domino	30	0	0	7	tr.	0	tr.	0	0	0	0	0
Sweet potatoes, cooked														
Baked, skinned	100	1 small	140	2.0	0.5	33	64	40	0.9	8100	0.09	0.07	0.7	22
Boiled in skin	100	1/2 medium	115	2.0	0.4	26	71	32	0.7	7900	0.09	0.06	0.6	17
Candied	100	1/2 medium	170	1.5	3.0	34	60	37	0.9	6300	0.06	0.04	0.4	10
Canned, vacuum pack	100	1/2 cup	110	2.0	0.2	25	72	25	0.8	7800	0.05	0.04	0.6	14
Tomatoes														
Fresh	150	1 medium, 2 x 2-1/2 in.	35	1.5	0.3	7	140	20	0.8	1350	0.09	0.06	1.1	35
Canned or cooked	120	1/2 cup, solids and liquid	25	1.0	0.2	5	124	7	0.6	1080	0.06	0.04	0.8	20
Tomato juice, canned	180	6 oz., 3/4 cup	35	1.5	0.2	8	169	13	1.6	1440	0.09	0.05	1.4	29

Food	g	Measure												
Tomato purée, canned (sauce)	120	1/2 cup	50	2.0	0.2	11	104	16	2.0	1920	0.11	0.06	1.7	40
Tongue														
Beef, fresh, simmered	100	3-1/2 oz., cooked	245	21.5	17.0	0.4	61	7	2.2	—	0.05	0.29	3.5	—
Canned or cured, beef, lamb, etc.	100	3-1/2 oz., cooked	265	19.5	20.0	0.3	57	—	—	—	—	—	—	—
Tuna, See Fish.														
Turkey, roasted (flesh only)														
Light meat	100	3-1/2 oz., 3 slices (3-1/2 x 2-1/2 x 1/4 in.)	175	33.0	4.0	0	62	—	1.2	—	0.05	0.14	11.1	—
Dark meat	100	3-1/2 oz.	205	30.0	8.0	0	61	—	2.3	—	0.04	0.23	4.2	—
Turnips, white, boiled, drained	75	1/2 cup, diced	20	0.6	0.2	4	70	26	0.3	tr.	0.03	0.04	0.2	17
Turnip greens, boiled, drained	75	1/2 cup	15	2.0	0.2	3	70	138	0.8	4730	0.11	0.18	0.5	52
Veal														
Cutlet, broiled	100	3-1/2 oz.	215	27.0	11.0	0	60	11	3.2	—	0.07	0.25	5.4	—
Shoulder, oven braised	100	3-1/2 oz.	235	28.0	13.0	0	59	12	3.5	—	0.09	0.29	6.4	—
Vinegar, cider	15	1 tbsp.	5	tr.	0	0.9	14	1	0.1	—	—	—	—	—
Waffles (from mix) with milk and eggs	75	One, 4-1/2 x 5-1/2 x 1/2 in.	205	6.5	8.0	27	31	179	1.0	170	0.11	0.17	0.7	tr.
Walnuts, English	100	1 cup, halves	650	15.0	64.0	16	4	99	3.1	30	0.33	0.13	0.9	2
	15	2 tbsp., chopped	100	2.0	10.0	2	1	15	0.5	10	0.05	0.02	0.1	tr.

Food	Weight gm.	Approximate Measure	Calories	Protein gm.	Fat gm.	Total Carbohydrate gm.	Water gm.	Calcium mg.	Iron mg.	Vitamin A I.U.	Thiamine mg.	Riboflavin mg.	Niacin mg.	Ascorbic Acid mg.
Watercress, raw	10	10 average sprigs	2	0.2	tr.	0.3	9	15	0.2	490	0.01	0.02	0.1	8
Watermelon, See Melons.														
Wheat germ, crude	10	1 tbsp., rounded	35	2.5	1.0	5	1	7	1.0	0	0.20	0.07	0.4	0
Yeast														
Baker's moist	12	1 cake, compressed	10	1.5	0.1	1	9	2	0.6	tr.	0.09	0.20	1.3	tr.
dry, active	8	1 tbsp.	20	3.0	0.1	3	tr.	4	1.3	tr.	0.19	0.43	2.9	tr.
Brewer's (debittered)	8	1 tbsp.	23	3.0	0.08	(3)	tr.	(17)	1.4	tr.	1.24	0.34	3.0	tr.
Yogurt, See Milk.														

appendix C

Desirable Weight for Women (Age 18 and over)*

Weight in pounds according to frame†

Age 18				Age 19			
Height (with shoes on) Feet Inches	Small Frame	Medium Frame	Large Frame	Height (with shoes on) Feet Inches	Small Frame	Medium Frame	Large Frame
4 11	97–104	103–111	110–120	4 11	98–105	104–112	111–121
5 0	98–106	105–113	112–122	5 0	99–107	106–114	113–123
5 1	100–108	107–115	114–124	5 1	101–109	108–116	115–125
5 2	103–111	110–118	117–128	5 2	104–112	111–119	118–129
5 3	106–114	113–121	120–131	5 3	107–115	114–122	121–132
5 4	109–118	117–125	124–135	5 4	110–119	118–126	125–136
5 5	112–121	120–128	126–138	5 5	113–122	121–129	127–139
5 6	116–125	123–133	131–143	5 6	117–126	124–134	132–144
5 7	119–129	127–137	135–147	5 7	120–130	128–138	136–148
5 8	122–132	130–140	138–151	5 8	123–133	131–141	139–152
5 9	126–136	134–144	142–155	5 9	127–137	135–145	143–156
5 10	129–140	138–148	145–159	5 10	130–141	139–149	146–160
5 11	132–143	141–151	148–162	5 11	133–144	142–152	149–163
Age 20				Age 21			
Height (with shoes on) Feet Inches	Small Frame	Medium Frame	Large Frame	Height (with shoes on) Feet Inches	Small Frame	Medium Frame	Large Frame
4 11	99–106	105–113	112–122	4 11	100–107	106–114	113–123
5 0	100–108	107–115	114–124	5 0	101–109	108–116	115–125
5 1	102–110	109–117	116--126	5 1	103–111	110–118	117–127
5 2	105–113	112–120	119–130	5 2	106–114	113–121	120–131
5 3	108–116	115–123	122–133	5 3	109–117	116–124	123–134
5 4	111–120	119–127	126–137	5 4	112–121	120–128	127–138
5 5	114–123	122–130	128–140	5 5	115–124	123–131	129–141
5 6	118–127	125–135	122–145	5 6	119–128	126–136	134–146
5 7	121–131	129–139	137–149	5 7	122–132	130–140	138–150
5 8	124–134	132–142	140–153	5 8	125–135	133–143	141–154
5 9	128–138	136–146	144–157	5 9	129–139	137–147	145–158
5 10	131–142	140–150	147–161	5 10	132–143	141–151	148–162
5 11	134–145	143–153	150–164	5 11	135–146	144–154	151–165

*Courtesy of Metropolitan Life Insurance Company.
†Your frame is indicated by your bone size (wrist girth). Use this guide to determine body frame: Large = 6.3"–6.8" Medium = 5.6"–6.2" Small = 4.6"–5.5"

Age 22

Height (with shoes on) Feet Inches	Small Frame	Medium Frame	Large Frame
4 11	101–108	107–115	114–124
5 0	102–110	109–117	116–126
5 1	104–112	111–119	118–128
5 2	107–115	114–122	121–132
5 3	110–118	117–125	124–135
5 4	113–122	121–129	128–139
5 5	116–125	124–132	130–142
5 6	120–129	127–137	135–147
5 7	123–133	131–141	139–151
5 8	126–136	134–144	142–155
5 9	130–140	138–148	146–159
5 10	133–144	142–152	149–163
5 11	136–147	145–155	152–166

Age 23

Height (with shoes on) Feet Inches	Small Frame	Medium Frame	Large Frame
4 11	102–109	108–116	115–125
5 0	103–111	110–118	117–127
5 1	105–113	112–120	119–129
5 2	108–116	115–123	122–133
5 3	111–119	118–126	125–136
5 4	114–123	122–130	129–140
5 5	117–126	125–133	131–143
5 6	121–130	128–138	136–148
5 7	124–134	132–142	140–152
5 8	127–137	135–145	143–156
5 9	131–141	139–149	147–160
5 10	134–145	143–153	150–164
5 11	137–148	146–156	153–167

Age 24

Height (with shoes on) Feet Inches	Small Frame	Medium Frame	Large Frame
4 11	103–110	109–117	116–126
5 0	104–112	111–119	118–128
5 1	106–114	113–121	120–130
5 2	109–117	116–124	123–134
5 3	112–120	119–127	126–137
5 4	115–124	123–131	130–141
5 5	118–127	126–134	132–144
5 6	122–131	129–139	137–149
5 7	125–135	133–143	141–153
5 8	128–138	136–146	144–157
5 9	132–142	140–150	148–161
5 10	135–146	144–154	151–165
5 11	138–149	147–157	154–168

Age 25 and Over

Height (with shoes on) Feet Inches	Small Frame	Medium Frame	Large Frame
4 11	104–111	110–118	117–127
5 0	105–113	112–120	119–129
5 1	107–115	114–122	121–131
5 2	110–118	117–125	124–135
5 3	113–121	120–128	127–138
5 4	116–125	124–132	131–142
5 5	119–128	127–135	133–145
5 6	123–132	120–140	138–150
5 7	126–136	134–144	142–154
5 8	129–139	137–147	145–158
5 9	133–143	141–151	149–162
5 10	136–147	145–155	152–166
5 11	139–150	148–158	155–169

glossary

ABDUCTION: Movement away from the midline (median axis) of the body.

ACCELERATION: Change in velocity, expressed in units of distance and time.

ACTIVE EXERCISE: A movement initiated by the muscular effort of the individual; the opposite of passive exercise.

ADDUCTION: Movement toward the midline of the body.

AEROBIC: Requiring the presence of oxygen. When applied to exercise, this term implies that the requirements of the exercise are fully supplied.

AFFERENT NEURON: Nerve cells that conduct impulses to the brain and spinal cord.

AGILITY: The ability to change direction rapidly and easily.

ALL-OR-NONE LAW: A term used to describe the response of muscle fiber to stimuli. When the stimulus is applied above the threshold level, the fiber responds totally.

ALVEOLI: The tiny terminal air sacs of the lungs where gas exchange (O_2 and CO_2) with the pulmonary capillaries takes place.

ANAEROBIC: Occurring in the absence of oxygen. When applied to exercise, this term implies that the oxygen requirements of the exercise cannot be met which results in an oxygen debt.

ANTHROPOMETRY: Measurement of the body and body parts.

ARTERIOSCLEROSIS: Hardening of the arteries, including a variety of conditions that cause the artery walls to become thick and inelastic.

ARTICULATION: A joint between two bones.

ATHEROSCLEROSIS: A reduction of the internal diameter of the arteries, through the buildup of fatty substances (such as cholesterol), which makes the inner wall of the artery rough and thick and interferes with circulation. (A variety of arteriosclerosis.)

ATROPHY: The wasting away of tissue. When applied to muscle, it means lack of use or a condition caused by disease.

AUTONOMIC NERVOUS SYSTEM: That component of the nervous system that controls essentially nonvoluntary responses such as those of the smooth muscles, heart muscle, and glands.

BALANCE: The ability to maintain equilibrium, to hold a body position.

BALLISTIC MOVEMENT: Rapid movement of the body limbs initiated by strong muscular contraction and carried through by the limbs' own momentum.

BASE OF SUPPORT: Those body part or parts in contact with the supporting surface.

BIOMECHANICS: The study and analysis of human movement involving the application of mechanical principles to both internal and external bodily actions.

BLOOD PRESSURE: The pressure (in millimeters of mercury) that exists in the arteries of the body because of the force of contraction of the heart and the amount of resistance to the flow of blood. It is generally quoted as two numbers, 120/80 (normal for 20–25 year olds), the first number referring to the pressure as the ventricles of the heart contract and force blood through the arteries (systolic), and the second number to the pressure when the ventricles are relaxed (diastolic).

BODY IMAGE: The perception that an individual has of her own body in terms of its appearance, function, capacity, and performance qualities. There are usually two components of body image: the *ideal* image, or what the individual would like to be, and the *actual* image, what the individual thinks she is.

CALISTHENICS: Set exercises that are performed with the aim of improving the strength, endurance, and flexibility of the body. Progressive calisthenics are exercises in which the level of difficulty of the exercises is increased gradually as the individual improves.

CALORIE: The amount of heat liberated from food substances. High-calorie foods require more time to "burn off" as energy; what is not used as energy by the body may be stored as fat.

CALORIE BALANCE: This occurs when energy intake and output are equal.

CAPILLARIZATION: Possessing capillaries.

CARDIAC MUSCLE: A special type of muscle found only in the heart.

CARDIAC OUTPUT: The amount of blood pumped by the heart per minute.

CARDIOVASCULAR DISEASE: Any disease involving the heart and blood vessels.

CARDIOVASCULAR-RESPIRATORY ENDURANCE (Organic Tone): The ability of the body, through the capacity of the heart, lungs, and circulation to supply oxygen, perform strenuous, continuous activity for long periods of time.

CARDIOVASCULAR SYSTEM: The body organs involved in extracting oxygen from the air and transporting blood and its contained oxygen to the tissues and back to the lungs to eliminate the carbon dioxide that was taken up by the blood from the tissues. This system includes the heart, the lungs, and all the blood vessels.

CENTER OF GRAVITY: A theoretical point within the body about which the gravitational forces on one side equal those of the other side. Any change in body positions or the body parts will cause the center of gravity to shift.

CHOLESTEROL: A fat-like substance important in the body's metabolism. It is largely responsible, when stored in the inner walls of the arteries, for reducing blood flow by reducing the diameter of the blood vessels.

CIRCUIT TRAINING PROGRAM: An exercise program involving several different activities, each keyed to a particular body function, that are performed in rotation. The individual performs a set number of repetitions at each exercise station and tries to complete the entire program (circuit) within a set time. It is a progressive exercise program, the number of repetitions are increased or the circuit time is reduced as the individual improves.

COLLATERAL CIRCULATION: Additional or supplemental blood vessels that increase circulation to a part of the tissue.

CONCEPT: A mental construct developed through analysis of experience, isolating the common attributes of the objects or the events.

CONCEPTUAL SCHEME: Essentially a controlling idea for the organization of content (concepts and supporting data and experiences). A conceptual scheme is derived from a pattern of concepts.

CORONARY ARTERIES: The arteries that supply blood and blood-transported nutrients to the heart muscle.

CORONARY OR CARDIAC RESERVE: The ability of the heart to increase its output by increasing its rate or stroke volume or both. (Stroke volume is the amount of blood pumped by the heart per beat.)

CORONARY HEART DISEASE: Atherosclerosis of the coronary arteries.

DEGENERATIVE DISEASE: A disease continuing for a long time involving gradual deterioration and impairment of function of the tissue or organ affected.

DYNAMIC STRENGTH: Maximum force that can be exerted by a muscle or group of muscles in isotonic contraction.

DYSMENORRHEA: Painful menstruation or cramps.

ECTOMORPH: One of the three main classifications of body types. An individual whose predominant component of physique is linearity. An extreme ectomorph is tall, thin, thin-boned, and angular in appearance.

EFFERENT NEURON: Nerve cells that conduct impulses from the spinal cord and brain to muscles and glands.

EFFICIENCY: Accomplishing a given task with minimal expenditure of energy.

ELASTIC TONE: Free and easy joint motion. See *flexibility*.

ENDOCRINE SYSTEM: The body system responsible for the secretion, into the blood or tissue fluids, of chemical substances known as hormones.

ENDOMORPH: One of the three main classifications of body types. An individual whose predominant component of physique is roundness and who tends to store fat. An extreme endomorph is short, fat, and flabby and has a prominent abdomen.

ENDURANCE: The capacity to sustain an activity over a long period of time. Cardiovascular-respiratory endurance depends upon the strength and efficiency of the heart, lungs, and circulation to supply oxygen. Muscular endurance depends on strength of the skeletal muscle, and local blood supply.

ENERGY COSTS: Energy expended is generally expressed in terms of Calories used per Minute and is measured by collecting the subject's expired air (oxygen consumption) during an activity. Tables may be used to determine the caloric equivalent of 1 liter of oxygen (the conversion of oxygen consumption to energy expenditure in calories). In the literature, the energy cost of activity is often expressed in these terms. Liter of oxygen = 4.68–5.04 calories.

ESTROGEN: The female sex hormones responsible for control of the sex cycle, and for development of secondary sex characteristics during maturation.

EXTENSION: An increase in the angle at the joint between two body segments, either straightened or extended.

FASCIA: Connective tissue surrounding the outside of muscle.

FAT: A concentrated source of food energy consisting of three molecules of fatty acid and one molecule of glycerol. It can be stored in the body and used as needed.

FATIGUE: A reduced capacity for continuing to perform work as a result of a buildup of the by-products of exercise or from the subjectively perceived sensations accompanying continued emotional stress or mental work. A feeling of tiredness or disinclination to continue a task; the former is called physical fatigue, the latter psychological fatigue.

FLEXIBILITY: Also called "elastic tone." The range of joint motion.

FLEXION: The angle at the joint between two body segments is decreased; bending.

GENERAL ADAPTATION SYNDROME: The concept developed by Selye to describe the progressive manifestation of the reactions of the body to continued stress from any source. He identified three stages—the *resistance stage*, the *adaptation stage*, and the *exhaustion stage*.

HEALTH-PHYSICAL FITNESS: The attainment of a state of optimal efficiency of the body as reflected by measures of strength, flexibility, and cardiovascular-respiratory endurance.

HEART RATE: The number of times the heart beats (contracts) per minute.

HOMEOSTASIS: The normal balance of all the internal functions of the body. Internal physiological equilibrium involving the autonomic nervous system and the endocrine system.

HORMONE: A chemical substance produced by any one of the endocrine glands of the body, and transported in the blood to a specific organ or tissue where it helps to produce a certain effect. Hormones are commonly known as the chemical messengers of the body.

HYPERTROPHY: When applied to muscle tissue this term means an increase in muscle mass.

HYPOKINETIC DISEASE: Disease produced through a lack of physical activity and manifested in a variety of physical, somatic, and mental derangements.

INERTIA: Resistance to change of position or change of motion.

INTERVAL TRAINING PROGRAM: A method of training involving the development of the body's capacity to endure oxygen debt. It is training that utilizes the body's anaerobic metabolism by relying on short bursts of all-out work interspersed with brief rest periods.

ISOMETRIC: A term used to describe a muscular contraction in which the muscle remains the same length while tension is developed. No movement is produced by this type of contraction, called "isometric exercise." It is static contraction.

ISOTONIC: A term used to describe a muscular contraction in which the muscle shortens against a load or resistance, resulting in movement, called isotonic exercise. It is dynamic contraction.

KINESTHESIS: The sense of perception of movement, of position and weight in space. Sensitivity of receptors in joints, muscles, and tendons to change.

LAW OF CONSERVATION OF ENERGY: Energy is neither lost nor gained but only changed to a different form.

LEISURE: That portion of an individual's daily, weekly, or monthly life cycle that is devoted to doing those things he wishes to do for his entertainment or mental enrichment, for satisfaction and enjoyment, as distinct from those portions of the life cycle devoted to employment, eating, sleep, and necessary biological functions.

LIGAMENT: A tough band of tissue that connects bones.

LINEAR MOTION: Also known as translatory motion. Uniform motion of the body or an object as a whole with all parts moving in the same direction.

LINE OF GRAVITY: An imaginary line that falls vertically downward from the center of gravity to the surface-base of support.

LUNG: One of a pair of organs responsible for the transfer of oxygen from inspired air into the blood stream and for the exhausting of metabolic by-products, in the form of carbon dioxide and water, from the blood stream to be exhaled into the air.

MENSTRUATION: The monthly discharge of cells and blood from the uterus that occurs from the beginning of feminine maturity to the time of menopause, or change of life.

MESOMORPH: One of the three main classifications of body types. An individual whose predominant component of physique is muscularity. The extreme mesomorph is stocky, rugged, square shouldered, and heavily muscled.

METABOLISM: The complex chemical changes whereby the body converts food into tissue elements and energy.

METABOLITES: The result of the intermediate or final stage of the breakdown of foodstuffs in the body by metabolic action. Also, the by-products of metabolism within the muscle that result from muscular contractions.

MORBIDITY: The relative incidence of sickness.

MOTION: Movement or a change of position in contrast to rest or inactivity.

MOTIVATION: Being provided with a motive or reason for initiating conscious and purposeful activity.

MOTOR LEARNING: Learning related to the efficient and coordinated application of the muscles of the body to perform skilled movement tasks.

MOTOR PERFORMANCE: The ability of an individual to perform a variety of activities in such a way that the muscles are used in an efficient and coordinated manner. Measures of motor performance include power, speed, agility, and coordination.

MOTOR UNIT: The basic unit of skeletal muscle activity, consisting of a single efferent nerve fiber and the muscle fibers which it innervates.

MUSCLE ISCHEMIA: A deficiency of blood supply to the active muscles caused by an inability of the circulatory system to supply sufficient blood to sustain the constricting effects of isometric tension.

MUSCLE TONE: A condition of muscle firmness in contrast to flabbiness. Also used to describe optimal levels of strength and muscular endurance in skeletal muscles.

MUSCULAR ENDURANCE: The ability to continue performing certain specific muscular movements. The limiting factors are strength and local blood supply to active muscle tissues.

NEGATIVE ENERGY BALANCE: Energy outgo is greater than energy intake.

NERVE: A bundle of nerve fibers connecting the periphery with the central nervous system, and which contains sensory fibers (afferent) which carry impulses to the spinal cord and brain, and motor fibers (efferent) that stimulate the muscles into activity.

NEUROMUSCULAR COORDINATION: The neural control of muscular contraction in the performance of motor acts.

NEURON: A nerve cell.

NUTRIENT: The nourishing ingredients of food: proteins, carbohydrates, fats, vitamins, minerals.

OBESITY: An excessive deposition of fat in the body.

OLYMPIC GAMES: The modern revival of the ancient Greek sporting festival. The modern Olympic Games were initiated in 1896 and are held every four years, with competitions in summer and winter sports.

ORGANIC TONE: Optimal functioning of heart, lungs, and blood vessels. See *cardiovascular-respiratory endurance*.

OVERLOAD: A load or resistance greater than usually encountered in daily routine tasks.

OVERLOAD PRINCIPLE: The application of a resistance or load greater than that normally encountered by the individual.

OVERWEIGHT: An individual is regarded as overweight if her weight is in excess of the statistical average for age and height.

OXYGEN DEBT: The amount of oxygen that must be taken into the body during the recovery period following strenuous exercise. An individual contracts oxygen debt when the supply of oxygen is insufficient to meet the exercise demands. The oxygen debt is repaid during the recovery period at the end of exercise.

PARASYMPATHETIC NERVOUS SYSTEM: That part of the nervous system responsible for maintaining the state of homeostasis of the organism.

PASSIVE EXERCISE: A movement or action produced by a force other than the muscular effort of the person herself.

PERCEPTION: An individual's interpretation of sensation as received by her sensory organs from stimuli in her environment.

PERSONALITY: Personal characteristics or traits that reflect the dynamic integration of the attitudes, beliefs, and ideas of an individual, which are responsible for the pattern of her normal responses to stimuli.

PHARMACOPEIA OF EXERCISE: An exercise prescription chart indicating what kind and how much physical activity or specific exercise is recommended for a particular condition in a given individual, with counterindications and precautions listed.

PHYSICAL CONDITIONING: The improvement of the capacity of the body to function effectively under exercise stress.

PHYSICAL FITNESS: See *Health-Physical Fitness.*

PHYSICAL IMAGE: See *body image.*

PHYSICALLY EDUCATED PERSON: An individual who knows her self; knows the why and how of physical activity in modern living; has the skill to meet her personal needs and interests; and accepts self and the responsibility for developing and maintaining her physical potential.

PHYSICAL POTENTIAL: Represents high levels of energy or vitality in all life experiences, measured in terms of definitive descriptive characteristics which reflect the kind and extent of regular physical activity in mode of living (components are health-physical fitness, body shape, motor performance).

POSITIVE ENERGY BALANCE: Occurs when energy intake exceeds energy outgo.

POSTURE: The characteristic positions that an individual assumes while lying, sitting, standing, and walking and in performing other movements in work and play. *Standing posture* is the relative arrangement of the different body segments. Posture is rated desirable if there is a minimum expenditure of energy to maintain body balance and a minimum of joint-muscle strain in the performance of specific tasks.

POWER: A motor act of explosive muscular contraction, with force exerted by the muscular contractions for a short period of time. It is a composite of strength (muscular force) times speed (rate of muscular contraction).

PRONATION: The rotation of the lower arm until the palm of the hand faces downward. In the foot it is the rolling of the ankles inward with weight being supported on the inner border of the foot.

PROPRIOCEPTORS: The sensory receptor organs located within joints, around muscles, and stimuli arising within these tissues.

PSYCHO-SOCIAL TONE: Inner balance or emotional tone toward self and others.

RANGE OF MOTION: See *flexibility.*

RECREATION: An activity performed for pleasure. May also be interpreted as an activity performed that results in refreshment and relaxation; a recreating or re-energizing of one's self.

REFLEX ARC: The anatomical pathway that forms the basis of a reflex. It consists of a receptor, a sensory nerve fiber, a synapse, a motor nerve fiber, and an effector, such as a muscle or gland.

REINFORCEMENT: Approval, or disapproval of others for an individual's behavior or actions.

RELAXATION: A release or reduction of tensions.

RESIDUAL NEUROMUSCULAR TENSION: The amount of tension residing in the skeletal muscles at rest.

RESPIRATION: The sum total of all the processes in the body involved in the exchange of oxygen and carbon dioxide.

RETROGRESSION: Diminishment of performance during a rigorous conditioning regime that occurs before an improvement in performance begins.

ROTARY MOTION: Also known as angular

motion. The progression of the body around an axis with all parts of the body moving in an arc—a somersault.

ROTATION: The turning of a bone around its longitudinal axis as in the turning of the lower arm in pronation and supination, the upper arm inward or outward, and the trunk or head to the right or left.

SELF: An individual's perception of her own personal characteristics and behavior.

SELF-CONCEPT: See *self, perception,* and *body image.*

SKELETAL MUSCLE: Muscle tissue responsible for the movement of the limbs and body segments. Skeletal muscle is striated (striped) and is under voluntary control, as distinct from cardiac and smooth muscle.

SKINFOLD TEST: The lifting up of a fold of skin so that the underlying fat deposition may be measured to assess an individual's degree of fatness.

SMOOTH MUSCLE: Muscle tissue occurring in the walls of the hollow organs of the viscera. This type of muscle tissue is not striped and is not under conscious mental control.

SPECIFICITY: A concept that each conditioning regime is prescribed to achieve desired effects. The body adapts or responds in specific ways to each exercise stressor.

SPEED: The ability of the body to move quickly. When applied to a body part, the quickness of movement.

SPOT REDUCING: Commonly known as an attempt to reduce or eliminate fat deposition in a specific body area by massaging, electrically stimulating, or exercising the muscles in a specific way.

STABILITY: The ability or ease with which the body maintains balance.

STAMINA: See *cardiovascular-respiratory endurance.*

STANCE: A posture or position of readiness for performance of specific tasks.

STATIC STRENGTH: The maximal force that can be exerted by an isometric contraction.

STEADY STATE WORK: A condition in which the oxygen required by the body is equaled by the oxygen utilized in performing the task.

STRENGTH: The maximal force that can be exerted under a specified set of circumstances.

STRESS: The total psycho-soma response elicited by a stressor on the body, whether that stressor is psychological or physical; the body's reaction to stress-producing stimuli or stressors.

STRESSOR: Any agent or enviornmental influence that is capable of eliciting a stress response from the individual and forces a system or systems of the body to perform at a high level of function.

STRETCH REFLEX: The reflex contraction of a muscle that follows its stretching.

STRIATED MUSCLE: This refers to skeletal muscle, or voluntary muscle, whose contraction produces movement of the total body or body segments or maintains body position.

STROKE VOLUME: The amount of blood that is expelled from the heart on each beat.

SUPINATION: Rotation of the lower arm until the palm faces upwards. Movement is backwards and away from the body's midline. Some other joints are also capable of supination.

SYMPATHETIC NERVOUS SYSTEM: That branch of the nervous system that is responsible for preparing the body for flight from a dangerous situation or for preparing to respond to an emergency.

SYNTHESIS: The integration of facts and concepts or ideas into a complex whole.

TENDON: The connective tissue tying or attaching a muscle to a bone.

THERAPEUTIC: Pertaining to treatment, with agents having medicinal, healing, or curative properties.

TONUS: A term describing a state of slight, sustained continuous muscular contraction even when the muscle is completely relaxed.

VASCULAR: Of or pertaining to the blood vessels. See *capillarization.*

VITAMIN: Organic substance in food that is essential in small quantities to normal body function.

index

Muscle *(continued)*
  ischemia of, 74
  physiology of, 77–80
  skeletal, 75, 280–83
    composition of, 78
  types of, 77
Muscular contraction, types of, 75
Muscular endurance, 11, 28, 68–69, 73, 77, 79–80, 81, 82–83, 96
  appraisal of, 28–29
  definition of, 77
  specific exercises for, 29
Muscular hypertrophy, 81
Muscular power, 11, 68–69, 73, 77, 79, 80–82, 83, 96
Muscular strength, 11, 28, 68–69, 73, 75, 79–80, 81–83, 96
  definition of, 77
  dynamic strength programs for, 280–85
  specific exercises for, 28, 82–83
  static strength programs for, 280–85
Muscular tone, 11, 68–69, 73, 77, 80, 81, 82, 192
  definition of, 77

Nerve
  afferent, 78
  All or None Law, 79
  components of, 78–79
Nervous system
  autonomic, 247
  sympathetic, 247

Obesity
  as chronic disease, 232
  coronary heart disease and, 246
  emotional influence on, 237
  family influence on, 236
  health, illness and, 233
  influence of social factors on, 237
  personality and, 235
  prevalence of, 232–33
  See also Overweight
Overload, 68–69, 71, 80, 82
  dynamic flexibility programs and, 280–85
  specific type of, 69
  static flexibility programs and, 280–85
Overweight, 232–36
  A.M.A. statement on, 232–33
  caloric balance and, 235–36
  coronary heart disease and, 246
  eating patterns and, 171–72
  health risk of, 233
  illnesses associated with, 233
  longevity affected by, 233–34
  psychological and personal effects of, 235
  racial differences and, 232
  socio-economic class differences and, 232
  See also Obesity
Oxygen debt, 100–1
Oxygen utilization, 102

Participation
  body image and, 40–42
  personality factors and, 42–43

psychological reinforcement and, 43
  social influence on, 43–46
Performance
  body image and, 40–42
  personality factors and, 42–43
  psychological reinforcement and, 43
  social influence on, 43–46
Personality
  performance and participation, influence of, 41–43
  women competitors and, 41–43, 54
Physical activity
  benefits of, 9
  importance in daily life of, 7–8
  medical reasons for, 8–9
  personal reasons for, 10–11
  positive approach to, 11
  psychological factors influencing, 40–43
  sociological factors influencing, 40, 43–46
  technology and, 7–8
Physical conditioning
  for cardiovascular-respiratory endurance, 162
  goals of, 67, 69–70
  for menstrual function, 210–11
  for muscular endurance, 139, 147, 151, 166
  for muscular strength, 139, 147, 151, 166
  programs for
    calisthenics, 153–60
    circuit training, 147
    dynamic strength, 280–85
    interval training, 166
    progressive calisthenics, 151
    specific competition training, 166
    static strength, 280–85
    weight training, 139
    See also Exercises for specific purposes
  relative merits of
    endurance programs, 100
    flexibility programs, 89
    strength programs, 280–85
  for relaxation and release of tension, 252
Physical education
  meaning of, 3
  personal programs for, 5–6, 219
    goals of, 6
  program content, 4–5
  program development of, 269
Physical inventory, 13–14
Posture
  appraisal of, 21, 22–27
  control of, 186
  habit patterns of, 193
  individual differences in, 187–88
  techniques in body alignment, 188–191
Pronation, 87
Psychological factors influencing participation and performance, 42–43

Range of motion, *see* Flexibility
Recreation
  emotional stability through, 256–57
  stress release through, 256–57

Relaxation
    programs for development of capacity for, 257
    stress or tension release through, 255–58

Self
    acceptance of, 3
    awareness of, 3
    concept of, 40–42
    image of, 4, 13, 40–42
    optimal development of, 3
    total, 4
    unity of, 10
Skeletal structures, 85–86
Skinfold
    measurement of, 15, 18–19
    standards of, 15–16
Sleep, 258
Smoking, coronary heart disease and, 241
Social factors influencing participation and performance, 39
Specificity, concept of, 68–69, 72–73
Spot reducing, 185–86
Static strength program, 280–85
Stress
    adaptation and, 252–53
    endocrine system and, 253
    fight or flight syndrome, 254
    General Adaptation Syndrome, 253
    hormone response to, 253
    hypokinetic disease and, 253–54
    relaxation and, 255–58
    release through exercise, 255–58

Supination, 87
Stretch reflex, 89

Technology, 7–8
Timing, force and, 110
Tone
    muscular, 11, 68–69, 73, 77, 80, 81, 82, 192
        definition of, 77
    sympathetic, 247
    vagal, 247

Vascularization, 81, 96–97
    exercise and, 246
    heart and, 97, 246

Warming up, activities for, 73
Weight
    fatness and, 15
    principles of control of, 169
    tables of, 15, 310
Weight training
    benefits of, 139
    program of, 82–83
    program of exercise of, 140
    specific exercises for, 141–45
Women
    femininity and, 54
    international competition and, 56–58
    Olympic competition and, 44, 58–60
    school and college competition for, 55–56
    sports organizations for, 55–57
    youth programs for, 60–62
Work, rhythmic patterns of, 116

Youth, competitive programs for, 60–62